Irish nurses in the NHS

Irish nurses in the NHS
An Oral History

Louise Ryan, Gráinne McPolin
and Neha Doshi

FOUR COURTS PRESS

Set in 11.5pt on 13.5pt CentaurPro by
Carrigboy Typesetting Services for
FOUR COURTS PRESS LTD
7 Malpas Street, Dublin 8, Ireland
www.fourcourtspress.ie
and in North America for
FOUR COURTS PRESS
c/o IPG, 814 N. Franklin St, Chicago, IL 60610.

© Louise Ryan, Gráinne McPolin and Neha Doshi and Four Courts Press 2025

A catalogue record for this title is available from the British Library.

ISBN 978-1-80151-163-6

All rights reserved. No part of this publication may be reproduced, stored in or introduced into a retrieval system, or transmitted, in any form or by any means (electronic, mechanical, photocopying, recording, or otherwise), without the prior written permission of both the copyright owner and publisher of this book.

Printed in England by Short Run Press Ltd, Exeter.

Contents

	LIST OF ILLUSTRATIONS	6
	ACKNOWLEDGMENTS	7
1	Introduction	9
2	Re-writing history: researching migration stories	17
3	'I up and went': stories of nurse recruitment	35
4	'What an adventure!': arriving in Britain	62
5	'On the wards': nurse training begins	84
6	'Let free for the first time': the social lives of student nurses	110
7	'The world is my oyster': developing and changing careers over time	136
8	'You're OK, even though you're Irish': experiences of being Irish in Britain	161
9	'Under the radar': reflecting on the contribution of Irish nurses to the NHS	187
	APPENDICES	
1	The anonymous interviewees, ordered by date of interview	209
2	Undertaking interviews across geographical locations	211
3	The project outputs	216
	BIBLIOGRAPHY	220
	INDEX	226

Illustrations

Plates appear between pages 128 and 129

1. Mary Hazard, 1952
2. Nora and Tony Hayward, 1954
3. Teresa Doherty, 1955
4. Josie Caulfield, 1959
5. Noreen Schierz and nurse cohort, 1961
6. Dee Cokeley, 1965/6
7. Bernie Naughton and nursing students, 1966
8. Ethel Corduff, 1966
9. Lorna Keating, 1972
10. Maureen Ryan, 1974
11. Phil Ellen Donovan, c.1975
12. Geraldine Hilder, 1970s
13. Betty Graham, 1986
14. Betty Halfpenny, 1990s
15. Eddie Mulligan, 1994
16. Group photo of Irish nurses outside Lewisham Hospital, 2022
17. Group photo, Luton Irish Forum St Brigid's Day event, 28 January 2023
18. John Redmond, 2023
19. Group photo at Liverpool Institute of Irish Studies, June 2023
20. Group photo at Irish Embassy, London, film premiere, February 2024

FIGURES

Cork Examiner (now the *Irish Examiner*), 1949	44
Sligo Champion, 1954	46

Acknowledgments

We would like to express our heartfelt gratitude to the forty-five Irish nurses who took part in our oral history project and who allowed us to tell their stories through this book, and in our other outputs such as the podcast series, documentary film and photo exhibitions.

This book, and our wider research project, would not have been possible without the support of the Irish Government Emigrant Support Programme, colleagues at the Irish Abroad Unit and the consular missions of London, North of England and Scotland which enabled us to connect with Irish nurses who migrated to Scotland, England and Wales.

The Irish Nurses and Midwives Organisation granted initial seed-funding for which we are very grateful; this signified the starting point of our journey. We would like to thank our partners at the London Irish Centre for their support from the beginning of our project and by hosting several dissemination events. We especially want to acknowledge the generous support of Mary Kerrigan and Fionuala Pender. We would like to thank the Institute of Irish Studies, University of Liverpool, for their generosity and Irish Community Care Liverpool and the Liverpool Irish Centre who gave us the opportunity to tell the story of the nurses who migrated from Ireland to Liverpool. We are grateful for a grant awarded by the Burdett Trust for Nursing which enabled us to curate a portrait exhibition along with the photographer Fiona Freund and her colleague Lise Meyrick.

We wish to thank Dr Tom McGorrian, Buckinghamshire New University and director Mohamed Ali Elota whose determination, creativity and enthusiasm brought the Irish Nurses in the NHS story to the big screen. Thanks to Kelly Crichton for her insightful skills in public relations marketing and branding, especially for the podcast series.

We are grateful to colleagues at the EPIC Museum Dublin, The Migration Museum Lewisham, the Museum of the Home, Huddersfield Irish Centre, Irish World Heritage Centre Manchester, Leeds Irish Centre, Irish Arts Foundation in Leeds, Abbey House Museum, Luton Irish Forum, the *Irish Voice* newspaper in Scotland, and the Royal College of Nursing for welcoming the Irish Nurses in the NHS project into the public narrative.

The writing of this book was facilitated by Louise's study leave from the School of Social Sciences and Professions, London Metropolitan University, and a visiting professorship at University College Cork in 2023. Thanks to both institutions for their support. A special thanks to Dr Breda Gray for her comments and advice on early drafts of Chapter 2.

We would like to thank Four Courts Press for giving us the opportunity to tell the remarkable stories of the Irish nurses in the NHS. A special thanks to Martin Fanning and an anonymous reviewer for their helpful feedback on the early drafts. The two newspaper advertisements from the 1940s/1950s are reproduced with permission of the Irish Newspaper Archives.

We would like to thank our families who have been a constant support behind the scenes of this project.

The forty-five nurses who took part in this research were (in alphabetical order):

Rosanna Anderson, Ann Brennan, Madeline Brett-Richards, Rosaleen Burke, Noreen Capplis, Annie Casey, Josie Caulfield, Dee Cokeley, Peggy Conaty, Mary Cook, Ethel Corduff, Rita Corley, Marian Davies, Teresa Doherty, Phil Ellen Donovan, Mary Dowling, Ann Ferguson, Betty Graham, Betty Halfpenny, Nora Hayward, Mary Hazard, Geraldine Hilder, Lorna Keating, Therese Lawton, Elizabeth McCluskey, Ann McGeever, Margaret McGuire, Olive McKeown, Rosemary McLoughlin, Tina McNulty, Eddie Mulligan, Bernie Naughton, Marie O'Sullivan, Annie Paul, Anne Ranshaw, John Redmond, Margaret Robson, Maureen Ryan, Peggy Sarsfield, Anne Scriven, Noreen Schierz, Rita Simmons, Eileen Walsh, Breda Watling, Connie Wood.

We thank them all.

Finally, we want to say that it has been an absolute privilege to celebrate the Irish nurses in the NHS and to have their voices heard at last.

CHAPTER 1

Introduction

I was born in March 1947 in the big snow, and I didn't have any midwife, doctor or anything, in attendance because the snow was so heavy that nobody could get there. I was the fifth of six children. I was the fourth daughter on a farm ... and we're still all alive and well and healthy. We were brought up in rural, agricultural Ireland, and we didn't have an awful lot but it didn't seem like that at the time. We had adequate. We had lots of fun amongst ourselves and I can remember life being tough and there always was lots of work to do.

Off to school, not very advanced at school because that was how it was. So, at 15 and a half, 16, I left school, went to work in one of the local factories, and can't remember that I enjoyed it very much ... Ah, it was making hats. I could still tell you how to make hats ... it was very monotonous and physically demanding work, but not very interesting ... And that might have been one direction that my life, my career could have taken. Fortunately, it didn't ...

I was always ambitious and I wanted to escape ... I certainly was a dreamer. I had aspirations ... the options available to me were very, very limited ... I probably could have got married. I probably could have gone into a convent ...

... one of the friends, her sister was a nurse in Kent, and the stories! ... It was a very good experience that she had, and it seemed as if, well, here was a profession, here was access ... She told me, or she obviously fed back through my sister, that they were recruiting Irish nurses, and I made contact with them, wrote a letter ... and was surprised, almost immediately, got back a reply saying that there were vacancies there and offering me a place. (Bronagh, began nurse training in England in 1965)[1]

Following the establishment of the National Health Service (NHS) in 1948 and, given the urgent need to rapidly expand the number of nurses, there was an active campaign to recruit thousands of young Irish women, and men, as trainee nurses. Advertisements were placed in national and provincial newspapers

---

1 Bronagh, as with all the interviewees named, is a pseudonym.

and recruitment officers travelled to every town in Ireland interviewing potential student nurses. At a time when nurse training in Ireland[2] was not only very limited but also extremely expensive, the chance to train for free, and to benefit from live-in accommodation, in British hospitals, proved highly attractive (Ryan, 2007). Furthermore, as we can see in Bronagh's story, above, for ambitious young women, who wanted to pursue a career but faced limited prospects in Ireland, at that time, moving to Britain to train as a nurse seemed quite a straightforward route into exciting new opportunities.

As a result of this mass recruitment, by the 1970s, tens of thousands of Irish-born nurses were working in British hospitals (Walter, 1989; Daniels, 1993: 5–6). Irish nurses quickly gained a reputation for being hard workers, but also friendly and chatty with patients. Moreover, as young people, away from home for the first time, they also had the chance to enjoy the fun and freedom of life in cities like London and Liverpool. Of course, it was not always plain sailing and these Irish migrants also encountered challenges such as homesickness and loneliness, but also prejudice and hostility, especially during the years of the IRA bombing campaigns throughout England. Indeed, in later chapters we will hear more of Bronagh's experiences, particularly after she moved to live in Birmingham in the 1970s around the time of the infamous pub bombing.

Given that the great waves of Irish recruitment to the NHS took place many decades ago, those pioneering Irish nurses are an ageing population. Sadly, many of the NHS recruits from the 1940s–50s are no longer around to tell their stories. Indeed, we are sad to say that two of the nurses who participated in this study have since passed away. Therefore, there is an urgency in gathering as many stories as possible, before it is too late.

Of course, it is important to acknowledge that Irish nurses were working in Britain prior to 1948. In fact, there is a long history of Irish migrants working as carers across British society (Corduff, 2020) including, for example, during the Second World War (Muldowney, 2007). In the course of doing our research, we heard many stories about young Irish women who migrated to Britain to work as nurses during the Second World War. For example, Freida Winters from Co. Laois who went to work in Barnsley and Maeve White from Cobh, who nursed in London – both now deceased.[3] In this book we focus specifically on those who were recruited into nursing following the establishment of the NHS.

2 The opportunities for nurse training in Southern and Northern Ireland were somewhat different and will be discussed in more detail later in the book.   3 We are grateful to all those who got in touch with us during this research to share stories of their late mothers, especially the Winters family and the White family.

Introduction

This book draws on the rich oral history narratives of forty-five participants. As we can see in the case of Bronagh, above, their stories are rich and evocative, painting vivid pictures of past events. Because we were especially keen to hear the voices of the older generation, we focused our recruitment on research participants who trained as nurses in the 1940s through to the early 1970s. Hence, most of our interviewees are now retired and entering advanced older age. Indeed, many were in their 80s and several were over 90 years of age. Interestingly, some of our younger participants, in their late 60s and early 70s, were still working, part-time, despite being over retirement age. While we had intended to hear the stories of women, two men – both psychiatric nurses – were also interviewed, as discussed in more detail below. Therefore, through these forty-five sets of stories, we learn about the remarkable contribution that Irish nurses have made over seven decades, from the inception of the NHS in 1948 right up to the present day.

The book is part of a wider, three-year project led by Professor Louise Ryan, at London Metropolitan University, and Gráinne McPolin, a freelance radio producer and former nurse (who lives in Ireland), with research assistant Neha Doshi, a PhD student at London Metropolitan University. The project's primary aim is to record and relate the hitherto untold stories of Irish nurses in Britain's National Health Service, through the media of photography, audio and film recording and the printed word.

HOW THE PROJECT CAME ABOUT

This research builds upon two earlier projects. In the early 2000s, Louise Ryan undertook a small study of Irish nurses (2007, 2008), which has become widely cited and regarded as pioneering research in understanding the role of Irish migrant women in the NHS.

In 2021, a radio documentary entitled *Angels of Mercy*, produced by Gráinne McPolin, was broadcast on Ireland's Newstalk Radio, to wide acclaim. The programme was runner up in the 2021 New York radio awards and winner of the 2022 Clarion International Women in Media Award. That programme ignited interest in the history of Irish nurses in Britain and listeners indicated their desire to know more about this important chapter in the story of Irish migration. Gráinne McPolin was a nurse for over 30 years, half of that time spent working in the NHS, and she brings that life experience to the project. Louise Ryan was a contributor to that radio documentary and at that point she and Gráinne decided to develop the project further, seek funding, and preserve the stories of Irish nurses.

The oral history project secured a small amount of seed funding from the Irish Nurses and Midwives Organisation. The interviewing began in London, in March 2022, when the London Irish Centre came on board as a partner to support the initial stage of the study – which focused upon nurses in the London area. Following a grant from the Burdett Trust for Nursing in summer 2022, we were able to add a photographic dimension to the London project.

From the start, we were keen to extend the project beyond the capital, to look at the experiences of nurses who trained and worked in other cities throughout Britain. In 2021 we began conversations with the Liverpool Institute of Irish Studies[4] about the possibility of doing some interviews in Liverpool. Later, in summer 2022, we were delighted to receive funding from the Institute which enabled us to include nurses from Liverpool in our oral history project.

Also in summer 2022, we were very pleased to receive a substantial grant from the Irish Government's Emigrant Support Programme (Irish Abroad Unit) to expand the project still further to include Irish nurses across Britain including Scotland.

OUR RESEARCH METHODS

Through our rich oral history interviews with forty-five participants, we aim to understand:

- why they left Ireland as teenagers to train as nurses
- their experiences of travelling to Britain and encountering new people and places for the first time
- how they got on during their initial nurse training and how their careers developed over time.
- the role of social networks of friends, family and colleagues as sources of support and sociality for these migrants.
- how they negotiated their Irish identities in Britain, particularly during decades of heightened political tensions.
- The extent to which they felt appreciated as nurses and whether or not they think the contribution of Irish nurses to the NHS is well known and understood in wider British society.

We welcomed participants from the whole island of Ireland[5] if they chose to identify as an Irish nurse. Hence, our participants come from every province in

---

4 We are grateful to Dr Maev McDaid for brokering an introduction to Professor Peter Shirlow at the University of Liverpool.   5 It is worth clarifying terminology. We refer to the whole

Ireland. We have participants from as far north as Tyrone and Down, and as far south as Cork and Kerry, from Sligo in the west to Dublin in the east, and every county in between.

We decided to focus this research on Irish people who are still living in Britain. We are aware that many Irish nurses, after working in the NHS, returned to work and live in Ireland (see also Ryan and Doshi, 2024). Indeed, this was the experience of Gráinne as she returned to nursing in Ireland after working in the NHS. However, given the constraints of time and resources, we decided not to interview nurses who had returned to Ireland.

It is noteworthy that two of our participants are men. We had not intended to interview men but when the opportunity was suggested by the Irish community organizations, we jumped at the chance to hear the voices of male nurses. Interestingly, both of these men, who worked as psychiatric nurses, told us that psychiatric hospitals often had many Irish male nurses. So clearly, there is more work to do on the story of Irish male nurses in Britain.

ETHICAL ISSUES AND CONFIDENTIALITY

Our research project received ethical approval from the Research Ethics Committee at London Metropolitan University. All data were processed in full compliance with General Data Protection Regulations (GDPR). Interviews were subject to informed consent. Participants are anonymized across data collection, audio transcription, analysis and writing up. Participants were expressly asked if they wished to be named (first name only) in the podcasts and the photographic exhibition (see appendices) in line with Oral History Research protocol and the guidelines of the Oral History Society (2021).

Many of the stories shared with us involved sensitive information and, in order to ensure that no harm or distress is caused, inadvertently, to other people or to our participants, we made the decision to exercise caution and remove all real names. Therefore, for the purpose of this book, we have given all our research participants pseudonyms to protect not only their identities but also the identities of others including hospital staff, patients, relatives and friends. A table of all pseudonyms and years of arrival in Britain is included towards the

---

island of Ireland to mean the Republic of Ireland and Northern Ireland. Throughout the book different terms are used such as Northern Ireland/ the North of Ireland – to respect different ways of referring to the six counties – and the Irish Republic/ the South of Ireland – to refer to the 26 counties. Therefore, we also refer very deliberately to Britain (meaning England, Scotland and Wales). We do not use 'UK' as that term technically includes Northern Ireland and so it would be inappropriate and contradictory to refer to nurses from Northern Ireland

end of this book (see Appendix 1). The pseudonyms were chosen with care to ensure that no new name is the same as the real of any other participant, and also to ensure that the names are culturally and generationally appropriate. We have also removed the names of hospitals. While some readers may be disappointed that actual hospitals are not named, we had to exercise caution and be guided by ethical protocols to ensure that no confidential information, about particular hospital staff or patients, was accidentally divulged.

DATA ANALYSIS

The interviews were audio recorded, with permission of the participants, and fully transcribed by a professional transcription company.[6] All transcripts were given identity codes, and names were removed, to protect confidentiality. Transcripts and recordings were transferred via a secure, password protected data-sharing portal.

Following transcription, all transcripts were cross-checked against the original recording, to ensure accuracy. To support this labour-intensive work, we hired a part-time research assistant, Neha Doshi. The process of data analysis was undertaken using the NVIVO software package, a well-known tool to support qualitative analysis. All coding and analysis were undertaken by Louise and Neha.

STRUCTURE OF THIS BOOK

In the next chapter (Chapter 2), we present a brief overview of the existing literature on Irish migration and, in particular, we discuss the body of research on Irish women's migration to Britain. In this way, we situate our book within the existing literature and highlight the contribution that we are making through our rich oral history of Irish nurses.

Thereafter, all the chapters flow through the chronology of the participants' migration stories. Chapter 3 relates the nurses' stories of recruitment and, like Bronagh's narrative at the start of this chapter, we hear how and why they decided to pursue nurse training in the NHS.

Chapter 4 recounts their experiences of leaving home and making that initial journey to Britain. We hear funny and also moving stories as they embarked

moving to the 'UK'. 6 We employed real people – from 'Transcribe It' – not AI, for transcription purposes. We are grateful for the great care that these transcribers took with our precious data.

upon their big adventure, had new experiences and encountered a few mishaps along the way.

Chapter 5 presents the stories of training, wearing their new uniforms and adapting to the rigors of working on the wards. We hear about the matrons who ruled over hospitals and could not be defied. But we also hear about young students who sometimes bent the rules and had fun despite the pressures and demands of training. Of course, Irish nurses were not the only migrants working in the NHS and we also hear about their encounters with people from different nationalities and ethnicities.

Chapter 6 focuses on the social scene. Living in the Nurses' Homes, these young students made new friends and together they could explore the amusements that British cities had to offer. From the music scene in Liverpool, to the dance halls of swinging London, we hear about how these young nurses worked hard but also played hard and enjoyed themselves during their free time. We also learn about some of the risks they faced as young people living away from home and without the protective gaze of their families.

Chapter 7 discusses their careers, post-qualification. It is remarkable how many participants married young. In the 1950s–1960s, for women, marriage and children often proved incompatible with careers. However, nursing offered the opportunity to continue working part-time, usually on night shifts. As we will hear, the extent to which careers could be developed, over time, depended on the support of partners, childcare and the opportunities to pursue additional training within the NHS.

Chapter 8 explores their experiences not only as nurses but also as Irish migrants in Britain. While they had been actively recruited to work and deliver vital health service to British society, that does not mean they received a warm welcome. Irish people encountered a range of negative stereotypes and in some cases open hostility that underlined their position as migrants. Moreover, during the period known as 'the Troubles' and heightened political tensions, Irish people, including nurses, experienced explicit forms of suspicion and animosity. This chapter uses the rich oral history narratives to consider how Irish professionals, such as nurses, navigated these tense and difficult situations.

Chapter 9 draws the book to a close by considering if the enormous contribution of Irish nurses to the NHS is fully appreciated within British society. Most of our participants described feeling appreciated, on an individual level, by patients and colleagues. Nonetheless, several expressed the view that more needs to be done to ensure that the overall contribution of tens of thousands of Irish nurses to the NHS is better understood and acknowledged more widely in society. Indeed, one participant said that she was motivated to take part in our project specifically to ensure that Irish nurses' contribution is researched and recorded for posterity. As some of our participants stated, Irish nurses have been somewhat taken for granted and so their contribution has not received the public recognition that it truly deserves. We hope that this book and our wider project will rectify that situation.

We wish to express our heartfelt thanks to all the nurses who gave their time so generously to this research project. This is their story and we hope we have done them proud.

CHAPTER 2

Re-writing history: researching migration stories

Although women have made up a large proportion of migrants leaving Ireland, during the nineteenth and twentieth centuries, until recent decades that story has been largely untold. In this chapter, we present an overview of Irish migration and, in particular, we highlight some key texts that have helped to shine a light on women's migration. In so doing, we show how oral history studies have been crucial in telling the hitherto under-researched story of women's migration from Ireland, especially in the twentieth century.

We then move on to focus on nursing and migration. We present a brief overview of the academic research on Irish nurses in Britain and also highlight some life writing by Irish nurses themselves who spent long careers in the NHS. Then we present a short discussion about using oral history to tell the stories of Irish nurses. Oral history interviews provide opportunities to explore aspects of historical experience that are rarely recorded in official texts (Thomson, 1998a). Nonetheless, as discussed later in this chapter, doing oral history research also raises some questions about how the past is remembered and retold after a significant passage of time.

We end the chapter by looking more widely at overseas recruitment into the NHS and consider why the British health service, since its inception in 1948, up to the present day, has been so reliant upon migrants, particularly in the field of nursing. Therefore, this chapter aims to set the scene and provide a jumping off point for our own oral history research with Irish nurses in Britain.

UNDERSTANDING IRISH MIGRATION

Migration has been a defining feature of Irish society throughout the nineteenth and much of the twentieth centuries (Akenson, 1993; Delaney, 2000; Jackson, 1963; Redmond, 2018; Walter, 2002). Indeed, as Arensberg (1937) observed, migration has formed part of the history of rural life, farming, inheritance and economic survival.

From the late nineteenth century up to the 1920s, the vast majority of migrants from the southern 26 counties of Ireland went to the US (Kennedy, 1973). Indeed, such was the volume of Irish migration, that by the mid-1920s,

43% of Irish-born men and women were living overseas, over one million in the US alone (Kennedy, 1973). This made Ireland unique with the rather dubious accolade of having nearly half of its native-born population living abroad (Redmond, 2018).

During the early 1930s migration declined briefly because of the international economic depression, which meant that the numbers going to North America decreased dramatically (Jackson, 1963). However, as the economic situation overseas improved, Irish migration increased again in the mid-to-late 1930s. It is noteworthy that the majority of migrants were then going to Britain (Jackson, 1963). By 1951, there were an estimated 722,000 Irish-born people living in Britain (Redmond, 2018).

As Britain's nearest colony, Ireland has long been its traditional labour reserve. As Hickman and Walter (1997) have shown, in their detailed report on the Irish in Britain, the colonial relationship between these two countries has impacted on Irish migrants in particular ways. On the one hand, Irish people had many social and political rights in Britain including freedom of movement stemming from the Common Travel Area[1] (B. Ryan, 2001). On the other hand, the colonial legacy has reproduced many negative stereotypes of Irish inferiority and dependency (see Walter, 2002; Ryan, 2008; Hickman and Ryan, 2020).

Given its huge prevalence, it is hardly surprising that emigration has been depicted in many popular Irish songs, poems, stories and paintings. However, within those cultural representations, especially during the nineteenth and twentieth centuries, there was a marked tendency to depict the migrant as male, while women were depicted as the weeping mothers, sisters and sweethearts left behind (Travers, 1997).

It is necessary to go beyond these images to uncover more diverse, complex and personal stories of migration experiences. Contrary to the popular image, one of the most striking characteristics of Irish emigration has been its uniquely high proportion of female migrants (Rudd, 1988; O'Sullivan, 1997). Statistical data reveal the preponderance of women in Irish migration and demonstrate that between 1871 and 1971 women outnumbered their male migrant counterparts (Travers, 1997: 146). Moreover, these female migrants tended to be young, mostly in their late teens and early 20s, and single (O'Sullivan, 1997). Thus, unlike other nationalities where women tend to migrate as part of family groups, Irish women usually migrated as young, single individuals.

1 Under the terms of the Common Travel Area, there is free movement of citizens between Ireland and Britain. The arrangement dates back to the establishment of the Irish Free State in the 1920s. However, immigration restrictions were imposed during the Second World War and continued into the early 1950s. So free movement between the two countries was not always guaranteed. Since the 1950s, the CTA has meant that citizens of both countries have mutual rights

During the early/mid-twentieth century the high numbers of women leaving Ireland provoked much political debate and concern (see Ryan, 2003). Jenny Beale (1986) noted the irony:

> At a time when politicians were praising family life in rural Ireland, when de Valera[2] was exalting the countryside 'bright with cosy homesteads', the people of the west were streaming away, leaving the traditional way of life as fast as they could (Beale, 1986: 35).

Indeed, by the mid-1930s, there was growing moral panic about the number of young people leaving Ireland and in these public debates it was the sight of so many young women migrants that provoked the loudest concerns.

In 1936 the *Irish Independent*, the biggest selling national daily newspaper, published a series of feature articles on 'Irish girl emigrants'. Written by regular columnist Gertrude Gaffney, the articles were based on a fact-finding mission in several British cities.

Gaffney emphasized that most young Irish women did well in Britain and earned decent wages, mainly working in domestic service. However, she drew attention to the 'rapidly growing minority' who experienced poverty, loneliness and desperation in unfamiliar cities, far away from their friends and relations. In an extensive analysis of these articles, Louise Ryan (2002a; 2003) notes that they were remarkably frank and open in exposing the challenges encountered by young Irish women and girls who migrated alone to British cities. Gaffney wrote that an 'astounding number of girls' arrived in Liverpool docks with no money and no job. Many were as young as 16, and, without training for any particular occupation, some of these young women were taken advantage of and got into difficult situations. Coming from rural districts in Ireland, they were ignorant about the ways of the world, as Gaffney put it. Gaffney concluded that the root of the problem lay in the general lack of preparation and training among young Irish women arriving in Britain. Rather than trying to prevent emigration, Gaffney suggested that it was more sensible to accept this reality and ensure that the young women were appropriately prepared and trained for what lay ahead.

During the 1930s, the plight of the 'emigrant girl' also exercised the Catholic hierarchy. For example, Dr James Joseph McNamee, bishop of Ardagh and Clonmacnoise, in a fiery sermon condemned what he described as 'the rising stream of emigration of young girls to Great Britain in circumstances of dubious advantage to their welfare, temporal or spiritual'. He said that girls were attracted

---

to travel, settle, work, study and vote.   2 Eamon de Valera was Taoiseach (prime minister) of the Irish Free State/Irish Republic for several terms of office during the 1930s, 1940s and into the 1950s. His particular brand of conservative Catholic nationalism shaped Irish society for decades.

'by the fascination of the garish distractions of the city, and by the hectic life of the great world as displayed before their wondering eyes in the glamorous unrealities of the films'. Cinema, he argued, was breeding a discontent with 'the prosaic placidity of rural life' ('Alarming evil', *Irish Independent*, 8 February 1937, also cited in Ryan, 2003).

Despite the rhetoric of the Catholic Church, at that time, we should not, of course, assume that Irish women were helpless and passive victims who were simply carried along on a wave of migration or lured by the false promises of romantic films. Indeed, women's decisions to emigrate were based on a number of related factors (Jackson, 1963; Walter, 2002; Gray, 2004). Migration decisions were often motivated by harsh economic realities. It was not only that employment was scarce but also the types of low paid jobs available in Ireland, especially for women, proved unattractive (Jackson, 1963). Compared to life in rural Ireland, pay and working conditions were considered to be far better in England. Furthermore, women in rural Ireland were particularly likely to emigrate because of 'their exclusion from inheriting land' and 'the custom of large dowries' (Fielding, 1993: 19). Young, unmarried women in rural Ireland experienced very low social status (Kennedy, 1973) and, within the conservative political climate of de Valera's Ireland, women's rights were limited and their employment opportunities restricted (Beaumont, 1997; Connolly, 2001).

The link between these social conditions and women's migration was not lost on some observers at the time. By the 1950s several public voices, including, for example, the Irish Housewives Association, were articulating the view that women were leaving Ireland, in their droves, because of their low status and inferior position in Irish society (Travers, 1997).

As Nicola Yeates has argued: 'The social roles prescribed for women; essentially as wives and mothers – restricted their opportunities for economic independence in Ireland' (2004: 85). Therefore, Irish women's emigration was motivated by a quest for social as well as financial independence (Walter, 2002; Gray, 2004).

A curious phenomenon of nineteenth- and twentieth-century Irish society was that, while women had low status, limited employment opportunities within a strictly conservative moral environment, which curtailed their social freedoms, there appeared to be no restrictions on their freedom to leave and migrate abroad:

> A convergence of economic and cultural imperatives had created the paradoxical situation whereby Irish women who stayed in Ireland faced a life of domination by fathers, brothers, and – for the minority who were

able to marry – husbands, and yet were free in one important respect: there were few impediments to their leaving (Daniels, 1993: 4).

In fact, emigration can be seen as a sort of 'safety value' in twentieth-century Irish society; a way of letting off steam and diffusing social tensions. Moreover, emigration was also a way of exporting/concealing some social problems, as we will hear in later chapters, such as unwanted pregnancy (Garrett, 2000). This phenomenon has been described by Joy Rudd (1988) as Ireland's 'invisible exports'.

Nonetheless, concerns about the large numbers of young women leaving the country continued to be raised, in some quarters, in the post-war period. In the 1950s, the Irish government set up a commission to investigate levels of emigration and the related problem of rural depopulation. The Commission published a long and very detailed report in 1955. Explaining the high levels of migration from rural Ireland, the Commission stated: 'It is not actual want or poverty, but a desire to secure an improved economic and social status, which urges such people to seek the apparent attractions of a changed environment' (Commission on Emigration 1955: 137). As the Commission noted, in Ireland there was an established tradition of emigration and this resulted in relatives and friends in Britain, and elsewhere, acting like magnets in encouraging and facilitating the migration of others (Commission on Emigration 1955: 138). The extent to which friends and relations abroad acted like 'magnets' points to the 'culture of migration' and the role of social networks, especially female networks, in perpetuating migration flows (see Ryan, 2007; Ryan, 2023).

A pervasive 'tradition' or culture of migration may mean that migrating abroad becomes normalized and taken for granted (Ryan, 2007). In addition, this culture of migration also creates transnational networks, made up of family and friendship ties, forging a direct link between those abroad and those back in Ireland (Gray, 2006; Delaney & MacRaild, 2007). Thus, a culture of migration and the existence of transnational networks are likely to be closely interconnected, each one fuelling and reinforcing the other. Nonetheless, it is possible for one to exist without the other. For example, a particular individual may not have any close friends or relatives who have previously migrated but may be influenced by the wider culture of migration in society (Ryan, 2007). These are issues we will revisit later in this book as we present the stories of our participants and we consider the role that networks of kith and kin played in their emigration decisions.

Given the preponderance of female migration, and the concerns that it provoked among political and religious leaders at various moments in the twentieth century, it is surprising that there has been limited academic research on this topic until recent decades. As Daniels noted in the early 1990s, women's 'historiographical invisibility (is) profoundly unjust' (1993: 4). Indeed, the omission of women migrants from Irish history results in a 'flawed understanding' of migration (Travers, 1997: 147). In the next section we discuss some important contributions to advancing understanding of Irish women's emigration.

ACROSS THE WATER: RESEARCHING IRISH WOMEN IN BRITAIN

The omission of women from histories of migration is not unique to Ireland. Within migration studies more widely there has been what Eleonore Kofman (2004) terms 'historical amnesia' about the prevalence of women in international migratory waves. As a result, the novelty of the so-called 'feminization of migration' in recent decades has been exaggerated. In other words, recent claims that women are now suddenly migrating in very large numbers across the globe are built on the assumption that women did not migrate very much in the past.

Therefore, understanding the history of female migration matters not only in understanding the past but also in informing how we make sense of current migration patterns. Paying attention to the Irish case demonstrates that female migration is certainly not a new phenomenon. For example, as discussed below, after the Second World War, large numbers of young women from the Caribbean and Eastern Europe as well as Ireland were recruited to fill specific roles in the British labour force (Phoenix & Bauer, 2012; McDowell, 2013).

The omission of Irish women from histories of migration matters for several reasons. First, if we do not include women's experiences, then there are gaps in our knowledge of emigration from Ireland and the wider implications for Irish society as a whole. Second, if Irish women are missing from wider, international analyses of migration, then the range, diversity and complexity of women's migration patterns over time are also not properly understood.

However, the significance of Irish women's migration for British society and economy is still not properly understood. In fact, as discussed below, with a few notable exceptions, much of the research that has been undertaken is by Irish academics, including Irish researchers working in Britain. Among mainstream British migration studies, the enormous contribution of Irish women still needs to be fully researched. As Bronwen Walter (2002) explains, while the Irish male migrant is immortalized in the 'Mick' and 'Paddy' stereotypes of navvies and construction workers,[3] Irish women, despite their prevalence, have been largely invisible in Britain.[4]

---

[3] The contribution of Irish men to Britain's post-war construction has been researched by Ultan Cowley. [4] In a fascinating paper, Tony Murray (2017) discusses the contrasting visibility and

Given the lack of information about Irish women's experiences of migration, some pioneering women researchers began to undertake new research in the 1980s. These studies used oral history methods to record the voices of women migrants and so add important new insights on this heretofore under-researched topic.

In their path-breaking book *Across the water*, published in 1988, Lennon, McAdam and O'Brien note the 'resounding silence' about Irish women's migration. Given the absence of any systematic research about Irish women's experiences in Britain, those authors were prompted to come together to write this book based on rich oral history interviews and insightful photographs. In so doing, they sought to gain an understanding of women's migration stories 'as perceived from the inside' (1988: 11).

Similarly, in her influential book, *Models for movers* (first published in 1990 and re-issued in 2015), Ide O'Carroll also used oral history interviews and photography to relate the stories of Irish women who migrated to the US. Like Lennon et al., O'Carroll was also prompted to write her book because she was 'shocked by the absence of Irish women's voices in accounts of Irish migration' (2015: 2). Meanwhile, on the other side of the globe, Angela McCarthy (2005) has used migrant letters to unearth the stories of Irish migrants, including many women, who went to New Zealand in the late nineteenth and early twentieth centuries.

Since the pioneering work of Lennon et al. and O'Carroll, there has been a number of important contributions to the history of Irish women's migration, especially to Britain. As Bronwen Walter (2002) has argued in her influential theorization of the Irish presence in Britain, Irish people have been simultaneously viewed as insiders and outsiders. The anomalous position of Irish migrants is also defined by whiteness, Europeanness and use of the English language, although these attributes were also complex and contested.[5] The apparent ease with which Irish citizens have moved across national boundaries between Ireland and Britain belies many of these underlying complexities. British government attitudes to Irish migrants have often been less than sympathetic and the exclusion of Irish migrants from anti-immigrant legislation has usually been the result of internal government debates and careful political negotiations (Delaney 2000; Ryan 2001). As Walter's research shows, popular British attitudes towards and stereotypes about Irish migrants reveal these ambiguities.

invisibility of navvies and nurses.   5 Of course, the whiteness of Irish migrants has been contested especially in the nineteenth century. There is extensive historical research on how the Irish were racialized and only gradually 'became' accepted as white over time (see Gerber & Kraut, 2005). Furthermore, it is important to note that not all Irish migrants to Britain are white and in recent years the Irish-born population has become increasingly diverse (see King-O'Riain, 2021).

The ambiguous position of Irish migrants in 1950s Britain is discussed by Marc Scully (2015). Although not focusing specifically on female voices, many of the participants in Scully's focus groups are women and offer fascinating insights into perceptions of Irish migrants in the post-war era within British cities like Birmingham.

Another, important contribution to understanding migration experiences within particular locations is Sharon Lambert's (2001) oral history of Irish women who migrated to Lancashire between 1922 and 1960. By focusing on one specific county, in the north of England, Lambert also shifts the lens to the experiences of Irish migrants in less researched geographical contexts. An early and perhaps lesser-known contribution to the story of Irish women's migration is by Russell King and Henrietta O'Connor. Published in 1996, the paper draws on 50 in-depth, life history interviews with Irish women who were living in and around the Leicester region of England.

Breda Gray's book, published in 2004, focused on more recent women migrants from the 1980s across key sites including London and Luton. Using focus groups, she offered sociological analysis of how her participants negotiated their identities as women and as Irish migrants in British society especially against the backdrop of the socio-political context of the period.

Also using a sociological lens, in combination with oral history techniques, Louise Ryan's early work involved interviews with 1930s women migrants (2002b). Conducted in the early 2000s, her interviews with twelve women, in advanced older age, helped to capture the stories of women who migrated during the inter-war era to work in domestic service in England. Interestingly, these twelve women had left Ireland against the backdrop of growing political concerns, discussed above, about the 'emigrant girl' and the moral panic about the high numbers of young Irish women leaving the recently created Irish Free State. The oral testimonies of the women interviewed by Ryan help to reveal valuable insights into why they left and what motivated them to stay in England throughout their adult lives.

Following on chronologically from Ryan's oral history interviews with 1930s migrants, Mary Muldowney's (2007) oral history interviews with women who migrated to Britain during the 1940s helps to add another piece to the story of Irish migration. The women in Muldowney's book contributed to the British war effort at a time when the Irish Free State remained neutral. Her research adds new understanding of the little-known story of Irish women's war work. Yvonne McKenna's (2003) rich oral history research with Irish nuns focused attention on a group of women who travelled throughout the globe and are, to some extent, 'forgotten' migrants.

As Breda Gray has argued (2015), the women who take part in oral history interviews are often unaware of the significance and wider appeal of their personal stories. Their stories often go beyond or complicate the official, public accounts of history by, for example, shining a light on issues that may be ignored or under-represented in formal historical texts.

In a similar vein, Joanne Devlin Trew notes:

> Stories and memories of individual lives offer insights from social, psychological and geographical perspectives on larger historical contexts by uncovering hidden histories or by supplementing the available documentary evidence (2016: 1–2).

Later in this chapter, we discuss oral history techniques in a little more detail and reflect on our own use of this research method.

To understand migration from Ireland to Britain, it is necessary also to include the perspective of those moving from the North of Ireland. In her powerful book *Leaving the North*, Trew (2016) draws on rich interview material to tell the stories of both Protestant and Catholic migrants who left their homes to move to Britain. While technically not 'international migrants' because they were moving within the borders of the United Kingdom, nonetheless, their migration also involved many similar experiences to those migrating from the South of Ireland. Although that book is not specifically about women, it does include many powerful stories by women who left Northern Ireland around the time of the Troubles.

We are very mindful of Trew's admonishment that accounts of 'Irish' migration often focus only on those leaving the Irish Free State or later the Republic of Ireland. She emphasizes the necessity to include Northern Ireland in that story. Inspired by this argument, we have deliberately taken a 'whole island' perspective and included participants from both sides of the border.

As noted in this section, over recent decades, there have been several important and highly original research studies that have added new knowledge to the story of Irish women's migration to Britain. Nonetheless, despite these important contributions, writing in 2018, Jennifer Redmond observed that there remains a dearth of research on Irish women's migration and more work needs to be done. In this book, we contribute to the story of women's migration by focusing on one group – Irish nurses in the NHS.

RESEARCHING IRISH WOMEN'S CONTRIBUTION TO BRITISH SOCIETY: NURSING IN THE NHS

Although, as noted earlier, Irish women have tended to be largely invisible within British society, there is one notable exception – the Irish nurse. Walter (2002) argues that nurses are exceptional for two key reasons: First, unlike many other Irish migrants in Britain, especially in the 1970s–80s, Irish nurses had a very positive image and reputation as hard-working carers in the NHS and, of course, the NHS is the most highly valued institution in British society.[6] Second, while many other Irish women were invisible in British society, the image of the Irish nurse is relatively more common in popular culture.

Looking at popular British TV programmes, over the last four decades or so, the character of the Irish nurse is clearly apparent in several hospital dramas. Brenda Fricker, who later won an Oscar for her role in *My Left Foot*, began her career playing an Irish nurse in the long-running British TV series *Casualty* and also had a brief role as a nurse in the soap opera *Coronation Street*. Sorcha Cusack played an Irish staff nurse, for several years, on *Holby City*, another popular TV series, and more recently a younger member of that famous Irish acting family, Megan Cusack, played an Irish student nurse on the very successful TV drama *Call the Midwife*.

The image of the Irish nurse is not just a cultural stereotype but it actually reflects statistical trends. During the Second World War and throughout the post-war period, Britain consistently drew on Ireland, along with other former colonies, as a source of trained and trainee nurses (Murray, 2017; Daniels, 1993; Yeates, 2004). During the 1960s, 11% of all nurses recruited to hospitals in the south-east of England were born in the Irish Republic (Walter, 1989). By the 1970s there were 31,000 Irish-born nurses in Britain, constituting 12% of all nursing staff (Daniels, 1993: 5–6).

According to the census in 1981, 17% of all Irish-born women employed in Britain worked in medical services, which was similar to the African Caribbean-born female group but significantly higher than the white British female population (Walter, 1989). Census data are useful because, as Walter notes, the actual number of Irish nurses employed in the NHS is difficult to determine precisely because of limited and sporadic ethnic monitoring. Thus, census data reveal that Irish women made up a very significant proportion of nurses within the NHS and that very high numbers of Irish-born women were employed right across British medical services.

---

6 https://www.thelancet.com/journals/lancet/article/PIIS0140-6736(22)01182-5/fulltext.

To generate much-needed information about Irish nurses, Walter undertook a survey in 1988 with mainly students and young, newly qualified nurses.[7] Hence, they tended to be 1980s arrivals, though some were second-generation, born in Britain to Irish parents (Walter, 1989). The survey explored the experiences of these Irish nurses, especially against the highly charged political backdrop of the 1980s. The results from that survey provide useful background for our own research, although our participants were much older and mainly from an earlier wave of migrants.

Another important contribution to the study of Irish nurses is Mary Daniels' project from the early 1990s in which she interviewed seventeen Irish-born nurses and midwives working in the Wirral near Liverpool. Her participants, from both the North and South of Ireland, migrated to train and work in the Wirral in the 1950s–1960s (Daniels, 1993) and thus are closer in age to our participants, as will be discussed in later chapters.

Adding to the body of work on Irish nurses in Britain, in 2005–6, Louise Ryan undertook a qualitative study with 26 nurses, mainly in the London area, who had migrated in the 1940s–80s (Ryan, 2007). As well as adding to our understanding of why and how those women joined the NHS, Ryan's work also explored their experiences of marriage, family life and motherhood as Irish women in Britain. That research, which became highly cited in the academic literature, contributed to analyses of how Irish women forged social networks and built their lives both as nurses and mothers and how they navigated their Irishness in contexts that were sometimes hostile and unwelcoming (Ryan, 2008).

That body of academic work by Daniels, Walter and Ryan provides an important foundation to the new research undertaken by us in this book. Those earlier, local studies in London and on the Wirral focused on particular waves of migrant nurses. Our book takes a broader geographical and historical view by including participants from across Britain and spanning seven decades of experience within the NHS.

In addition to that academic research, it is necessary to acknowledge accounts written by Irish nurses themselves.[8] We have drawn upon four books written by Irish nurses who spent their careers in the NHS. All four of these women were also participants in our oral history interviews.

7 This survey was largely based in a few hospitals in west London. 127 Irish nurses took part. These were mostly young, the vast majority aged under 26. We are grateful to the archivist at London Metropolitan University, Cathy Phillpotts, for finding the original survey data.   8 Tony Murray (2017) discusses the memoir written by Mary Morris about her nursing experiences during the Second World War but this falls outside the scope of our study of the NHS. We also note the fictional account of Irish nurses written by Maeve Kelly – *Florrie's girls* (1989) – and are

Published by Harper Element in 2015, *Sixty years a nurse* is written by Mary Hazard with Corrine Sweet. The book is an autobiographical account of one of the longest serving NHS nurses. Having left Tipperary in 1952, at the age of 17, Mary continued to work in the NHS for the next sixty years and eventually retired at the age of 79 in 2015. Her remarkable contribution was recognized with an award from the NHS on its seventeenth anniversary. The book is a vivid account of the social landscape of the time, packed full of stories of antics in the Nurses' Home, hospital life, interactions with patients and fun in London during the Swinging 60s.[9]

Elizabeth McCluskey's autobiography entitled *I did it my way* was independently published in 2017. This is the story of Elizabeth's journey from Co. Fermanagh to Britain in the 1960s. The book begins with a detailed account of growing up in poverty in rural Northern Ireland. Elizabeth travelled to London with her sister and began her nurse training in 1964. Against the backdrop of the Civil Rights Movement and the Northern Ireland Troubles, she vividly describes the discrimination she encountered in London at that time. The book is a mix of stories of her life as a nurse, mother, Civil Rights campaigner and traditional Irish dancer.

Ireland's loss Britain's gain, Irish nurses in Britain: Nightingale to millennium, published by Rainbow Valley Books in 2021, is written by Ethel Corduff, originally from Kerry, who was a nurse in the NHS for forty years. The book takes a long historical view and offers a detailed account of nursing in the context of Ireland and Britain from the nineteenth century up to the millennium. The book is based on many years of painstaking research by Ethel. It includes chapters on the important role of Irish nursing nuns and connections with Florence Nightingale, Irish-trained nurses in Britain between 1881 and 1921, Irish nurses during both the First World War and the Second World War and continues right up to the Celtic Tiger[10] era in Ireland of the 1990s and the early 2000s.

An Irish nurse, published independently in 2022, is an autobiographical account of Maureen Ryan's life as a nurse in Essex. Maureen, originally from Co. Leitrim, initially trained in Derry before pursuing nurse training in England. Arriving in Oldchurch Hospital, Essex, in 1953, she remained there for the rest of her career. The book describes her career as a psychiatric nurse, including progression to ward sister and nursing officer in the NHS.

---

grateful to Tony for drawing this to our attention.   9 For an extended discussion of this book see Murray, 2017.   10 The Celtic Tiger refers the decade of tremendous economic growth in Ireland during the late 1990s up the global financial crash in 2008.

ORAL HISTORY RESEARCH AND UNDERSTANDING NARRATIVES

Oral history can be defined as a technique that seeks to preserve accounts of historical events by recording the stories of those who participated in those events (Sommer & Quinlan, 2018). As Joanna Bornat (1989) has noted, reading historical documents in archives seems very dull in comparison with speaking to the actual participants in historical events.

Indeed, we enjoyed all the interviews immensely and felt privileged to meet women and men who had lived through so much history. However, it is necessary to reflect on the process of retelling and recording the past. It may be tempting to think that the researcher arrives, recording devices at the ready, to tap the rich vein of narratives that have lain buried for decades in the interviewee's memory bank. However, we are aware that our participants are not offering snapshots of the past (Ryan, 2006). They were not living records of historical events. Memory is the raw material of oral history but remembering is not a passive process. Oral history researchers are not attempting to capture the past, instead they are interested in how the past is represented and retold.

Stories of past events involve memory work; somethings are remembered, while others are forgotten. Moreover, there are also decisions about what is shared and what is concealed and untold. In other words, what is shared with a researcher is not necessarily all that is remembered (Gardner, 2002).

It is important to emphasize that oral historians are not necessarily concerned with assessing the accuracy or veracity of memories. As Mary Chamberlain (1997) argues, the stories participants share with us are 'cultural constructions' – shaped by particular contexts, attitudes and experiences. In other words, interviewees do not simply describe the past but actively interpret and make sense of it from the perspective of the present day. Similarly, Alastair Thomson (1998b) points out, 'we "compose" memories which help us to feel relatively comfortable with our lives ... We seek composure, an alignment of our past, present and future lives'.

Our participants were usually reflecting back on the distant past, such as their nurse training forty or fifty years ago. Revisiting past experiences, from the standpoint of their present selves, can trigger new interpretations and evaluations. Rather than simply reporting the past, they are actively re-assessing the significance of particular incidents or relationships through the benefit of hindsight (Brannen, 2013). As Sinead McDermott (2002) explains, memory work is not simply about embalming the past as 'a perfect, irretrievable moment' but rather it creates new understandings of the past (p. 390).

It is noteworthy, as mentioned earlier, that some of our participants had written memoirs and so tended to have prepared a clear narrative structure highlighting particular events, with defined dates. However, for the vast majority of our participants, talking about the past, in a clear chronological order, was a relatively new experience. Thus, their narratives tended not to follow a clear sequential structure. Many were quite hazy about dates, including some quite significant dates, as will be noted in Chapter 4. Stories were told through interconnections of particular places and people rather than neat sequences of time. The narratives tended to jump around, moving back and forth in time, and often involving a large cast of characters including relatives, friends and work colleagues.

Constructing a 'retrospective story of a life' raises practical questions about the chronological structure (Henderson et al., 2012: 25). As researchers, it was sometimes challenging to keep up with who was who and when certain events had taken place. It is important to acknowledge our role as researchers in the interview process. We were not simply passive recorders of stories. Instead, we actively participated in the memory work. The dynamic relationship between the interviewer and interviewee may impact on the content and form of the narrative (Ryan, 2023). We asked questions, prompted and probed particular stories, sought to clarify dates and events, and thus we sought to impose some sequential structure.

Therefore, the process of remembering is not always spontaneous. Moreover, people may have a stock of particular anecdotes and funny stories that they have told many times, shared with friends, honing and polishing them in the process of retelling (Ryan, 2006). We encountered a fascinating example of how some of our participants, who were friends, had honed some stories over time to the extent that they had become a shared narrative, as we will demonstrate in Chapter 4.

Hence, being aware of how stories can be shared and enhanced among family and friendship networks, we sought to include as much variety as possible in our study by interviewing different participants across a wide geographical and historical spectrum. For example, while many of our participants had sisters who were also nurses, we only interviewed two sisters among our forty-five participants.

While the key focus of our book is Irish nurses, of course, it is important to acknowledge that they were not the only overseas workers recruited to the NHS. In the next section, we briefly consider how and why so many nurses from around the world have been recruited to train and work in Britain's health service.

THE NATIONAL HEALTH SERVICE AND RELIANCE ON OVERSEAS RECRUITMENT

Nursing in Britain has long been reliant on overseas recruits. For example, during the Second World War, prior to the formation of the NHS, wartime shortages led to expanded avenues for nurse recruitment to allow for more convenient passage of 'foreign' nurses (Solano and Rafferty, 2007; Muldowney 2007; Corduff, 2021).

At the birth of the NHS in 1948, staff shortages were so critical as to threaten the institution's viability (Solano and Rafferty, 2007). Indeed, as Jinks et al. (2014) argue, nursing was unpopular as a profession and there were difficulties in recruitment leading to a 'woeful shortage of nurses' (p. 319). According to Nicola Yeates, the 'need to recruit overseas care labour to fill professional nursing posts in the NHS resulted from the failure to remedy what was perceived by British women as a poorly paid and less attractive occupation' (2004: 86). Moreover, nursing had to compete with other, better paid and more attractive, job opportunities for women in Britain 'such as secretarial work or teaching' (Jinks et al., 2014: 642). Hence, the British government launched a recruitment drive 'with a deliberate policy to attract qualified nurses and student nurses often from the former British colonies' (Jinks et al., 2014: 642).

The Nurses Act of 1949 eased the eligibility criteria, creating, in theory, few differentials between colonial and British-born nursing staff. Thus, significant numbers of recruits arrived from the colonies and former colonies (Spiliopoulos and Timmons, 2023), particularly the Irish from the 1940s through to 1980s (Ryan, 2007) and the Caribbean between the 1950s and 1960s – the so-called Windrush generation (Snow and Jones, 2010). Among the Caribbean recruits, Jamaican nurses were the largest group with between 3,000 and 5,000 working in the service by the end of 1965. By the mid-1970s, 8% of all student nurses and trainee midwives were born in the Caribbean (Snow and Jones, 2010).

In their detailed analysis of recruitment and training data from one hospital in Liverpool during the 1950s–60s, Jinks et al. note that from a sample of 641 recruits, over half, 350 were from 'Eire' (or the Irish Republic), with a further 7 from Northern Ireland, 8 from the Caribbean, 5 Nigeria and 3 Mauritius. By contrast, just over 1/3 (38%) were from England. These data are very revealing and clearly evidence the massive reliance on overseas recruits, especially from Ireland, when nursing was so unattractive to local, English-born women. Moreover, 92% of the recruits were female:[11] 'the incidence of male nurse recruits was usually small in number, apart from in specialities such as mental

---

11 In the dataset gender was not broken down by country of origin.

health nursing' (Jinks et al., 2014: 645). The fact that nursing was an overwhelmingly female occupation may also have contributed to its low pay and low status in Britain.

Driven by the labour shortages, across the economy, migration into Britain was made easier between 1948 and 1962, as colonial subjects were offered British citizenship through the 1948 Nationality Act. However, immigration restrictions were later imposed through the Commonwealth Immigration Act of 1968. Interestingly, nursing remained exempt (Jones and Snow, 2010). In fact, the health minister of the time, Enoch Powell,[12] infamous for his anti-immigration stance, actually supported the recruitment of overseas nurses (Jones and Snow, 2010). It has been argued that Powell's attitude towards migrant recruits into the NHS may be explained by his perception of overseas nurses as a source of cheap domestic labour (Kakissis, 2018). In any case, it remains clear that a) the contribution of overseas nurses to the NHS cannot be denied and b) even politicians ideologically opposed to immigration recognize the necessity of overseas nursing staff to preserve the NHS. Of course, because of the Common Travel Area agreement (B. Ryan, 2001), Irish migrants were not impacted by tightening immigration restrictions and thus remained an available source of migrant labour for Britain.

Britain's membership of the European Union, which came into effect in 1973, did not appear to immediately shift the reliance on nurses from former colonies; the proportion of EU nurse applications began rising significantly in the period between 2007 and 2016 (Perry, 2018). Meanwhile, nursing recruits from Ireland continued to remain a prominent source to the NHS until the 1990s, however, in recent decades the numbers have fallen off considerably (Buchan, 2002). During the twenty-first century, the growing Irish economy has meant that Ireland has not only seen a decline in emigration but also has become an attractive destination for incoming migration, shifting centuries' long patterns of mass, outward migration. Moreover, the shortage of nurses within the Irish health service has led to 'efforts by the Irish Department of Health to improve nurse retention, halt the outflow of nurses and encourage inward recruitment' (Buchan, 2002: 15). As a result of these changes, not only were Irish nurses staying in Ireland, but the country was, in fact, encouraging inward migration to meet capacity for the booming economy. Ireland's growing reliance on overseas nurses is clearly evidenced in the recruitment of Filipino nurses across Irish hospitals (Trinidad and Faas, 2024).

---

12 British Conservative MP Enoch Powell became notorious for his inflammatory anti-immigration speech in 1968.

Meanwhile, in Britain, NHS dependency on overseas nurses continues into the twenty-first century and a 2003 report found that '43.5% of nurses recruited to the NHS after 1999 were born outside the UK' (Simpson et al., 2010). Interestingly, the countries of origin have changed over time. For example, while the UK was within the EU, the NHS attracted large numbers of European nurses, especially from Spain (Buchan, 2007). Nonetheless, non-EU nursing recruits were also significant, with Filipino nurses being the largest group (Simpson et al., 2010).

Since the Brexit vote in 2016 and the UK exit from the EU in 2020, there has been a sustained fall in the number of nurses from an EU nationality working for the NHS (Spiliopoulos and Timmons, 2023; Baker, 2022). As well as the Philippines, other important sources of new nursing recruits are former British colonies including India, Nigeria, Zimbabwe and Ghana (Baker, 2022; see also Okougha & Tilki, 2010). Thus, irrespective of where migrants come from, it is apparent that the NHS's reliance on overseas staff has continued throughout its 75-year history and is likely to continue in the future.

CONCLUSION

In this chapter, we have presented a brief overview of the relevant academic literature on Irish migration, especially women's migration. Despite some important contributions to the study of Irish female migration, including several oral history studies, there is still a need for more work on this relatively under-researched aspect of Irish history (Redmond, 2018). Indeed, despite the huge numbers of Irish women who migrated to Britain in the twentieth century, there is little recognition within British society of the significant contribution made by these women migrants (Walter, 2002; Gray, 2004). Irish women have been largely invisible in studies of migration within British academia.

As we have shown in this review chapter, from its inception in 1948, the NHS struggled to attract British women into nursing and therefore relied heavily on overseas recruitment (Yeates, 2004; Jinks et al., 2014). Irish women made up one of the largest groups recruited into the nursing profession, especially during the 1950s–70s, constituting around 12% of nursing staff (Daniels, 1993).

Given the prevalence of Irish nurses, the lack of research on this important topic is somewhat surprising. In this book, we build on the pioneering work of Walter, Daniels and Ryan, as well as the writing by some Irish nurses, such as Mary Hazard, Elizabeth McCluskey, Maureen Ryan and Ethel Corduff. Based on original oral history research with our forty-five participants, we now seek to add new insights into the story of Irish nurses in the NHS and, in so doing, to advance understanding of this important but hitherto under-researched aspect of migration history. In the next chapter we begin with stories of recruitment and why our participants came to be attracted to nursing as a profession.

CHAPTER 3

'I up and went': stories of nurse recruitment

> My aunt, who lived near Middlesbrough, was on holiday with us as she usually came nearly every year and she said to me, she said: 'you know, you might wait forever for your call here. You should come back to England with us and apply to Middlesbrough General and do your general (nursing), do you not fancy that?' So, I mean I was seventeen-and-a-half and the world's your oyster and I just didn't think twice about it. I up and went. (Aisling migrated to Middlesbrough in 1950)

In this chapter, we hear the nurses' stories of migration. We begin by exploring whether they had always wanted to be nurses, if it was a 'vocation' since their childhood days, or if nursing was a career path they pursued for other, more pragmatic, reasons.

Then, we move on to explore the active NHS recruitment throughout Ireland and how that influenced migration decisions and pathways into nursing. We discuss the role of newspaper advertisements in promoting the idea of doing nurse training in Britain. We also look at the application processes and memories of being interviewed. But that is not to suggest that young people were simply plucked out of Ireland by the lure of NHS recruitment campaigns. Many participants, like Aisling above, had aunts, sisters and cousins who were also nursing in Britain. These relatives had encouraged our participants to travel across the Irish Sea and enrol in training programmes. Thus, we examine the interplay of different factors, including the quest for adventure, the lure of networks of friends and relations, and pragmatic decisions, against the backdrop of harsh economic conditions and limited opportunities for women in 1950s–60s Ireland. Thus, we build upon the wider academic migration research, discussed in Chapter 2, and, in so doing, advance understandings of why these young people left Ireland to become nurses in Britain.

'I ALWAYS WANTED TO BE A NURSE'

Some participants stated emphatically that, since childhood, they had always wanted to be nurses. As Aileen put it succinctly: 'I would say probably from my earliest memory I always wanted to be a nurse.'

For several participants, wanting to be a nurse was linked to particular childhood experiences. For example, Ruth, who came from a very large family of eleven children, 'always wanted to be a nurse.' As she explained:

> I think it probably came into the picture when I was at primary school, because if another child fell over in the playground or something, I was the one always to soothe them and actually make them feel better. I came from a big family as well, I came from a family of eleven. I was the third eldest, and there were eight younger children in the family, so I was quite used to nursing and looking after children. So, I think it was a natural progression to go into nursing and make nursing a career. (Ruth)

Similarly, Mairead, who grew up on a farm in Co. Sligo in the west of Ireland, observed:

> I did have experience of looking after my young brother who was seven years younger than me, and I thought he was mine. So, we had a farm, my mother would be out milking cows in the morning and if the baby cried I was the one that attended to him, and I kind of liked that ... I think it was sort of part of me, it was ingrained, it was in some part of my nature to look after people. (Mairead)

Jacky also grew up on a farm but rather than looking after people, it was caring for animals that inspired her into a career in midwifery:

> I witnessed the cows and the sheep, and they were all giving birth in the fields and as children we roamed those fields. I have one memory actually of being at home as a young child ... 10-ish. I had a new coat, I remember particularly a new brown coat. I saw this cow giving birth and I thought I can't leave this calf out here, it was a terrible day, raining and miserable. I wrapped this calf in the brown coat, brought the calf into the house. Needless to say, I thought I had done such a wonderful deed and I got into terrible trouble, separating the mother and the calf. (Jacky)

Julia, who also went on to train as a midwife, remembered her passion for caring even at a young age:

> I can remember with our dog, I used to put a pillowcase on my head and pretend it was a veil ... And I used to bandage our dog's tail and bandage his legs, and he sat there very quietly and let me do it, and if anybody said

they had a sore finger, I had to be allowed to bandage it. I don't ever remember wanting to be anything else but a nurse. (Julia)

Those participants who had a lifelong passion for nursing seemed to share an interest in looking after people and caring for others, even in their childhood. Bridget, who grew up in Co. Tipperary, had clear childhood memories of wanting to look after people: 'I decided I wanted to be a nurse very early on.' Similarly, Anita also stated that she had wanted to be a nurse since childhood. At 12 years of age, she used to spend time looking after her father who was seriously ill: 'I always had it in my head I would like to do nursing'. In particular, the uniform appealed to her: 'I just liked the idea of the uniform, I think'. (Anita)

Niamh recalled an abiding childhood memory where the idea of being a nurse and wearing the smart uniform first occurred to her:

> When my brother was little an ambulance came to take him to hospital and I remember the ambulance pulling into our street and I saw this nurse in the front of the ambulance and I thought, 'What a wonderful job. I would love to do that.' I was only maybe seven or eight years at the time but that thought kept in my mind. I kept telling my mum, 'I would like to be a nurse.' (Niamh)

While these particular women had a burning desire to be nurses, the pathways into training were filled with obstacles as nurse training in Ireland, at that time, was very expensive and oversubscribed.

'YOU COULDN'T AFFORD TO PAY': BARRIERS TO NURSE TRAINING IN IRELAND

It has been noted that nurse training opportunities in the Irish Republic[1] were extremely limited and expensive (Daniels, 1993). Across our interviews, it was repeatedly emphasized that becoming a nurse in Ireland was not possible because of limited training places, high costs, and the need for 'pull' to obtain a place. One participant summed up the challenges she encountered:

---

1 The health systems in Northern Ireland and the Republic of Ireland were significantly different. The NHS was being rolled out across the UK including Northern Ireland. However, it is curious that so few of our participants considered training in hospitals in the North. The experiences of those who did apply to Northern Irish hospitals will be discussed later in this chapter.

> I wanted to apply to Dublin to the Mater Hospital, but I looked into the costs of books and clothes, and everything was colossal so I couldn't afford to do that. So, my mum said she couldn't afford it. (Anita)

Similarly, Caitriona also pointed to the high costs of training in Ireland: 'The thing is in Ireland, you had to pay to become a nurse ... so, if you were from a poor family, you couldn't afford to pay.'

For Ruth it was not only the cost but the lack of available training places in Ireland that posed the biggest barrier: 'I actually applied to a couple of places in Ireland, but I found that they were very oversubscribed, and it was actually quite hard to get into nursing in Ireland.'

Because nursing was so oversubscribed in Ireland, there was a long waiting list and so it could take several years for applicants to get on to the course:

> I decided to do nursing, I was about 19, and then I made enquiries to train in Dublin, but you had to wait years, because nursing in Ireland then was so, so popular ... So I couldn't wait that long. (Angela)

Given, the shortage of available places, it seemed that 'pull' was required to get into nurse training in Ireland (see also Daniels, 1993):

> you could never get into training in Ireland unless you knew somebody already. There was very much a thing, well it's a bit like nepotism really isn't it, I suppose, you either had to know somebody or your father knew somebody or something, life wasn't easy ... (Sheila)

Jacky agreed that nepotism or 'pull' was essential to gain access to nurse training in Ireland: 'You had to know somebody ... pull.' Interestingly, although she spent most of her career working as a nurse in Scotland, she had actually trained in a hospital in the North of Ireland in the 1970s. She revealed how 'pull' worked in her case.

> How was it for me? It was an uncle who was a Harley Street cardiologist. He was friends (with) the matron of this hospital ... This matron had come back from London ... When I had expressed interest in doing nursing, he, this uncle, must've said, 'Oh yes, well I know somebody. I know the matron of this hospital in (city in Ireland), I shall give her your name and then you shall hopefully go through the interview process' which I was successful at. Each person had to know somebody ... there wasn't one of those girls in our group who didn't have some recommendation from somebody before they began the interview process (Jacky).

We interviewed some nurses, like Jacky, who had undertaken their initial training in Northern Ireland. Colette, originally from Co. Leitrim, applied to do nurse training in Derry. However, as a Catholic she encountered prejudice and discrimination that tainted her experience: 'I started my nurse training in Northern Ireland in Derry. Because I was a Roman Catholic I wasn't very happy, I got a lot of jibes or whatever you call it.' After 'about six months' she decided to give it up and follow the advice of a school friend who persuaded her to apply for nurse training in England instead: 'there was a lot to be said for working in Derry but I wasn't happy there to do my training, so I came to England'.

Dervla also began her initial nurse training in Derry in the mid-1960s, but after only a year, she decided to move to England and train there instead. Her reasons were not motivated by religion or discrimination but because she wanted to get away from a small town mentality. Her family owned a local business and was well known in the area:

> so I decided I had enough of the claustrophobic atmosphere because everybody knew my family so it was always being 'I know your dad, your mom, I know your aunties and cousins.' So, I felt too claustrophobic I wanted to go away somewhere where nobody knew me basically. (Dervla)

These two examples suggest that even when opportunities were available to train as a nurse in Ireland, the allure of moving away to Britain remained quite strong.

In addition, some, who had trained in Ireland, later moved to Britain to pursue specialist courses and more career opportunities. For example, Julia trained in Belfast in 1968:

> we had an English matron and she was encouraging all of us to do our midwifery. She said that you really were not a complete nurse unless you had your general, orthopaedics was an extra, and your midwifery. There were five of us that were friends, we tried to get into the Coombe and the Rotunda (Dublin), but both of them had long waiting lists and we were very impatient to get on with it while we were still in the training mode … our matron got us the name of some hospitals in Scotland. (Julia)

Given all the obstacles to training in Ireland, it seemed that looking across the Irish Sea to opportunities in Britain was the most viable alternative, as Aine explained: 'It was difficult to get in really in Ireland, quite hard to get in at the time, so I decided, "Oh well, I'll try England".'

So far, we have focused on those who had a dream, or passion, to become nurses. But it would be misleading to suggest that all our participants had aspired to a career in nursing. As discussed in the next section some 'fell' into nursing.

'NO THOUGHTS OF BECOMING A NURSE, IT JUST FELL THAT WAY'

While childhood dreams of being a nurse were a key feature of many nurses' stories, that was not the case for all forty-five participants. In fact, the numbers were fairly evenly split between those who always wanted to be nurses and those who had no prior aspirations towards the profession.

Eilish stated emphatically: 'No, I never even thought about it, to be honest'. Maeve also had no idea of becoming a nurse: 'None whatsoever. I think the careers advice in secondary school wasn't particularly helpful unless you were going into teaching. They never really mentioned nursing to me'. While Maeve had not been informed about nursing, while at school, this was not the case for all our participants. Fiona was encouraged to consider nursing by one of her teachers who was a nun:

> I really don't think I had a vocation, quite frankly, for nursing. Just towards the end of my schooling in 1973 it was one of the nuns that actually mentioned about interviews for Dublin to start training as a nurse and I thought it's probably better than an office job. I want to be with people. I want to be around people. That's where it all started really (Fiona).

Like Fiona, several participants stated that, as school students, they had no idea about future career options: 'Well I didn't know what I wanted' (Helen). This point was echoed by Kitty: 'No. We didn't know what we wanted to do, to be honest, but they were recruiting for nurses going abroad and whatever, so, that was lovely.' As will be discussed throughout this chapter, the active recruitment campaigns led by the NHS, across Ireland, often persuaded young people, who had no prior plans to pursue nursing, to take up the opportunity. As Fiona remarked: 'I thought, "Oh, well, let's give it a go".'

As a result, some participants said they became nurses almost by chance. Interestingly, two separate interviewees, who did not know each other, used exactly the same expression. Maeve said: 'I think I fell into nursing rather than having aspired to be a nurse'. Echoing those words Sinead stated: 'I had no thoughts really of becoming a nurse, it just fell that way'.

Sheila, who went on to enjoy a long and very successful career in the NHS (see Chapter 7), put it rather nicely when she explained that: 'I wasn't one of these children who said, "Oh I want to be a nurse".' Instead of pursuing nursing, she felt that nursing actually found her: 'I think that found me rather than me finding, me wanting, it'.

A few participants had actually wanted to pursue entirely different careers. After leaving school, Veronica worked in a bookshop for several years and had aspirations to pursue a career in literature. Aoife wanted to be a hairdresser but was actively discouraged by her mother: 'I wanted to do hairdressing and my mother said, "All you do as a hairdresser is wash people's dirty hair!"'

While many participants who had not especially wanted or even thought of a career in nursing went on to have thoroughly enjoyable careers in the profession, a few felt regrets. Linda never wanted to be a nurse, in fact, she really wanted to be an air stewardess and her dream was to work for the Irish national carrier Aer Lingus. This idea stayed with her for many years, even during her nurse training she was still tempted by the allure of air travel. Now, looking back, although having had a long nursing career, she often wonders if she should have tried to get a job with Aer Lingus.

Indeed, several participants actually saw nursing as a route to travel further afield. Sorcha pursued nurse training because she had a long-term goal of going to work in the US, to join her much-loved older brother. Ciara also stated that: 'I applied for nursing because I thought it would be a good opportunity for travel. So that's my main thing.' The perception of nursing as a pathway to travel was common among our participants. Having completed her training in Northern Ireland, Jacky was keen to work as a nurse overseas:

> a few of us decided we would like to travel, we just wanted to travel. We didn't really mind where we were going. Some people expressed Australia, New Zealand, wherever. We thought let's start looking a little bit closer to home. So, we looked at Britain (Jacky).

As we will discuss in Chapter 7, a number of our participants did get to experience nursing in countries like the US and Canada.

The appeal of nursing needs to be understood against the backdrop of Irish society in the 1950s–60s (see Daniels, 1993; Walters, 1988; Ryan, 2007). As noted in Chapter 2, for young girls growing up in Ireland in the post-war decades, career options were extremely limited (Travers, 1997; O'Carroll, 1990; Lennon et al., 1988; Redmond, 2018). As Aisling stated bluntly: 'you can imagine in the 1950s it was nigh impossible to get a job'. Caitriona explained:

'in our generation either you went into nursing or teaching or into domestic, as women'. Una reflected that so many people went into nursing 'mainly because there was nothing else they could do'.

Many participants had felt there was no future for them in rural Ireland. Maeve grew up in the west of Ireland in a large family of twelve: 'if I want to do anything for myself, I can't live in Mayo, in the countryside, so I have got to take some positive steps to get myself into a better place and that's what I did'.

Similarly, Miriam, who also came from a large family, was keen to get away and improve her life chances:

> getting away from the country life ... something more exciting ... I wanted freedom. I was the eldest of eight and I was always babysitting, looking after other ones. I just wanted to be able to not have any responsibility, I suppose. That was really my reason.

Rather than being attracted to nursing per se, several participants, including Miriam, stated that it was the opportunity to go to Britain, with security of a guaranteed job and accommodation, that especially appealed to them:

> I wanted to get away from home. I wasn't quite sure that I wanted to do nursing but at least I was somewhere that my parents would agree because there was accommodation ... that pleased my father no end that we would be well looked after (Miriam).

Orla summed up the appeal of nurse training in Britain succinctly when she said: 'It's a way of getting away actually without taking too many risks'.

Claire, noting the lack of career opportunities for women in Ireland, said that applying for nursing in Britain was 'probably a way of changing my life, yes, in my head I thought that ... So, it was more as a means to an end'.

As mentioned earlier (see Chapter 2), such was the growing public and political concern about the large numbers of young women leaving the Irish countryside, that a Commission was set up to investigate the root causes (Travers, 1997). The nurses in our study echo many of the underlying reasons noted by the Commission: the desire to get away from limited, traditional roles, in small farming communities and to find better opportunities and lifestyles elsewhere (Ryan, 2008).

We were interested to observe that several of our participants had grown up in the care system in Ireland. One of them explained that, although she had not thought about a career in nursing, pursuing nurse training in Britain was an ideal escape route: 'It was a route out.' For these young people, leaving institutional settings, without family support or the financial resources to pursue further study in Ireland, nurse training in Britain held a particular appeal as a route into a stable and secure career with the added incentive of guaranteed accommodation and payment while they trained.

As noted earlier, the fact that nurse training in Britain not only seemed so alluring but also so accessible to all these young Irish people reflects, at least in part, the enormous success of the NHS advertising and recruitment campaign throughout the whole island of Ireland during the 1950s–70s. In the next section we explore that recruitment process in more depth.

'THEY'RE COMING TO ME': NHS RECRUITMENT IN IRELAND

Since its inception in 1948, the NHS carried out a targeted recruitment process throughout Ireland. Advertisements were placed not only in the big national dailies, like the *Irish Independent*, but also in local papers in every province of the country.

These advertisements usually announced that the recruitment team would be in local hotels on particular dates and anyone interested in an interview should write to make an appointment. The advertisements were worded in a very enticing way. In addition, to being paid while training and having accommodation in the Nurses' Home, many advertisements also promised nursing students the extra incentive of paid travel back to Ireland for annual holidays.

Many of our participants recalled seeing these advertisements but, unsurprisingly given the passage of time, over fifty years or more, were vague about the precise details. As Pauline recalled: 'I must have seen an advert or something in the newspaper and I applied to England'.

Nonetheless, a few did remember exactly where they saw the advertisement for nurse training in Britain. Kathleen went to train in Liverpool in 1968: 'I remember the name of it, the *Northern Constitution* was the name of the paper and that's where the advert was'. Similarly, Aileen recalled 'in the *Sunday Press* at home and I saw the ad and I applied'.

Advertisements were also placed in Catholic newspapers. For example, Ruth vaguely recalled seeing the ad for nursing recruits in 'one of the Catholic newspapers', while Veronica remembered clearly that she saw the ad in '*The Universe*', the main Catholic newspaper: '*The Universe*, yes, and there were two hospitals advertised – one was in Eastbourne and another was in Stoke-on-Trent'.

NORTH LIVERPOOL HOSPITAL MANAGEMENT COMMITTEE
Walton Hospital, Liverpool 9
(1,400 Beds.)
STUDENT NURSES.

STUDENT Nurses are required for this hospital, which is a recognised training school for both general nursing and Part 1 Midwifery. It contains 1,400 beds, and Nurses obtain a very wide experience as all types of cases are admitted.

Nurses are given a three-year course of training required for admission to the General Section of the Register of the General Nursing Council, and the status of State Registered Nurse after the appropriate examination.

There is a Preliminary Training School and a large Tutorial Staff, and every facility provided to enable students to pass their examinations.

Training Allowances.
First year of training £200
Second year of training £210
Third year of training £225

Board, lodging, uniform and laundry etc., is provided, for which a charge of £100 per annum is made.

In addition, dependants' allowances will be payable to help those with family responsibilities.

Nurses reside in a comfortable Nurses Home, where separate bedrooms are provided, and many social and sports amenities. Travelling expenses, etc., from home to Hospital paid to candidates when reporting for duty.

Applications should be addressed to the Matron.

F. J. WATKINS, Secretary to the Committee.

North Liverpool Hospital Management Committee, 4th January, 1949.   7675

SUBSCRIPTION RATES

	£	s	d
3 Months		19	6
6 Months	1	19	0
12 Months	3	18	0

Cork Examiner

WEDNESDAY, JANUARY 12, 1949.

Cork Examiner (now the *Irish Examiner*), 1949

However, others stated that while they could not remember exactly where they saw the ad, there was common knowledge at the time that hospitals in Britain were actively recruiting for student nurses with very favourable terms and conditions: 'It was like general knowledge really' (Gretta).

As Maeve explained:

> I mean it was everywhere ... very wide advertisement in Ireland at the time ... and I think it may be on the radio originally that we heard it because we didn't really go and buy the paper, so the radio was on all the time, so it must have been by the radio we originally heard it. (Maeve)

Information about recruitment to nurse training in Britain seemed to be circulating around Ireland through various means: 'It seemed to be like word of mouth as well, you know, other friends, but there was also a campaign, an advertising campaign at that time in Ireland for nurses in England' (Kathleen).

The role of word of mouth is demonstrated by Sinead who was originally from Kerry. Having completed her Leaving Certificate,[2] she was doing a commercial course when one of the girls in her class got an interview for nursing training in Britain: 'she said, "Oh I've got an interview for nursing next week in Cork". I said, "Have you? How did you get that?" So she told me'. Sinead also applied and was invited for an interview. She remembered getting the train from Kerry to the hotel in Cork. Like several other participants, Sinead appreciated especially the ease of going to interviews in nearby towns and cities around Ireland:

> being honest, I had no thoughts about going to London, it was just the fact the interview was in Cork ... it was convenient. I didn't have to travel anywhere, I just had to get the train from Kerry to Cork, I got the train, went on my own. (Sinead)

Orla, originally from Cork, while noting the difficulty of getting into nurse training in Ireland, due to long waiting lists and high costs, emphasized the apparent ease of gaining access to nurse training in Britain:

> there were adverts and I wrote off to some of the places advertising nursing places and there was one group coming to interview at the Intercontinental Hotel in Cork and I thought, 'Oh that's great, I don't even have to find them, they're coming to me' and that's after I'd been for, I think, some of the local hospitals and was told there was this waiting list. (Orla)

---

2 Irish school examination undertaken at 17 or 18 years of age and equivalent to A-Levels.

PUBLIC NOTICES

GAME NOTICE.
Persons found trespassing on my lands at Fortland, Easkey, in pursuit of rabbits or game will be prosecuted.
Signed—
J. P. HIGGINS.

RUNWELL HOSPITAL, NEAR WICKFORD, ESSEX.

STUDENT NURSES & NURSING ASSISTANTS REQUIRED, 18 Years and Over.

The training period for Student Nurses is three years, during which allowances of from £255 to £280 a year are paid. Upon passing the preliminary qualifying examinations students receive a bonus of £40; a further bonus of £50 is paid on passing the final examination. A qualified nurse receives a salary of from £405 to £505 a year, and becomes eligible for promotion to a position with a maximum salary of £595 a year.

Nursing Assistants, who are not required to pass examinataions, receive from £280 to £425 a year.

There is a modern, well-equipped Nurses' Home with single bedrooms and good recreation rooms equipped with radio and television. The charge to student nurses and nursing assistants for full board, laundry and uniform is £108 a year.

Runwell Hospital is the newest Mental Hospital in England and the staff work under exceptionally good conditions. Facilities are provided for Roman Catholics to carry out their religious obligations; there is a Chapel and the Priest is an officially appointed Hospital Chaplain.

The Hospital is 40 miles from London and 13 miles from Southend-on-Sea, one of the largest resorts in England.

Many Irish girls have made very successful careers on the nursing staff.

The Matron will be pleased to answer enquiries from girls who are interested, or their parents.
T. FITZROY KELLY,
Secretary.

LOCAL APPOINTMENTS COMMISSION.

MEDICAL POSITION VACANT.

RADIOLOGIST, SLIGO COUNTY

ST. FRANCIS HOSPITAL, HAYWARDS HEATH, SUSSEX, ENGLAND.

Women (age 18-35) accepted as Student Nurses for training in nervous and mental nursing. Deals with all types of brain illness from minor nervous states up to conditions requiring major brain surgery. Fast electric trains to London and Brighton. First class residential accommodation. Full recreational facilities—games, dances, etc. Religious services and Catholic Nurses' Guild in Hospital. Annual cash training allowances commencing at £255 and the addition of dependants' allowances where applicable, also cash allowance of £40 on passing preliminary examination, and £50 on passing final examination. A deduction of £108 per annum in respect of board and lodging provided by the Hospital. Trained nurses qualified to hold posts up to £595 per annum. Travel vouchers supplied. Matron pleased to supply further details to applicants or parents.

LEITRIM COUNTY COUNCIL.

ERECTION OF THREE HOUSES AT KILTYCLOGHER.

Tenders are invited from competent contractors for the erection of three houses at Kiltyclogher and all works incidental thereto.

Full particulars and Forms of Tender may be obtained from R. H. Dowling, Architect, 8 Merrion Sq. North, Dublin, or the undersigned, on payment of a deposit of £5, returnable on completion of Bond or rejection of tender.

Sealed Tenders on the prescribed form only and endorsed "Kiltyclogher Housing," must be lodged with the undersigned not later than Tuesday, 23rd November, 1954, at 5 o'clock p.m.

The lowest or any tender not necessarily accepted.
By Order,
L. KEAVENY,
Co. Secretary.
Courthouse,
Carrick-on-Shannon.

Sligo Champion, 1954

Apart from the newspaper advertisements, the interviews by NHS recruiters in local hotels could also pique the curiosity of some teenagers. Finnuala was 18 years old and just finished school in the early 1970s. At that time, she had no plan to pursue nurse training in Britain. One Saturday afternoon, she and a friend went to Cork city to do some shopping.

> I was in town with my friend, and in the Metropole Hotel there was a sign that said, 'Do you want to come to London?' I went, 'Yes, of course!' 'Have you got the Leaving Cert?' 'Yes.' 'Come in for an informal talk.' So, we went in, and it was a Miss M, who was the head nurse at (London) Hospital.
>
> She sold it to us ... because there was nothing in Cork, and I came home and said to my mother, 'I'm going to be a nurse.' 'Oh, I'm so proud,' she said. 'Are you going to St Finbarr's?' And I said, 'No, I'm going to London.' She wasn't very happy, but in the end anyway, she relented, and that's how we made the steps to come here (Finnuala).

It may seem strange that girls of 17 or 18 years of age would pack up and leave Ireland simply on the basis of a recruitment campaign enticing them to go to Britain and become a nurse. As described by Finnuala above, the decisions sometimes seemed rather spontaneous and even surprised their families. These decisions need to be understood against the culture of migration in Irish society at that time (see Ryan, 2008). As noted in the previous chapter (Chapter 2), in a society where female migration was so prevalent and taken for granted (Walter, 2002; Gray, 2004), getting the boat to Britain seemed almost routine. The process was not necessarily straightforward though. While some, like Finnuala, happened upon the interviews for nursing almost by accident, others had to apply in writing and sit entrance exams. In the next section we look at the application process in more detail.

APPLICATION PROCESS

There is some variety in how people secured their training place in Britain. Several, like Orla and Finnuala, above, were interviewed in hotels in cities like Cork but others were interviewed in smaller towns around the country.

One of our oldest participants, Gretta, was recruited from a small town in 1948:

> Well I had a friend at home in Clonakilty. So we were talking and we both decided we should go ... and be a nurse ... There was a matron ... came to the local hotel and she would kind of interview you and make

arrangements if you really wanted it. So, we agreed, and we both went to the hotel and really it went from there.

Others had to travel to Dublin. Maeve, who grew up in the west of Ireland, recalled travelling, with her sister, across the country to attend the interview in Dublin:

> So we both applied. Because I had already got my results, my Leaving Cert results, I got accepted … So, we rocked off to Dublin, had our interview. I got accepted but (sister) had to wait for her results. When she got it, we were both accepted. (Maeve)

Some participants had only a very vague recollection of the interview itself. As Maeve reflected: 'I don't really remember much about it, no. I don't even remember what she asked me or anything. I mean if somebody said to me, "what were you asked?" I'd think, "Oh, I don't know".' Similarly, Claire could not recall any details about her interview: 'Very vaguely, extremely vaguely … It's weird, really vague.' Other participants were similarly hazy:

> all I can remember is my mother taking me on the train to Dublin to be interviewed by a matron who was a nun for a Catholic hospital in Surrey, to be interviewed for nursing. And I can't even remember what the interview was … anyway, I was successful. (Sheila)

Caitriona was recruited to work in a hospital in Manchester in 1960, a city where she still lived when we met on her 85th birthday. She did her nursing interview in one of Dublin's most famous hotels:

> The interview was in Ireland, in the Gresham Hotel … Yeah, it was very posh but the point was I think because they came from England and obviously, the English government was paying, we weren't paying anything. We didn't stay overnight, we were there for about three hours. (Caitriona)

Some people remembered odd snip-bits of conversation or funny remarks from the interview. It is noteworthy that many of these teenage girls had only a vague idea of what nursing would entail and now, looking back, with the benefit of hindsight, they recall how innocent or naïve they were at the time:

> Back in the day we had a business, my family were butchers … I remember even saying in my interview, 'Oh, my father's a butcher so I'm used to

blood!' I remember saying that in my interview, you know what I mean? 'Oh, okay!' that was my selling point, I think. (Sinead)

By contrast, others remembered the interview vividly as a somewhat unnerving experience. Aileen – from Co. Mayo – went for her interview to a hotel in Dublin. She was met by her aunt who was nursing in a Dublin hospital.

> I can tell you the biggest worry I had was, 'Where would my parents find the money to send me to Dublin for the interview?' And I went up and my Aunt was a nurse in Dublin at the time … she picked me up at the station and took me to this hotel. There was the lady interviewer – and that's the Head of Nursing and her associate was with her, Mrs F … This room full of like, I suppose, all my age and maybe older and some had their mammies and their sisters and their aunties, some were on their own.
>
> And she (Mrs F) said, 'Anyone who'd like to bring their mother or whoever with them into the interview, please do.' And I remember nearly having a heart attack, thinking, 'My God, Aunt come into the interview with me? She's going to tell (my parents) if I made an awful mess of that [laughs]. Whereas if I made a mess, I wouldn't really have to tell anyone, would I? And anyways, when they called my name, I tell you, I shot out of that chair and I was sitting in front of Miss M faster than … [laughs]. And then there was a knock on the door: Mrs F with my Aunt. Oh, God almighty (!)
>
> Anyways, she came in and in the end it was a godsend because herself and Miss M had trained in the same era, over here. So they really interviewed each other, had a nice chat [laughs] and Miss M ended up by saying, 'If you pass English and Maths,' she said, 'Come over in September, there'll be a place for you.' And that was it. (Aileen).

As this humorous anecdote reveals, relatives, especially aunts, often played a key role in the recruitment, application and interview process. In a later section, we will consider networks in more detail.

Curiously, for some applicants, the entire recruitment process was completed by post.

> No, we didn't actually attend any interviews. It was actually all done on paperwork and applications and education certificates. Whatever they looked for we sent along, like you did, and got accepted … It was all done by post very successfully. (Ruth)

The apparent ease with which people applied by post and were offered places on nurse training course seems quite remarkable.

> I wrote to a lot of hospitals. Everyone I wrote to I was accepted – one was Liverpool, Manchester and in Romford. I chose Romford, I went there in 1952 and I started in the October. (Colette)

Prior qualifications mattered and those with Leaving Certificates often found the whole process quite straightforward. In the Irish Republic, secondary school education only became free to all in 1967. Before that time, it was only the affluent middle classes and large farmers, who could pay for their children's education up to Leaving Cert level (see Daniels, 1993). After free secondary schooling was introduced, many of our participants, who applied for nurse training in the late 1960s and early 1970s, had been able to complete their education up to their Leaving Certificates.

For example, in the early 1970s, Eilish applied to a hospital in Leeds just before receiving her Leaving Cert results:

> Do you know, isn't it funny, I can't remember ever going for an interview, but it must have been done by letter, and then just wait for your results to come out. You would go with the guarantee that you could start your training, but you had to wait till your leaving certificate result came out.

However, Eilish was disappointed when her Leaving Cert results arrived:

> I didn't actually do as well as I thought I would have done in my Leaving Cert, and at that time they had two levels of training. They had the SRN,[3] which was the state registered nurse, and then there was SEN, which was the state enrolled nurse.
>
> I remember crying when I opened my results and I thought there's no way, I can't even remember what they were now, but I'm not going to get on to do the state registered nursing, but I did get in to do the state enrolled nurse, which was a two-year course. (Eilish)

As discussed later (see Chapter 5), Eilish did eventually succeed, many years later, in attaining her SRN qualification.

---

[3] SRN – State Registered Nursing, SEN – State Enrolled Nursing – will be discussed in more detail in Chapter 5.

However, completing the entire process by post meant that these young people were applying to hospitals they did not know and to geographical locations they may never even have heard of before. For example, Pauline applied by post to a hospital in Kent: 'I think they would be just names on a map, I'd have probably a vague idea that I was relatively near London.' A similar point was made by Bronagh who also applied by letter and did not know anything about the locality of the hospital: 'Didn't even know where it was ... My mother didn't know where it was. None of us knew where (it) was.' The reality of finding themselves in remote, rural locations, far from social amenities that they had expected to enjoy in British cities, will be discussed in a later chapter (see Chapter 6).

Moreover, the postal service was not always quite so reliable. One nurse explained that her application got lost in the post and she had to wait for months to be accepted on a training programme in Scotland:

> Three of us were accepted but two of the girls had gone ahead three months before me, because my paperwork got lost in the post. I was delayed and I was very upset at the time because it was the end of the world. I thought if that happens I may not be accepted now at all. Anyhow, I did come along three months later. (Jacky)

Overall, for those with good school results, the application process was largely straightforward. However, those without such certificates, or who did less well than expected, faced more challenging processes, as explained by Nessa. Having completed her education up to Intermediate Certificate (Inter Cert)[4] in Ireland, she applied in writing to a hospital in Yorkshire in 1957, just before her 18th birthday, without needing to do an interview or any entrance tests.

> Yes, we had to fill in an application form and we were, because we had done our Inter Certs, we were allowed to start because that was on the same lines as the O-Levels here. Now, some nurses that went over that didn't have Inter Certs and Leaving Certs, they had to sit an exam before they would be taken on as nurses. (Nessa)

As mentioned, earlier, Irish secondary school education only became free to all in 1967. Hence, it is unsurprising that many of our interviewees did not have Leaving Certificates when they applied for nurse training in Britain. Interestingly, not having a Leaving Cert did not preclude applicants from

---

4 An Irish school exam usually undertaken around age 16 and equivalent to GCSEs or O Levels.

nursing in the NHS, but they needed to sit entrance exams instead. We interviewed several nurses who described sitting entrance exams at British hospitals. For example, Miriam had to do an exam after her arrival in London and was anxious in case she failed the test and was sent home: 'it certainly focuses you because I was not going to go back home and say I didn't get an intelligence test'.

The exams were scheduled to take place a few months after her arrival, so Miriam was allowed to work in the hospital as an auxiliary (nursing assistant) while she waited.

> Once I'd seen Matron, the day after I arrived, she told me the exam was going to be on such a date and 'until then you will work here and if you fail the exam, you will be returning to Ireland at the end of that because we don't do any other training, it's SRN or nothing'. She said: 'make sure you read up on your English and your Maths because the exam is mainly English and Maths and you've got plenty of time to do it and I'm going to send you to a ward where there's an Irish sister and she will show you what to do and she will see if you're worth training.' (Miriam)

Luckily, Miriam passed the exam and soon afterwards began her training and we will hear more about that in Chapter 5.

Trisha, who applied to a hospital in Essex, also had to wait for months in order to sit the entrance exam but she decided to pursue another opportunity instead: 'and then you had to sit an exam when you came over to get in for training … they said to come over. I could work as an auxiliary nurse for the six months or whatever, which I did'. However, shortly after arriving in Essex, Trisha was encouraged to apply for nurse training at a London hospital and jumped at the chance.

> And then I met a very good friend, who's still my friend, from Tipperary and she said, 'Look, why don't we go and do it in (London hospital)?' Because she had worked (there), she was trained already. So I applied, and I got in. (Trisha)

Sean, one of our two male participants, had applied to do his nurse training in the North of Ireland, close to his hometown, but was turned down, so instead he applied to do his training in Yorkshire. He related the experience of sitting the entrance exam in Sheffield:

> the tutor pretended to lock the doors because he hadn't seen scores like that for years. Because there was full employment in Sheffield, in things like the steel industry and nobody was going to work for £7 a week in a psychiatric hospital, you know. (Sean)

This anecdote may partly explain why so much recruitment was undertaken in Ireland. In the context of full employment in cities like Sheffield, with thriving industry in the 1960s, it was very difficult to attract people into nursing. The tutor pretended to lock the door so that Sean and his friend did not leave. They were immediately offered places on the psychiatric training course.

Also in Yorkshire, Niamh applied to a hospital in Leeds in 1958: 'because I had no qualifications, I had to do an entrance exam'. She had to travel to Leeds to sit the exam.

> It was mostly English and Maths which I think I had a good basic knowledge of English and Maths from my primary education and there were six of us. There were four English girls, there was a black girl and there was me. At the end of the day, we were all called back for interview and the four English girls had failed and the black girl and me had passed … (Niamh)

Travelling to Britain to sit the tests also involved the worry, as mentioned earlier by Miriam, that if they failed they would have to return to Ireland. However, such was the demand for recruits that they were usually offered another form of nursing, such as auxiliary or enrolled nursing, if they failed the exams for state registered nursing (SRN). As Niamh explained: 'Well, actually, it did say in the letter that if I fail the exam, I could train to be an enrolled nurse'.

One nurse shared her experience of failing the test first time around: 'I applied to nursing when I was about 18, in Coventry. So, then they said to do an IQ test. Well an IQ test you have to prepare for, but nobody told me anything. Anyhow, I didn't get in' (Angela). However, she learned from this disappointment and prepared the next time around. When she applied to a hospital in London, a year later, Angela had no difficulties in passing.

As well as travelling to Britain to do entrance exams, a few participants had also travelled to British hospitals to do their interviews. Aisling arrived for her interview at a hospital in Middlesbrough in 1950. As noted, in the opening quote to this chapter, Aisling had an aunt living in that city who had encouraged her to come and pursue nurse training there.

> And I came over to Middlesbrough in 1950, September 1950, and I applied to (hospital) to do my general training. I went and had an interview and I was accepted straight away and I started my training in October of that year. I like to think, you know when you're 17 and half, you've got a load of confidence. (Aisling)

As Aisling's story illustrates, networks are a feature of many migration stories. As noted, in the previous section about newspaper advertisements, relatives such as mothers, sisters and aunts, as well as friends, often figure in the narrative as key players who facilitated or encouraged the application process. This is also the case in Fiona's account of her application to a hospital in south London.

> There I was out of school not knowing what I wanted to do, working in a supermarket getting cash in hand, basically, for my week's work in the supermarket. My aunt lived in London and she said, 'Why don't you think about interviewing?' They were interviewing in Dublin ... but because I was coming over to see her, they offered me an interview in London back in the end of '73 I think it was. Probably about October 1973. (Fiona)

ROLE OF NETWORKS

While networks ('pull') seemed to have been absolutely fundamental to securing nurse training positions in Ireland, this was not the case in Britain. The huge number of vacancies in British hospitals resulted in an open recruitment process. Nonetheless, networks did appear to be crucial in more 'indirect' ways for young Irish people considering the move to Britain. As noted by Ryan (2022; 2023), in analysing the role of social networks in accessing different kinds of jobs, social connections can operate in different ways in particular sectors of employment. For example, on the one hand, networks may play a 'direct' role in providing a job offer, such as 'pull'. However, on the other hand, networks can also play an 'indirect' role as sources of advice, information or encouragement that can enable and support someone in their job search.

Thus, it would be simplistic to state that newspaper advertisements or recruitment drives alone were responsible for this massive outflow of young Irish migrants into the NHS. Many stories about the recruitment process highlighted the key role played by other social ties, including relatives and friends. Hence, there was an interplay between NHS recruitment campaigns and the active support of social networks: 'It was the paper, I think my aunt found it in the paper' (Claire); 'my mother found an advert in the paper for student nurses' (Julia); 'my mother must have seen advertised that they were coming over from England recruiting for nurses' (Sheila).

It should be noted that a few participants said they had no pre-existing nursing networks at all. For example, Pauline explained that she didn't have any connections with anybody in nursing or any relatives in Britain who encouraged her migration: 'I came by myself'. Similarly, Colette did not know anyone prior to her arrival: 'I knew nobody there, not a soul'. As Orla put it: 'Because I hadn't ever known anybody who'd actually been a nurse in England ... so I really knew nothing about it.'

However, these stories were definitely in the minority as the vast majority of the nurses we interviewed had clear network ties which had enabled or encouraged their migration to Britain and in particular their decision to train as nurses. Interestingly, the descriptions of these significant others, who supported the migration process, were overwhelmingly female: aunts, sisters, friends and female cousins feature prominently in the narratives.

For example, Fidelma, from Roscommon, was influenced by her older cousin who had gone to Hertfordshire to do nurse training a few years earlier: 'my cousin had come over a few years before me, and I decided, right that's it, I'll apply ... she sounded as "oh it was great", and I thought yeah, I'll have some of that [laughs].'

Jane from Monaghan explained how a neighbour, home on holidays, actively encouraged herself and her friend to do nurse training in Liverpool and later arranged to meet them and show the way to the hospital: 'we were only young girls like, you know. So, she took us ... we wouldn't have known where to go or anything, we'd never been before to Liverpool or anywhere like that, so that's how we started out'.

The role of visitors, back in Ireland for holidays, as mentioned by Aisling in the opening quote to this chapter, was a recurring theme in the narratives. These visitors often played a significant role in encouraging teenagers to consider migrating to Britain or indeed to go to specific towns and cities. Another such story was narrated by Niamh:

> one day a couple appeared from Leeds. They were touring Ireland and they knew my father when he worked in Leeds in the 1930s ... my mother told them about me wanting to be a nurse so they gave my mother the address (hospital). That's what happened. (Niamh)

This visiting couple did not actually encourage the migration process or plant the idea of becoming a nurse. Niamh was already exploring opportunities to pursue nursing. However, by providing the address of a particular hospital they facilitated migration. In addition, the fact that Niamh's father had worked in Leeds during his youth may have helped to make this place seem more familiar and attractive.

Another participant, who had grown up in the care system, recounted how a friend returning from England, for the summer holidays, was a valuable source of encouragement to do nurse training. After leaving school, our participant was working in a shop and feeling bored and frustrated. She vividly recalled the day her friend came into the shop: 'and she says to me, "Why don't you come and do nursing?"' Up to that point, this participant had not considered nursing, her primary motivation was to leave Ireland where there were no career opportunities for her: 'you see, we didn't have a choice of what we did because we didn't have any money'. With the encouragement of her friend, she now began to perceive nurse training as a route to migration: 'To get over to England was a thing for us'. Without any money, nursing seemed the ideal option: 'With nursing you had accommodation, and you didn't have to pay for rent or anything, you got food, which was really just what we wanted'.

Friends and relations visiting Ireland for holidays often embodied the apparent glamour and success of the migrant life abroad. Carmel, who came originally from Donegal and migrated in 1954, told us how her aunts had influenced her decision to go to London and train as a nurse.

> At the time I had two aunts on my mother's side, both nurses, having trained here in England. The thing that used to fascinate me, and they often laughed afterwards when I joined nursing, was Auntie K when she came home. There were few cameras around, she was the only one who had a camera, and she used to have lovely red nails. I used to think, 'Wouldn't it be lovely to have lovely nails like that and be a nurse?'
>
> The silly thing that I was thinking about the nails, going into nursing. She often had a laugh afterwards. She said, 'You'll soon find out there'll be no time for your red nails when you're in nursing'. (Carmel)

This aunt then helped Carmel to apply to the same hospital in south London, where she had also trained, many years earlier. After Carmel started her training, this aunt continued to provide support: 'She was very kind to me when I came over. Every time I had time off, she lived so close to the hospital, I used to go and spend my time with her and her daughter.'

Eilish, who also came originally from Donegal, recalled the excitement surrounding the holiday visits of her older sister who was nursing in Leeds.

> Any time she got a holiday she was always back home in Donegal … (she) used to love coming home. And we used to love her coming, because she'd come back with a full suitcase and it would be going back empty, because we'd be borrowing her clothes and then getting her to leave them with us [laughs].

Similar to Carmel's story earlier, the glamorous visitor in effect recruited the teenage Eilish to work at the same hospital.

> I just applied to come to (Leeds hospital). I had no interest in going anywhere else, simply because I had (sister) here and then I knew that I would settle easier. (Eilish)

Nursing sisters appear to have played a key role in encouraging and enabling what is termed 'chain migration'. No family demonstrated this more than the case of nurses Aoife and Una, sisters whom we interviewed together in Liverpool. Out of a family of seven sisters, six had become nurses. With several older sisters already training in Liverpool, Una explained her motivation to join them: 'I thought I'm missing my sisters, it would be much better if I went over and I did this wonderful nursing with my sisters and that's what I did.' Although Una had the chance to do teaching training in Ireland, she chose instead to join her sisters and pursue nursing and so in 1963 she set off for Liverpool, soon followed by her younger sister, Aoife.

The prevalence of nursing in many Irish families was clearly illustrated by Aileen: 'Very big nursing family, an aunt was a nurse, my sister was a nurse … cousins are nurses – there's lots, lots of nurses. Great house to be in if you kind of felt a bit unwell [laughs]'.

Thus, for several participants, going into nursing seemed natural as they followed the example of older siblings and other female relatives. The story of Nessa, originally from Sligo, who trained in a small town in West Yorkshire, shows how family networks could overlap with and reinforce formal recruitment strategies.

> My sister was already a nurse – well, she'd just qualified. Back in those days, people from over here in the hospitals, they used to come and interview girls in Ireland to go to England to train. Now, I think that's what happened with my sister but I just, when I was ready to come, I just applied and came over with my sister and then started training. (Nessa)

NHS recruiters visiting Sligo had initially recruited Nessa's older sister, she then, in turn, facilitated the recruitment of her younger sister. Likewise, Nessa encouraged her friend to go nurse training with her in the same hospital. Thus, these connections between Sligo and the Yorkshire hospital strengthened over time.

This was not an isolated case. We found several examples of links between particular locations in Ireland and specific hospitals in Britain, usually reinforced by waves of chain migration among families and friendship networks, as noted in the case of Aoife and Una and all their sisters in Liverpool, and Nessa and her sister and friend in West Yorkshire. A similar pattern was noted in Luton, where numerous members of one extended family all settled during the 1950s–60s.

Yvonne explained: 'All my family were between London and Luton ... I'm the second youngest of nine, I had lots of support and almost several sets of "parents" because people were always looking after me, so I was very immature and probably irresponsible'. Because of all her relatives in Luton, including four of her older siblings, Yvonne had actually visited on several occasions during school holidays. Thus, unlike a lot of our participants, who had never been to Britain prior to enrolling on nurse training, Yvonne was very familiar with the locality. She applied to the local hospital because she knew her siblings, especially her older sister, would be on hand to support her.

In addition to networks of relatives in Britain who encouraged or facilitated migration into nurse training, other participants described how friends in Ireland had influenced their decision-making. For example, Ruth mentioned the role of her friend: 'I had another friend, I mean two of us actually went together. She was actually keen to go into nursing as well, and we had a good chat about it, and we actually went together.'

As discussed earlier in this chapter, Linda had no aspirations to be a nurse, on the contrary, her dream was to be an air stewardess. Nevertheless, she was encouraged to pursue nursing by her school friend:

> one of my best friends, she brought *The Independent* or one of the national papers into school one day, and she saw an ad for trainee nurses in (north London), and she said, 'Oh I want to go and do my nursing, I want you to go. Come with me, let's send away, let's apply.' So I said, 'Okay,' I went along with it, not really intending to take it up. (Linda)

This story shows how a newspaper advertisement and the encouragement of a friend overlapped and led to an application. Ironically, while Linda, despite her initial misgivings, did go ahead with the training course, the friend had a change of heart and pulled out.

While for some participants there appeared to be a straightforward link between a sister or friend or cousin and the decision to pursue nurse training in Britain, in other cases, there were multiple factors and numerous network ties at play. This is clearly illustrated in the case of Bronagh, whose story opens this book (see Chapter 1), who migrated to Kent in 1965.

Her sister had a good friend who was nursing in a hospital in Kent. Through her sister, Bronagh heard stories about how much this friend was enjoying her training:

> She told me, or she obviously fed back through my sister, that they were recruiting Irish nurses, and I made contact with them, wrote a letter, (brother-in-law) helped me to write the letter ... and was surprised, almost immediately got back a reply saying that there were vacancies there and offering me a place. (Bronagh)

This story indicates the role of different network actors, the sister, her friend and the brother-in-law who helped with the letter. So rather than one single person influencing or supporting the process, it is apparent that several people were involved. This story also reveals a high level of trust in the advice of the friend of her sister — whom Bronagh did not know personally. In fact, as noted earlier, Bronagh and her family knew nothing about this hospital or the town where it was located, it was simply a name on a map. Nonetheless they were assured by the encouragement of the sister's friend: 'we had this feedback that here was somebody who had a very good experience of nursing in a big hospital in Kent. And it all sounded interesting, exciting' (Bronagh).

The interplay of different relationships in someone's social network is also apparent in the story of Angela. Although she had two older sisters who were nursing in Britain, Angela was not initially sure that she wanted to join them. At the time she was working in her local town in the Irish Midlands: 'I was doing hotel reception, I knew that wasn't really for me'. Instead, she hoped to do nurse training in Ireland and made enquiries about applying in Dublin. However, the long waiting times and the high costs were discouraging, as noted above. In the meantime, she saw advertisements for vacancies in London but was very nervous about moving away from home to such a huge city. Interestingly, it was not her sisters who encouraged her to submit an application but her sister-in-law who could see how nervous and ambivalent Angela was feeling.

so my sister-in-law one day said to me, 'sit down, let's apply to these hospitals, these adverts.' I needed someone behind me, pushing me, and she's the one that said, 'Sit down, let's do this.' I just needed someone to give it a push to try really ... I thought, 'Oh God nursing, it's a bit nerve-wracking thinking I'm going to go to London.' So I just needed someone behind me to ... But I never regretted it. (Angela)

As discussed in Chapter 2, the vast majority of Irish migrants in the twentieth century were young and single (Travers, 1997; Redmond, 2018). Indeed, most of our participants closely conform to that pattern. However, two participants had a different, and more unusual experience, as they were part of family units who migrated with or to join parents. Thus, in both cases, family networks were fundamental to their reason for migrating and only later did they decide to apply for nursing.

Joseph, one of our two male participants, left Ireland in 1956 to join his family in Liverpool: 'I didn't exactly come over here to train as a nurse. When I came over here ... my mother and stepfather came over before me and my mother was expecting me to come over and join them'. Later on, while working as a tailor, Joseph[5] saw an advertisement for nurse training and decided to explore that opportunity.

Delia left Ireland, with her sister, in 1961, to join their father:

> He was over working on the British Rail. The idea was that when he'd have children old enough, he'd just take them over and deposit them, and they would send the money back that he sent while he was there. And he'd go back to his small holding. (Delia)

Initially, Delia got a job in an office in London but felt bored and wanted to pursue a more fulfilling career. She saw an advertisement for student nurses in a newspaper at the library. So, while both Joseph and Delia responded to newspaper advertisements for student nurses, they did so in Britain after they had already migrated to join relatives. We will hear more about their experiences as nurses in later chapters throughout this book.

CONCLUDING THOUGHTS

In this chapter, we have discussed why our participants decided to pursue nursing and what factors drew them to train in hospitals across Britain. Beyond

---

5 We were sorry to hear that Joseph passed away in 2024.

any simple 'push' or 'pull' explanation of migration, drawing on the rich narratives of our forty-five participants, we have discussed the complex interplay of multiple factors and influences.

Although there is no doubt that the active recruitment campaign run by the NHS, over many decades, targeted and enticed many Irish nursing students, that does not tell the whole story. The obstacles to nurse training in Ireland, including limited places and long waiting lists, as well as the apparent need for 'pull', were also contributing reasons for migration.

Furthermore, as this chapter has clearly shown, the long-established culture of migration in Ireland meant that most families had networks of friends and relatives in Britain who encouraged 'chain migration' (Ryan, 2008). For women, in particular, the lack of alternative employment opportunities in Ireland made migration even more attractive (Walter, 2002; Ryan, 2003). Migration seemed to offer freedom and a chance for a different way of life compared to the hardship on small family farms in rural Ireland (Lennon et al., 1988; O'Carroll, 1990). Against, this backdrop, even for young people who had no prior thoughts of becoming nurses, the offer of free training, guaranteed accommodation in Nurses' Homes, and the security of a job with good career pathways in the NHS, seemed especially appealing.

While this chapter has focused on our participants' experiences of recruitment and the application process, in the next chapter we hear about subsequent stages of their stories: leaving home, that initial journey across the Irish Sea, and first impressions upon arrival at their destinations.

CHAPTER 4

'What an adventure!': arriving in Britain

> ... the hospital must have paid for the tickets. All I know was I met these two girls, other girls who I'd never met before, in Cork and we were coming across on the Innisfallen which was the boat from Cork into somewhere in Wales ... So, these other two girls and myself, we sat on our suitcases on the Innisfallen. I can remember the water spraying up on us, I can remember that ... (Sheila, left Ireland in February 1961)

In the previous chapter, we heard how the participants had been recruited from Ireland to go and train in various hospitals across Britain. As noted, most of the recruits were around 18 years of age and had never been away from home before. In this chapter, we hear their stories of that initial journey from Ireland to Britain. Although they had applied for nurse training in British hospitals with varied levels of enthusiasm, when it came to actually leaving home for the first time, as we will see below, many felt sad, tearful and nervous about what lay ahead. Nonetheless, for most of these young people, there was also an enormous sense of adventure as they embarked upon a new chapter in their lives. For some, this was about fulfilling their long-held dream of becoming a nurse, while for others, it was about the opportunities to get away from rural Ireland and experience the bright lights and excitement of cities like London or Liverpool. However, as we will hear later in this chapter, their first impressions did not always live up to their expectations.

This chapter begins with memories of their initial journey to Britain including rough sea-crossings on cattle boats as well as some intrepid travel on aeroplanes.

'WHAT AN ADVENTURE': STORIES OF THE FIRST JOURNEY

Although it was a defining moment in their lives, some nurses had only vague recollections of that first initial journey from Ireland to Britain: 'that was in January, I can't remember the exact date' (Dervla); 'I'm really trying to think. I must have flown really but I honestly don't know how I got there either, it's all very vague' (Pauline); 'I can't remember how I came over, whether I flew or whether I went on the boat' (Trisha).

As noted in Chapter 2, memories of the distant past are shaped by intervening events (Thomson, 1998a; Brannen, 2013). Precise details about events that occurred more than 50 years ago can become hazy and imprecise. Considering that our interviewees travelled back and forth to Ireland at least once per year, for the rest of their lives, it is not too surprising that they cannot recall the exact dates and details of their first journey.

However, by contrast, others had very clear memories of the day, month and year of their first journey to Britain. In such cases, their memories were usually helped by the fact that the date held some particular significance, such as being close to their birthday, and hence was easier to recall.

For example, Bronagh remembered the date very clearly: 'on 12th March 1965, which was three days before my 18th birthday. I came on the Sunday and Tuesday was my 18th birthday'. Student nurses needed to be 18 before they could commence training, hence, many arrived on or just before this birthday. Fidelma recalled arriving in March 1966: 'I wasn't even 18 then. My birthday was in April'.

Aine remembered the date because it was unusual and stuck in her mind: 'two of my friends came with me as well, and we flew into Liverpool on the 29th February 1968, a leap year'.

For almost all these teenagers, it was not only their first time out of Ireland, but in several cases this was also their first trip alone outside their own towns and villages. While some, like Aine above, travelled with friends, others made the journey completely on their own.

Niamh described leaving Roscommon, on her own, at the age of 18, and making the long journey to Yorkshire via Dublin and Liverpool.

> ... June 1958, I set off by myself on the train to Dublin which I'd never been to before. Made my way to the North Wall to get the boat to Liverpool. Really, if I think about it now, I hadn't a clue. I was very naïve. I had never used a telephone. I had never seen a traffic light. When I got off the boat in Liverpool, I think somebody must have been watching over me because I met a lady as I was walking off the boat and she asked me where I was going and I said I was going to Leeds and she was from the Catholic Nurses Guild, would you believe it? ... She came with me into the station at Liverpool and put me on the train to Leeds. (Niamh)

Niamh recalled how she felt as she embarked on this momentous journey: 'I cried all the way to Athlone and then I thought to myself well there's no point in crying now because I'm going and that's it. I think I was naïve really and I just thought, oh, I'd be okay. When I think about it now, it was really brave of me'. For us in the twenty-first century, it does seem somewhat unimaginable that an 18-year-old would set off alone, without the aid of a phone, to make such a long journey to a completely unfamiliar destination. But, as Niamh explained, her naivety probably meant that she felt no sense of danger and somehow trusted that it would all be 'okay'.

Several young women explained that they had mixed feelings about leaving home. For example, Eilish set off for Leeds to join her sister in the early 1970s: 'Even though it was hard leaving home, it was exciting as well'. Moreover, her parents were relieved that the older sister would look after her: 'my mum and dad were happy that we were going to be with each other'.

For some of the nurses, leaving home was a deeply emotional experience and they still have vivid memories of how they felt on that particular day:

> I'll never forget it as long as I live. They brought me to the door. There were tears and tears and tears and tears and tears because being the only girl everybody was sad to see me go, I suppose, particularly my mum... My mother was heartbroken. (Fiona)

Similarly, Fidelma recalled: 'Oh, terrible, absolutely heart-breaking. Even now I think of it. When we actually came to be saying goodbye, that was it, I didn't want to go'. A few felt deeply nervous and anxious about leaving home and setting off for an unfamiliar destination. Helen explained: 'I was worried, worried sick ... I was nervous, yes, coming on the boat.'

Indeed, arriving in Britain, especially disembarking from the sea-ferry in the middle of the night, hardly inspired them with enthusiasm. Caitriona described her feelings upon arriving on the harbour in Wales on a cold January morning in 1960: 'when I arrived at Holyhead at 3 in the morning, if I could have gone back to Ireland, I would have gone back, it was so dark and so miserable'.

Like most of our participants Linda arrived on the sea-ferry from Ireland. She noted that many people are surprised when she mentions coming on a boat. To modern-day listeners, it seems like something from ancient history: 'Whenever I tell people I come over on the boat now they're like: "that was like not just one century ago, like a hundred centuries ago, you came on the boat!" and I really did come on the boat'.

Indeed, many of our participants had powerful memories of travelling aboard ships. Carmel, originally from the North of Ireland, travelled from Belfast by ship: 'I always remember how lonesome when we got off that big boat. We sailed from Belfast to Liverpool'.

Interestingly, several nurses, especially those who travelled from Dublin to Liverpool, came, not on passenger ferries, as might be expected today, but actually on cattle ships. These vessels were designed for carrying cargo, especially live animals, and usually only carried small numbers of human passengers.

Jane vividly recalled: 'oh it was awful, horrible … there was only like benches … it was like a cattle boat'. Sisters Aoife and Una, who were interviewed together in Liverpool, also recalled the animal cargo aboard their ship: 'the boats at that time came into Birkenhead and they used to call them the "cattle boats" … loads of cattle on them, very little people on them but lots of cattle on them'.

Those travelling from Cork usually made the journey on the famous *Innisfallen* which travelled from the port of Cork to Fishguard and later to Swansea in Wales. In fact, the *Innisfallen* was a name given to five different ships that made the journey from Cork through most of the 1900s. It is estimated that around one million people emigrated from Ireland, via Cork, on the *Innisfallen* ships.[1] Claire, originally from the west of Ireland, set off on the *Innisfallen* from Cork:

> I do remember that journey … I don't think I slept really but I could hear water running on the boat and I was like, 'We're going down' but somebody had left a tap on … You know, I could hear this.

Claire, despite her misgivings about the *Innisfallen* journey, was excited about the adventure: 'It was an experience because obviously where I initially come from, a little village in the west of Ireland … Yes, what an adventure!'

Similarly, Sheila who, as noted in the opening quote of this chapter, also sailed from Cork on the *Innisfallen*, did not recall feeling particularly upset. Instead, she embraced a spirit of adventure: 'Maybe I looked on it as an adventure because I'd never been anywhere, I just can't remember being terribly sad'.

Among our participants there were several who had grown up in children's homes. For these young people, nurse training offered an escape route out of their unhappy lives in Ireland. As one woman stated emphatically: 'I was so glad to get out of Ireland, and I swore I'd never go back.' While, in fact, she did go back to visit Ireland many times in later life, her strongest emotion as she embarked on that first journey was one of relief to get away.

Across all the forty-five interviews, many nurses talked about this spirit of adventure and embarking on their journey without thinking too much about the risks. As Bronagh explained:

---

1 https://www.irish-ferries-enthusiasts.com/innisfallen/.

> So I was 17 and yeah, very limited experience and had a very sheltered upbringing, so totally oblivious to this big wide world out there ... I had no experience of what I might even encounter that I might be frightened of. So, it all just seemed exciting.

Similarly, Miriam described her feelings upon leaving Ireland: 'I remember it so well because I suppose the adrenaline is going. I'd never been on an aeroplane, I'd never been to London, but none of that fazed me.'

Although they may not have been 'fazed' by the idea of setting off to Britain, several did experience a few mishaps along the way. Veronica, originally from Co. Kerry, worked in Dublin as a childminder, before deciding to pursue a career in nursing. Thus, unlike many of our participants, she had the experience of living in a big city in Ireland before embarking on the journey to Britain. In 1964, she set off quite confidently on her long journey. Nonetheless, she had a mishap on her way to the hospital in Staffordshire. Having travelled from Kerry, via train and sea-ferry, she then had to change trains at Crewe. After the long overnight journey, she decided to have breakfast in the café at Crewe Station. Before heading to the café, she put her suitcase on the train. However, as she sat in the café enjoying her breakfast, she was stunned to see the train pull out of the station with her suitcase on board. Despite her shock, she had the presence of mind to run and find the station master and quickly explain what had happened. Luckily, he arranged to have her suitcase taken off at the next station.

Reflecting back on why she put her suitcase on the train and then went off to the station café, Veronica explained that, at the time in Kerry, there were only a few trains per day going to big cities like Dublin. Moreover, her local station was a terminus, and so the train would often sit in the station for a long time before its scheduled departure. Hence, it was common for people to put their suitcases on board, while they mingled on the platform or went to purchase refreshments. At a busy inter-change like Crewe, she was not expecting trains to pull in and out of the station with such speed. This example illustrates how the experiences and expectations that these young people brought with them from Ireland did not always fit the reality of life in the British context. As we will see in the story of Ruth below, they could find themselves in tricky situations during their journey.

In 1968, Ruth and her friend, both aged 18, set off with a sense of adventure but were surprised by an event that occurred in Swansea.

> two of us actually went together. She was actually keen to go into nursing as well, and we had a good chat about it, and we went together. We went from Cork to Swansea ... We probably couldn't afford the plane fare,

because plane fares were quite expensive at the time. We went from Cork to Swansea, and we got off the boat in Swansea … We decided we'd get off and explore, so we'd got a B&B. And the lady in the B&B rang the police and thought we'd run away from home, because we obviously looked quite young. … We didn't think at the time, we thought we were well able to look after ourselves and quite confident. We were well put out that somebody should have called the police and thought we'd run away from home.

The police turned up, and luckily we had paperwork to show, yes, that we were actually getting the train the following day and we were going down to (hospital), via London obviously. But the officer gave us a talking to, as well, because they obviously thought that we were a bit young to be out on our own I suppose, or travelling on our own. (Ruth)

This story underlines the youth of these female migrants as they arrived in Britain to take up very responsible roles as student nurses. Within weeks they would be working on wards, administering care to sick patients. The story also suggests the innocence of these young women and how 'oblivious' (as Bronagh said) they were to potential risks.

As Caitriona, who travelled to Manchester, remarked: 'I was 18, you were very 'green' as I would call it now and, of course, you were very innocent in those days from Ireland, you wouldn't be street wise'.

These young arrivals were often completely unprepared for the new experiences that awaited them. For example, Linda travelled to Britain on the sea-ferry and was sick all the way; she humorously added: 'so that was something to look forward to on the next trip'. She recalled arriving in London and encountering an escalator for the first time: 'remember seeing escalators and we didn't know what to do … we asked somebody, "Do we sit down?" I can remember asking! We just didn't know! We were so naïve'.

It might be tempting to assume that while earlier migrants travelled by ship, more recent arrivals flew by plane. But our data show more varied patterns depending partly on geographical location and family resources. Arriving in London in 1952, Bridget was one of our older interviewees, however, family finances meant that she was able to travel by plane: 'they took me to Dublin to Collinstown Airport which is Dublin Airport now … I'd never been on a plane in my life and there was just a curtain between the pilot and the people, and we landed at Northolt, there was no Heathrow'.[2]

---

[2] In fact, Heathrow was opened in 1946 but it was not officially renamed Heathrow Airport until 1966.

Finnuala and her friend flew from Cork into Heathrow Airport in the early 1970s. They were very excited about getting the plane but had not thought about how to make their way from Heathrow to the hospital. Having no understanding of the geography of London, or the distance from the airport, on the outskirts of west London, into the city centre and then on to the hospital in south-east London, they had assumed that after arriving at Heathrow they could easily catch a bus to the hospital. Again, as noted in the case of Veronica's mishap at Crewe Station, they brought their knowledge and experience from Ireland and assumed it would apply to the British context. From Cork Airport, there is one bus route into the city centre, so Finnuala and her friend were completely unprepared for the scale and complexity of public transport from Heathrow to various parts of London.

> ... my mother said, 'How are you going to get from Heathrow?' I said, 'We'll get a bus'. I had visions of getting on the bus, next stop down, you know, turn around the corner. She said, 'Oh, that's a good idea'.
>
> We arrived at Heathrow. We'd made no plans, because we thought we were going 'to London', so we arrived at Heathrow ... But there was a priest picking up his niece – who came off the flight, and we were standing there and he said, 'How are you getting to the hospital?' and we said, 'We don't know', and he said, 'Come on, I'll take you.' So that was pure luck ... and he brought us. Looking back now, how kind was that? (Finnuala)

Orla travelled alone from Cork to Heathrow in the early 1970s and then had to navigate the convoluted journey from the airport to the hospital in far off south London.

> I got the train, the connections weren't as good as they are now and I got a train to West Brompton, Brompton Station, and then a bus to Charing Cross and when I arrived in Charing Cross on the bus there was a train strike and I remember sort of having to carry my suitcases a long way and this lovely man came along, he was a real gentleman, just helping me with my suitcases and said, 'Can I get you a taxi?' and he did, he booked me the taxi. I was chuffed and then the taxi went all around south London. (Orla)

In several of these stories it is noteworthy that strangers often provided vital help such as the woman who helped Niamh to get the right train at Liverpool Station, the man in Charing Cross Station who carried Orla's suitcase and found her a taxi or the priest who drove Finnuala and her friend all the way to their hospital. Perhaps their 'naivety' and 'innocence' led them to seek and accept help from people they met along the way. Miriam summed this up rather succinctly when she referred to 'the follies of youth'.

However, as discussed in the following section, they did not all need to rely on the kindness of strangers, several nurses had relatives living in Britain who were waiting to welcome them.

'MY AUNT MET ME': THE ROLE OF NETWORKS IN FACILITATING THE JOURNEY

While some young women travelled alone, many others were accompanied by friends, as noted in some of the stories above (e.g., Ruth), or siblings. For example, Carmel travelled from Belfast with her brother: '(he) was going to Birmingham so we were parting at Crewe. He was leaving me at Crewe, and I was coming on to Euston'. Upon arrival at Euston, she was met by her aunt and uncle: 'as I went out, they were meeting me there, and then took me back to their nice flat. And I think on the Monday morning she took me up to the hospital to be introduced to the matron and start my training.' As discussed in Chapter 2, the culture of migration in Ireland meant that many families had extended networks of friends and relations scattered across British cities including London, Liverpool and Leeds. These network ties could encourage and facilitate migration, as discussed in the previous chapter on recruitment.

However, as noted elsewhere (see Ryan, 2023), network ties are not necessarily dependable sources of support and companionship. For example, friends may prove unreliable and, indeed, several nurses talked about friends who had planned to move to Britain and later pulled out. Ciara had done initial nurse training in Ireland before moving to Scotland, in the early 1970s, to study midwifery:

> Two of my friends were meant to come with me, that I'd trained with and shared a house with, and by the time we were to go, they'd both met the men who are now their husbands, and they didn't come. So, I came on my own. (Ciara)

As noted in Chapter 3, aunts were often pivotal to supporting and enabling migration and reinforcing the significant place of women in Irish migration history (Ryan, 2008). Like Carmel above, several participants mentioned how aunts were waiting to greet them upon arrival in Britain.

Claire was met by her aunt: 'I was quite lucky in the sense that my aunt lived in Oxfordshire, so I then got the train and she met me off the train and then a few days later, she came with me to (hospital)'.

As discussed in the previous chapter, Aisling decided to apply for nurse training in Middlesbrough, because her aunt and uncle lived in that city; she was not actively recruited in the same way as other participants. Instead, she had applied directly, by letter, to a particular hospital. Therefore, she needed to go to the hospital for an interview. Although she travelled alone, she knew that her aunt was waiting to welcome her at the end of her journey: 'I came to Middlesbrough; I travelled myself, I came over by myself and my aunt met me when I arrived and I stayed with her while I went to have my interview'.

Despite the fact that many participants had relatives and friends in Britain, they were keen to communicate with their parents back in Ireland. Maintaining contact with their close networks of family and friends in Ireland was very important for most participants and, despite their great 'adventure' in Britain, most continued to visit Ireland on a regular basis throughout the decades, as will be discussed in later chapters. However, staying in contact with people in Ireland was not easy, especially during the 1950s–70s. Few families had access to telephones during those days, so most participants relied on letter-writing. Communication was slow and took considerable effort and, thus, was very different from the sorts of instant contact, via various apps, video messaging and free calls, that we tend to take for granted today.

Sheila recalled writing a letter to her mother to say she had arrived safely in London: 'which she got another week later! We had no telephones or nothing. Absolutely nothing'. Sinead explained that communication with home was even slower when she arrived because of a postal strike: 'could not write to my parents to say I'd arrived, could not ring them because there were no phones, it was actually months before I could contact them'.

So far, we have focused on their initial journey and first arrival in Britain; in the next section we consider their reactions and experiences while navigating new and unfamiliar environments.

'A TERRIBLE CULTURE SHOCK': FIRST IMPRESSIONS IN NEW PLACES

Upon arrival in Britain, many of the nurses spoke about experiencing a deep culture shock. Moving to new places, particularly in the 1950s–70s, when Ireland still felt very different from Britain, socially and culturally, could confront these teenagers with surprising new experiences.

Linda, who arrived in 1972, shared her early memories: 'What I remember too was sitting on a bus and all the fruit stalls, that was so new to me, you know now, the fruit is everywhere, and I'd look out and there was fruit everywhere and I thought, "Oh my God, that's fantastic."'

By contrast, those who arrived in the early 1950s had a markedly different impression. Bridget arrived in London in 1952 and was shocked to discover that rationing[3] was still in place:

> there was still rationing in England, we had to line up for our butter and sugar rations ... We used to go for our little dish of butter to the housekeeper and a little pot with sugar in it. The tea we didn't (but) sugar and butter was rationed still in 1952, yes.

Her initial experience of life in London did not meet her expectations: 'My vision of England was partying all night and dancing and all this which was a terrible culture shock to me'. (Bridget)

Bridget was not the only one to feel somewhat disappointed upon arrival in Britain. As noted in the previous chapter, Gretta was directly recruited from her small town in west Cork, to work in a London hospital in 1948 and hence can be seen as a pioneer recruit to the NHS. However, arriving in post-war London, she was shocked by the run-down state of the old Victorian hospital: 'I thought the wards were shabby.' The building was 'old' and the complicated and disorganized layout meant patients and students were 'very confused'.

First impressions were shaped by prior experiences. Helen[4] was also one of our oldest participants, having been born in 1930, and was a sprightly 92 when we interviewed her. Growing up in a very poor family in Ireland, she shared a small house with her many siblings and parents. She had never had a room of her own. Upon arriving in Liverpool in 1951 she was very pleasantly surprised by the Nurses' Home:

> it was really like a hotel ... the Nurses' Home was really lovely. And of course, the big dining hall, it was just lovely, it was like a hotel. We got breakfasts and all the different ones doing their different jobs, we even had girls that worked on the tables and all that. (Helen)

Similarly, Pauline was also impressed by the facilities at her Nurses' Home: 'we lived on a long corridor, we'd all have separate rooms but we had a shared kitchen and bathroom ... and we had a lovely Welsh cleaning lady came in and tidied up and stuff.'

---

3 Rationing of key staples like butter and sugar continued until the mid-1950s https://teachingresources.web.ox.ac.uk/files/rationingresource-updated8may2020pdf. 4 We were delighted to meet her again almost a year after our interview, when she attended our dissemination event in Liverpool, in June 2023, accompanied by her son, shortly after her 93rd birthday.

However, some new arrivals were not impressed by all the rules and regulations:

> you were only allowed so many late passes a week and every Nurses' Home had a home sister and you had to check in when you came in. So, you were all checked in and it was very much like a continuation of school, it was a bit like, I suppose, a boarding school really. (Sheila)

The strict rules of the Nurses' Home, and the ways these young students managed to circumvent them, will be discussed in a later chapter (see Chapter 6). For now, returning to their stories of arrival, several expressed an initial sense of disappointment in their new surroundings.

As mentioned in Chapter 2, oral history interviews can elicit a stock of stories that have been well honed, in retelling, over time. We interviewed a few nurses who knew each other and trained at the same hospital. Although each of these women was interviewed separately, we were intrigued to observe striking similarities when they described their first impression of the training hospital.

First, we interviewed Orla who described in great detail her first view of the hospital in south London as she arrived by taxi:

> approaching (hospital) and it was indicating into this very old building. I thought, 'That's a weird looking place' and on one side there were high-rise buildings ... and it was a female taxi driver and she said, 'Oh, this is the hospital here'. I said, 'Are you sure?' She said, 'Yes'. I said, 'Is it not the more modern building?' and she said, 'No'. My heart sank! I remember feeling very upset and thinking, 'Oh jeepers, if this is what it's like I probably won't be staying for long!' (Orla)

Then, sometime later, we interviewed her friend, Fiona, and she suddenly started to relate her first impressions upon arrival at the same hospital.

> Driving along the high street thinking that great big block of flats was our fabulous hospital, three big, huge flats. We did a right turn into this very Victorian old building thinking, 'Oh my goodness. What have I let myself in for?' (Fiona)

Later, we interviewed another participant, Finnuala, who had trained at the same hospital in the early 1970s:

> As we drove up (the) High Street, the hospital was on the right, but on the left was three big – they were council flats, but they were very impressive high-rise, three of them ... and we thought, 'Oh, that must be (hospital)'. And then the taxi turned right, and we went to, it was, 'Oh my God!' It looked like Hogwarts![5] ... Really depressing building.

The remarkable, almost word-for-word, similarity in the descriptions provided by Finnuala, Orla and Fiona is worthy of some reflection. As noted, these three had become friends during their nurse training and were still in touch today. It is likely that they had reminisced together many times and, in the process, probably subconsciously, honed the features of their stories until it became a shared narrative. This is not in any way to undermine the importance of their stories. On the contrary, using insights from oral history research, we understand that anecdotes of past events are often shaped by intervening conversations and reflections over time (Ryan, 2006; Henderson et al., 2012). This shared story of arrival at the hospital in south London is a clear example of what Chamberlain (1997) means when she refers to narratives as 'cultural constructions'.

Angela also felt an initial sense of disappointment. Upon arrival in London, she and her friend were met by her brother, and he later escorted them to the hospital. But the strict rules were imposed from the beginning:

> Anyway, my brother took us both to (the) hospital the next day ... He wasn't even allowed in with us, he wasn't allowed up to my room, even though he was my brother, he wasn't allowed, they were very strict. (Angela)

In the storytelling tradition, Angela vividly and humorously described an unnerving experience during her first night at the Nurses' Home. She was not familiar with central heating systems because her family had never had it in Ireland.

> I remember my first couple of nights in one particular Nurses' Home ... going into bed and the noise (!) It must have been, now when I think, the boiler. I was stuck to the bed for the night thinking there was somebody under the bed ... I'm thinking, 'Oh my god, there's somebody under my bed. I'm not getting out.' I was petrified, absolutely ... because we weren't used to central heating or whatever noises you might hear with it, at the time. That sticks in my mind. (Angela)

---

5 Hogwarts is a reference to the huge old castle in the Harry Potter stories.

That hospital was located in a quiet and rather rundown suburb in south-east London, very far from the bright lights and bustle of central London: 'Well I thought nursing in London it was so romantic and so wonderful.' But the hospital, on the outskirts of the capital, did not meet Angela's expectations: 'the building it was so grey and dismal and you thought, "Oh my God, this is not London?" We'd visions of being in London, being in Central London, you know.'

Angela shared the story of a fellow student who travelled with her to the hospital. That young woman's family owned a boutique in Ireland and her suitcase was full of lovely, glamorous clothes: 'she was awfully, awfully, very smart'. However, the old-fashioned hospital in a poor neighbourhood of south London was very far removed from the glamour this young woman had anticipated: 'That poor girl who came with me, she lasted two weeks … Straight back to the boutique'.

Several nurses expressed surprise about the poor, deprived and shabby neighbourhoods they encountered. This was very far from their vision of life in Britain. Pauline described Liverpool as 'a quite a dump really, a dump of a city' – though she noted that it had changed enormously over recent decades, but when she had arrived it was very deprived. Kathleen made a similar observation:

> when I came to Liverpool in 1970, I just thought it was still after the war. It looked really derelict, especially where I was living and the road into town, it was all terrible, really, really, hadn't been restored at all in any shape or form. (Kathleen)

This contrasted sharply with her expectations of Liverpool. She recalled how she and her brother had watched the Beatles on TV and this shaped her impression of what life in Liverpool might be like.

> I remember The Beatles, before I left Ireland, and my brother, we were looking at these four lads on the, we must have had a television, and I remember our reaction and then when I was going to Liverpool I thought this is wonderful, I'll see these four boys. I'll see these four lads and I'll go dancing in The Cavern.[6] (Kathleen)

Despite her disappointment at not meeting the Beatles and her realization that Liverpool was quite poor and rundown, Kathleen still appreciated the

---

6 The Cavern Club was a famous venue where the Beatles and other well-known Liverpool bands used to play in the 1960s.

freedom from the religious discrimination she encountered back in her native Northern Ireland.

> the freedom, the expression, there was nobody 'were you Catholic-Protestant, Irish or not Irish', they didn't seem to be, particularly Catholic-Protestant which we had at home a lot, the Catholic-Protestant divide at that time. (Kathleen)

Another culture shock for the young arrivals were the very particular regional accents they encountered. These would have been quite unfamiliar to most participants because at that time, regional accents rarely appeared on radio or TV, for example, because the 'received English' of the BBC tended to be the norm. Joseph, one of our few male participants, upon arriving from Dublin in the 1950s, initially found the Liverpool accent hard to fathom.

> It was strange at first ... I felt very strange and the Liverpool accent, I couldn't understand them and they couldn't understand me. They have difficulties and I had difficulty to understand them. (Joseph)

Jane arrived in Liverpool in 1954 and initially felt very nervous and unsafe:

> I never went out on my own really, I never wanted to go out on my own really because it was not a place to walk up and down on your own really, I thought it was always, really, you felt like you were looking over your shoulder all the time really. (Jane)

By contrast, Una expressed the view that Liverpool was an especially friendly city: 'I just notice how welcoming and how friendly and everything, everyone just intermixes, you don't know them but yet they intermix with you.' Moreover, Liverpool was regarded by many participants as a very Irish city. As Aine put it succinctly: 'it's full of Irish'. As a result, Una stated: 'I think people are very sympathetic to the Irish in Liverpool'.

As discussed in Chapter 3, Una and her sister Aoife were part of a family of nurses and had a strong connection with Liverpool where their older siblings had also trained. When we interviewed them together in Liverpool, they had the following exchange:

> Aoife: there's a lot of Irish in Liverpool. If you talk to people, they'll have somebody connected with the Irish and there's a lot of Irish in it.

> Una: There's not many people you'll meet that haven't real connections to Ireland or Irish in their family and they'll all tell you about their mothers and their grandmothers and their grandfathers, won't they?

As noted above, many participants in Liverpool and London were shocked to discover very poor and rundown neighbourhoods. In Glasgow, Jacky had a similar reaction:

> (hospital) was actually in one of the poorer areas of Glasgow, it was in its original format, it would've been almost considered the Poor House. It was in the industrial heartland of the city where all the shipbuilding had happened and just on the cusp of change, where industrialization was changing, and you could see the remnants of that. There still were shipyards open but things changed in those next number of years. It was quite a poor area actually ... It was an eye-opener for us really. (Jacky)

Nonetheless, Jacky found Glasgow to be a very friendly and welcoming city: 'The Glaswegian people and the women and the families were, well are, wonderful people and very friendly. The friendliness was amazing and we never felt in any way treated differently from, if you like, the other Scottish girls.'

Of course, newly arrived Irish student nurses were not only encountering the local English or Scottish population. As discussed later in this chapter, they were also encountering other ethnic minorities and migrants from around the world.

'THEY TOOK ME UNDER THEIR WING': FROM HOMESICKNESS AND LONELINESS TO NEW FRIENDSHIPS

Some people were initially very unhappy, homesick and found it very hard to settle into their new environment. Aoife, despite coming to join her older sister in Liverpool, still felt unhappy and tearful.

> I hated it! I never stopped crying, my sister said to me one day, 'If you don't stop crying I'm going to send you home'... I missed Ireland, I don't know why but I did miss Ireland ... It did take me a while. Maybe when I went to PTS[7] I settled because there were a lot of Irish girls in our PTS and I think maybe then was when I settled. (Aoife)

---

7 This a reference to preliminary training school and will be discussed in more detail in the next chapter.

Similarly, in London, Carmel initially felt very lonely and tearful.

> But it was sad. Obviously, I missed mum and my brothers. I had left four brothers behind, so it must have been quite sad ... The hospital wasn't far from Clapham Junction, and every train I heard go by I wished I was on it going back home again ... I used to be so lonely.

Fidelma who trained in Hertfordshire in the 1960s also described the sense of loneliness experienced not just by herself but also by other new arrivals around her:

> Bit sad too. Could be a bit lonely sometimes. Bit upsetting when you heard someone in the next room crying because they were homesick, which happened a lot, and that kind of unsettled you, but we had good times, and we all had fantastic social clubs, social life. We were looked after. (Fidelma)

The 'fantastic' social life of these young student nurses will be discussed in detail in Chapter 6. For now, it is important to acknowledge the initial sadness and loneliness that many endured as teenagers far away from home for the first time.

Niamh arrived in Yorkshire in June 1958 and remembered it as a 'very, very lonely period because I did not know anybody'.

A nurse in London described feeling especially isolated on Sunday afternoons:

> Sundays were always very lonely in London, and I remember on a Sunday afternoon if I was off on a Sunday walking up to Waterloo Station, just to meet people. I often talk about that still to this day, I used to just go up to see people, just walk up along the York Road and go and get some sort of takeaway for myself and just walk around Waterloo to meet people. (Sorcha)

One indication of feeling more relaxed and confident is learning to navigate new places (Trabka, 2019; Ryan, 2003). Several spoke about gaining an understanding of the public transport system and exploring their new environment. Linda recalled: 'I think I adapted fairly quickly to be honest. I think because you're young, isn't that right? I learned to hop on the bus within a couple of days ... and I knew what to do and pay.'

Learning to navigate public transport was a sign of growing confidence in a new city:

> I have two uncles in north London, so I came to one of them, Uncle J. And he had an English wife, E, and I would say in terms of practical things, E really was the one that [laughs] told you a bit, gave you a bit of a talking to. She would have been very practical, very helpful and a rather lovely person ... like the trains and the buses and Undergrounds and all of that and E took the time to take me around on the Underground, show me how to read the maps. Still to this day ... if I was taking anybody now, I'd do exactly the same thing. Get lost a couple of times, sit down, figure it out, you know, and you'll soon find your way. (Aileen)

Despite her initial loneliness, Sorcha also soon discovered ways to enjoy London: 'I remember walking through Green Park up to the West End. I mean that was just such a great feeling and seeing all the nannies with the big prams in Green Park. It was lovely, I mean walking past, you know, that lovely walk up through St James' Park and Green Park and then through Mayfair and up to the West End, yeah.'

As noted earlier, Jacky had initially found Glasgow rather poor and rundown, but soon discovered the beauty of the Scottish countryside.

> We travelled up to the islands and we went to music festivals and we certainly made the most of our time off which was great because we'd come back and over time, the staff and the Scottish and Glaswegian nurses and colleagues would say, 'Where have you been now?' We would be telling them about these islands and places and girls in our own group, because we'd trained with the Scottish girls, they were amazed because they had no idea of half the places we were. (Jacky)

As mentioned in the previous section, Jane had initially found Liverpool rather a scary place. But making friends with other students in the Nurses' Home was a turning point: 'I had the other girls with me, I wasn't so bad, like between us we managed alright'.

After their initial loneliness and homesickness, many nurses described how meeting other Irish students at the Nurses' Home helped them to feel more settled.

> Yes, very homesick for a while, and then I made friends. Matron was very kind. There were two Irish girls and they were older than me ... they had

done two years. P was from Westmeath, and M, who became a great friend of mine, she was from Monaghan. And because I was the youngest there as well, I was just 18 in May, and I was starting my training in June, so they were already allocated to a double room. So, matron gave us a bigger room and put the three of us in together, so we became great friends. (Carmel)

Niamh, who was initially very lonely when she first arrived in Yorkshire, described the lovely surprise that greeted her on the first day she entered the dining hall at the Nurses' Home:

I walked into this dining room and sat down at this table. There were three other girls sat at the table and one girl said to me, 'Are you Irish?' I said, 'Yes.' And they were three Irish girls, weren't they? It turned out they were from not far from where I lived in Roscommon. They were from Mayo. They took me under their wing. (Niamh)

The Nurses' Home was usually seen as a very warm and welcoming place where these Irish teenagers were quickly made to feel at home: 'I ended up, in Birkenhead, in the Nurses' Home, full of Irish nurses and had a lovely time, a whale of a time. They're looking after me' (Kathleen).

Similarly, Colette, who arrived in Essex in 1952, recalled: 'But once I was there, you were given your room, your bathroom, everything, it was very nice, you feel very secure to be honest ... very secure. All the rest of them, they were all Irish, so I felt very much at home'.

Interestingly, the word 'security' was also used by Caitriona, who went to train in Manchester in 1960:

the security of the Nurses' Home, that was very important because you had your own room and you had showers and your washing was done for you and all that, so there was a lot of security in those days for a young girl or a young boy coming over from Ireland. (Caitriona)

Another nurse also mentioned high levels of security at her Nurses' Home in Leeds:

When I first came in 1974 there was always a lady sitting at the reception, and she used to check who was coming in, and you'd sign your name in and out, and you weren't allowed to take boys up to the bedroom and things like that. (Eilish)

Although, as mentioned earlier, Finnuala felt a sense of disappointment when she first arrived at the old Victorian hospital (like Hogwarts!), she also noted that meeting new friends in the Nurses' Home helped her to settle. She remembered that a group of new arrivals went out for a treat to cheer themselves up.

> Really kind of depressing building. Anyway, we were there then, so went in, got our rooms, and then we had the chat. We must be in at night, no men allowed in, and all that kind of stuff. Then we made friends, we all went out, and we had a Kentucky Fried Chicken. That was the start of my career in London. (Finnuala)

Although, many participants mentioned meeting other Irish students in the Nurse's Home, of course, they were also encountering students from all around the world. In the next section, we discuss their initial encounters with ethnic diversity.

'A MUCH MORE DIVERSE CROWD': ENCOUNTERING ETHNIC DIVERSITY AND NEW CULTURES

For many of these young, newly arrived students, encountering ethnic diversity was a totally new experience. Sinead explained how, upon arriving at the Nurses' Home, she met the first black woman she had ever encountered in her life.

> we went in to this Nurse's Home, a very nice Nurses' Home, and we were met by this lovely West Indian woman who was from Birmingham, we'd never met anybody before, she was black and, you know, so friendly and she took pity on us and she took us to the canteen, showed us where the food was. She helped us out, she was just brilliant ... she was just lovely. (Sinead)

Their perceptions of ethnicity were shaped by prior experiences and expectations in Ireland. For example, some participants who came from cities like Dublin and Belfast had met black and Asian medical staff. Mairead, who had lived in Dublin, explained how her prior experiences confused her perceptions of ethnic diversity in London:

> So, I used to be going round on buses looking at people, people watching and kind of naïve looking back, very naïve, because the only people of

colour that we ever saw in Dublin were either doctors or medical students. So, I would be looking at people on buses and thinking, 'She's not wearing very nice shoes for a doctor,' I thought everyone was either a doctor or a medical student, I was that green. (Mairead)

Similarly, Julia contrasted the ethnic diversity she had known in Belfast with her new experiences in Glasgow:

> When we were in Belfast ... there was also a couple from India ... they had family working as consultants or doctors in Belfast. When we came over to Scotland, we had a much more diverse crowd. There were people from everywhere. I think it was twenty-two in our group, and out of that I would say there probably was only about eight or nine of us that were actually from Britain/Ireland. The rest were from different parts of the world. We had Jamaica, we had India, we had Pakistan, we had a Spanish girl. There were a lot of people that we had never met the cultures before. (Julia)

The ethnic diversity of the nursing cohort was mentioned by many of our participants. Miriam described her memories of arriving at the Nurses' Home in London in 1969:

> I arrived at the nursing home. It was a nursing sister that used to be the home sister. She opened the door, she said, 'Oh, a new girl from Ireland.' She opened another door and she screamed down this corridor, 'B, please come.' This little girl came popping out of her room and came up and we met and there was a whole lot of Irish girls, Malaysian girls, Trinidadian girls, Jamaican girls and we all became a group of friends together and that's how I started my nursing career. (Miriam)

As Miriam went on to explain, encountering diverse ethnicities, especially in the Nurses' Home, often resulted in new cultural experiences, particularly in relation to food.

> the Malaysian girls would cook ... we had a little kitchen for about every 10 rooms and they would cook and they would say, 'I've got some food if you would like.' We'd cook bacon, cabbage, Irish stew, and the Malaysian girls would come with their peppers and everything and put it into the middle of our Irish stew because it was 'completely tasteless', we used to be told. We used to defend it as if it was manna from heaven. (Miriam)

Nessa, in Yorkshire, stated that all the students, regardless of ethnicity, helped out and supported each other: 'we stuck together. There was no difference in colour because we'd all left home and that was it.'

While many nurses described the ethnic diversity, solidarity and lack of discrimination, particularly in hospital settings, this was far from universal. Violent racism, anti-immigration rhetoric and xenophobia were also features of Britain in the 1960s–80s. One nurse who was training in a hospital in south-east London described her first encounter with so-called 'race riots'.

> It was scary because, it must have been summer of 74, when we had the National Front march through (south London) and I mean there were battles and fights and most of them ended up in the hospital in our care. That was 'anti' everything and we were very, very scared. Again, didn't impact on us because we were well protected and well supported. That was my first six months in nursing. (Fiona)

The issues of racism, discrimination and violence will be discussed again in Chapter 8.

CONCLUDING THOUGHTS

This chapter presented stories of the initial momentous journey to Britain as these young people left home for the first time and embarked upon a new adventure that would change their lives. It is important to emphasize that these journeys took place over fifty and, indeed in several cases, over sixty or even seventy years ago. Travel was far more rudimentary in those days and the voyage on a cattle boat may seem almost unimaginable to modern-day readers. Moreover, in the days before mobile communication and advances in technology, these young travellers were effectively incommunicado throughout their journey, as their families did not have access to telephones. Thus, as parents waved goodbye to their teenage offspring, they knew that no news of their safe arrival would come through for days if not weeks.

While most of them had set off with a sense of adventure, the extent of homesickness and loneliness should not be underestimated and may even have surprised some of the young people themselves. Nonetheless, arriving as students and living in the Nurses' Homes gave these young migrants ready access to secure accommodation and a network of new friends. While many were drawn to fellow Irish migrants, they were keen also to forge new links with student nurses from around the world and explore new cultures and even to try new types of food.

These are themes that will be explored in subsequent chapters, especially when we discuss social life and friendships (Chapter 6), but first we need to get down to business and focus on the busy life of these young students as they commenced their nurse training.

CHAPTER 5

'On the wards': nurse training begins

> The training was very, very practical ... We were taught how to make a bed. How to make our nice envelope corners on the beds. How it was all very neat and tidy. We were told how to wash a patient, how to roll them. The importance of making sure that the patient was washed in a dignified way. Then we went off out onto the wards for a couple of weeks and we practised what we learned. So, it was very much learn, practice, learn, practice. (Maeve arrived in London in 1972)

In previous chapters, we discussed how the young student nurses were recruited from Ireland and then how they made the arduous but exciting journey to Britain for the first time. In this chapter, we now focus on their nurse training and the start of long careers in the nursing profession. We hear stories about the rigor and demanding nature of that training, as well as the strict and regimented discipline on hospital wards. They describe the exactness of their uniforms which denoted not only their professional identities as nurses but also their rank and level of training within the very hierarchical structure of the hospitals.

These stories, ranging from the late 1940s to the early 1970s, span key decades in the history of the NHS and offer fascinating, moving and, at times, humorous accounts of nurse training. For these young Irish people, many of whom had never before left their hometowns, hospitals held many surprises and shocks as well as fun and comradery.

'YOU CAN'T BEAT HANDS-ON': STARTING NURSE TRAINING

It is important to emphasize that the new recruits, arriving from Ireland, were very young and often had little idea of what to expect when they embarked on their demanding and intensive nurse training programme:[1]

---

[1] As mentioned in chapter 3, some participants had done initial nurse training in Ireland. For example, Julia and Ciara trained in hospitals in Northern Ireland but later went to Britain to train as midwives. However, the vast majority of our participants did all their nurse training in British hospitals.

> I started in September, beginning of September, and I was 18 in the October, so just a month shy of my 18th birthday. But I was the youngest in the group and ... we were very naïve, of course we were. We didn't really know what to expect. (Aileen)

Finnuala vividly recalled starting her training on 2 January, just days after she and her friend had arrived from Cork:

> We went on the 29th December 1972, and then we started on the 2nd January. We were taken over to the education centre. I mean that sounds posh – it wasn't. Of course we were introduced to the tutors, they gave us a test on what we would have to do, and about studying, and then they told us that we would be visiting the wards. (Finnuala)

Like Finnuala, most of the nurses began their training within days of arriving, so they had little time to adjust to their new environment. Sinead began her training on the day after her arrival and was so nervous that she was physically sick.

> I started the next day, I can remember ... we had to go then to the School of Nursing and we went in this van, I'm not joking, like a white van with seats on the side here and on the side there, and all I remember is I got off the van and I got sick on the pavement!
>
> I do suffer with travel sickness, I still do, but I got out, I think it was a combination of nerves and everything, I mean I thought: 'my god, it's so embarrassing'. At least I didn't get sick in the van, I vomited right outside the van. And that was that, my first day of nursing! But from then on, the driver, who was absolutely lovely, let me sit up the front so that was great. (Sinead)

Although our participants underwent their training from the late 1940s through to the early 1970s, it is apparent that the format of that training did not change much during the period. The programme was hospital based and very practical with short periods of classroom-based teaching in between.

Reflecting back on her training in the early 1950s, Carmel explained: 'We had six weeks of what we called PTS, preliminary training school, where we had mostly theory. They were very nice instructors. It was Monday to Friday, and then they put us on the wards on Saturday morning for four hours'.

Trisha, who began her training in Essex, in 1969, before transferring to a north London hospital, summarized the structure of the training:

> It was very good. We worked in blocks. We went on the ward for so many weeks, and then we went into the classroom and did so many weeks. And it went on and on, did exams throughout, which was good. It was great. (Trisha)

While the overall structure of the training remained very similar during those decades, recollections of how long the teaching blocks lasted varied between the nurses. Sinead, who trained in the 1970s, recalled: 'we had eight weeks first of block and then we were on the wards'. Ruth, who trained in the late 1960s, stated: 'I think we did about a month before we hit the wards.'

In Liverpool, Joseph, who also trained in the 1960s, described the emphasis placed on practical skills:

> it was hands on, on the ward and then block training, every so often you'd get two or three weeks academic, and that went on for three years. Halfway through you got, well about twelve months before the three years were up, you had an intermediate test and then after three years you had the main test, you know, finals. (Joseph)

Like many other participants, Joseph observed how his training differed considerably from how nurses have been trained in recent decades: 'nursing has changed and a lot of it is done in university, it's considered a university course'. As mentioned throughout this book, participants frequently expressed the view that their training was better than the current, university-based system. Fidelma, who trained in Bedfordshire in the 1960s, also valued the old ways of 'hands-on' nurse training:

> we did blocks, like you used to go into school for blocks ... But I think that was a good way really. I know now it's all university based and everything, but you can't beat hands on. You learn far more hands on. (Fidelma)

Although our participants were positive about the quality of their training, most stated that it was very demanding: 'it was hard' (Aine); Aileen referred to a 'huge amount' to do; 'it was hard work obviously' (Claire); 'it was really tough' (Sinead).

Training aimed to instil discipline especially in relation to punctuality and respect. Kitty, who trained in Liverpool in the late 1950s, related one incident that stayed clearly fixed in her memory over the decades:

> I remember one day, I hadn't long been doing my training, and I was late coming back to the lecture … However, at the end of the lesson the tutor called me over and he told me off for being late … And I thought, oh my god, I was annoyed with myself but it's as well that it happened at the beginning of my training and that I didn't make that a habit. It's just the way the things went. So that was good. The discipline and the training and the respect for everybody. (Kitty)

Miriam remarked that some days she was tempted to give up and go home but the comradery of her fellow students helped her through:

> Was it all rosy? No. There were lots of tears shed on the way but we had a group of us, we were all in the same boat and we'd go back to our rooms and think about whoever had given us a bad day. Many times, yes, I was going to go back home.

Miriam went on to describe her tutors and how demanding they could be:

> Once the PTS started, we did six weeks in nursing school where we had tutors. We had two English tutors and a German lady and, honestly, the German lady taught us more about life and about nursing and she really encouraged us. She wasn't an easy person, like she would throw something at you. One time, I wrote an essay and she walked down the room … and she threw the paper at me.
>
> But she taught us if you can't look on the bed and see your mother, your sister, your brother, then walk away. You're not meant to be for nursing. Be true to yourself because if you have empathy with the person in the bed, if it's a young girl and she's not coherent, it could be you after an accident, so give her the love and the care that you would want somebody to give you. She was very grounded. She was very strict but if you had a problem you could go to her and she would listen and she didn't judge. There was no judgement at all with her. She was wonderful.
>
> Then we had another tutor who used to read. We might as well open an anatomy and physiology book and just read it because her lectures were, 'blah, blah blah', all on the same tone. We somehow got through. Who knows how? (Miriam)

The account of a tutor throwing an essay at a student may be shocking to those of us who have teaching experience in the twenty-first century but it underlines the strict, demanding and hierarchical learning environment in those earlier times.

Finnuala remembered initially struggling to understand the accent of one particular tutor: 'We couldn't understand him, he'd say like, "The eso-phagus," that was the oesophagus!' Another tutor instilled a real sense of caring for the patients: 'Miss M, who was African. She was lovely ... she went on about caring for the patient'. However, Finnuala got a bit bored in the classroom and was keen to get on to the wards: 'and I thought, "I want some action, this is all quite boring!" Anyway, that came afterwards'.

As mentioned in Chapter 4, the cultural diversity of British cities often came as a surprise. Moreover, given the massive recruitment of overseas medical personnel (Yeates, 2004; Solano & Rafferty, 2007), many hospitals had staff from around the world. As noted by Finnuala and Miriam, their tutors were often ethnically diverse, with unfamiliar accents, so the recently arrived young Irish students had to adjust quickly to their new environments. This also created opportunities for new, diverse friendships.

'A NICE LITTLE COMMUNITY': COMRADERY AND ETHNIC DIVERSITY

Finnuala, like many other participants, emphasized how comradery among the students helped to overcome the challenges of their training: 'We all gelled then and looked out for each other. It was a nice little community amongst us all.'

The ethnic make-up of community among the students depended in large part upon the diversity of 'the set' or cohort. In many hospitals, because of recruitment campaigns, the student group contained large numbers of Irish migrants (Jinks et al., 2014). A nurse who trained in south London, in the early 1970s, remarked that:

> I think most of the set, I would say, was primarily Irish. There were very few English girls that I remember. Irish, Chinese and a few Indians but the vast majority in every one of the sets when I trained were Irish nurses. (Maeve)

Similarly, Aine, who trained in Liverpool in the 1960s, noted there were: 'loads of Irish nurses ... and Welsh'. Linda, who trained in a north London hospital in the early 1970s, described her set as 'mainly Irish' but with some ethnic diversity:

> We did have some English girls, but I could count them on my hand, about three or four. There were girls from Jamaica, a couple of girls from Trinidad, there was one girl from Malaysia. (Linda)

The ethnic diversity of the student cohorts, or sets, depended in part on the geographical location of the hospitals. It is apparent that hospitals in large cities tended to be much more diverse, while hospitals in more rural or suburban areas tended to attract fewer migrant nurses. Sinead trained in a hospital outside London, in a leafy suburb. There were few Irish nurses in her group. In fact, unlike most other participants, Sinead observed that most of her class were English, though there were a few other migrants too.

> a lot of English girls funnily enough in my set. There were three Irish girls and there was an Indian girl ... and there were two West Indian girls, so, if I remember correctly that was our set. And funnily enough the Irish girls and the Indian girl and the West Indian girls all became kind of a group and we all became quite friendly ... (in) the School of Nursing, it was mostly actually English girls and they were so confident, they used to sit up the front and have their hand up, answer questions. (Sinead)

Sinead stated that Irish recruits tended not to be attracted to that particular hospital because of its suburban location. Most Irish students, she said, preferred hospitals in more urban environments. It is interesting that in a 'set' made up mostly of English girls, especially those who appeared to be so confident in the classroom, all the migrant students stuck together and became 'quite friendly'.

Similar observations were made by Ruth who trained in Hampshire: 'There was not that many Irish, because being (Hampshire) it was actually a good bit out of London'. Indeed, Ruth's set was small: 'I remember our group, I think it was actually quite a small group then. There were fifteen of us, which is quite small. I think there was a couple of Filipino girls, and I think a couple from the Caribbean and a few English girls.' As will be discussed in more detail in Chapter 6, Ruth socialized with the Caribbean students and described going to numerous parties together.

Although Linda's set was 'mainly Irish', she formed close friendships with a Malaysian and Trinidadian student and recalled going on holiday together: 'we had a great time, and we still have pictures showing us on horseback, would you believe' (Linda). The extent of socializing and friendships among the student nurses will be discussed in more detail in Chapter 6.

'IF YOU LOOK THE PART, YOU'RE HALFWAY THERE': NURSES' UNIFORMS

For these young students, a key part of becoming nurses was putting on the uniform.

> I always remember the first day putting the uniform on, and one of the tutors said, 'Remember you have your uniform on you now, you have to be confident. Inside', she said, and I'll never forget this, 'you're probably very nervous, but you have to portray that you're looking very confident, if you don't the patients won't be confident in you.' That was very true, that was the first bit of advice that I got with the uniform. (Angela)

Several nurses described how putting on a uniform gave them confidence. For example, Kitty described how the uniform helped her to feel more like a nurse: 'you feel better in a uniform ... It gives you authority ... I think if you look the part you're halfway there'. Finnuala similarly remarked that once she put on the uniform: 'you felt like you were confident.'

Many nurses, despite the passage of time, were able to describe their early uniforms in immense detail. For example, Aisling who trained in the English Midlands in the 1950s vividly recalled the uniform she wore as a student:

> we wore a pink dress, a pin up apron, a starched white cap, black shoes and stockings which you supplied yourself. You had your uniform supplied – 2 dresses for each of us; you got half a dozen aprons, and the laundry was done on site for you. You put your laundry out and it was done and came back to you all lovely and starched aprons. (Aisling)

The precision and cleanliness associated with the uniform was highlighted by many participants. 'If you had one spot on your apron, you had to go to the Nurses' Home and change it straight away.' (Bridget) This precision even extended to the seams on the black stockings, as recalled by Aoife who trained in Liverpool in the 1960s.

> of course, you had to have black lace up shoes and black stockings and they all had seams up the back, didn't they? You had to have them straight, your seams had to be straight and if you had a ladder in them or a hole in them, oh, you were in real trouble! (Aoife)

While the rules were very strict, these young students did sometimes find ways to circumvent them. During our interview with Aisling, her daughter was present and reminded her mother to tell us about the suspender buttons. As noted in Chapter 2, some of these stories are well-honed anecdotes that participants had shared with family and friends many times over the years. Having been reminded by her daughter, Aisling told us how she and her fellow students used to find alternative ways of mending their stockings:

> we didn't wear tights – tights hadn't become fashionable in 1950 – so we used to wear black stockings and you wore a suspender belt with your black stockings. You know the little buttons at the end of your suspender belt? Well, we were always losing them so we used codeine tablets instead of buttons to fasten the suspenders (laughing out loud) you had to go to the cupboard to get your codeine tablets (laughing …). (Aisling)

The uniforms not only denoted identity as a nurse but, rather like a military uniform, they also indicated one's rank and seniority.

> we knew exactly from the uniform who everybody was. The patients knew who everybody was … A white belt was a first-year, a purple belt was second-year, a gold belt was a third-year, a blue uniform was a qualified nurse, a navy was a sister. (Aileen)

Achieving these markers of rank was mentioned, with pride, by many participants: 'you got the belt and the buckle, and you were proud of that and your fob watch and everything, you know, that kind of thing' (Linda). This point was echoed by many other nurses:

> You did an exam at the end of the first year and you got a belt at the end … you were going to do an exam for your blue belt. Then you got a blue belt with a navy stripe in it for your third year and you felt as if you could take on the world, you had got to year three. (Miriam)

Another participant recalled:

> it was lovely when you got a different colour belt because you'd gone up a bit … and I think it was a good incentive too, because it kept you focused, because you knew you had to work and you had to achieve certain things. (Fidelma)

Several nurses mentioned one specific part of their uniform that they especially appreciated: 'my navy cape with the red lining and the criss-cross. They were so lovely in the wintertime, they were brilliant' (Ruth); 'an absolutely wonderful woollen cape with red fleece inside for the winter' (Pauline); 'I wish I kept my cape, that lovely navy cape with the red lining' (Fiona).

However, another part of the uniform was remembered less fondly: 'The uniform, I loved it, apart from the hat, I couldn't make the hat properly. I couldn't make it stick together properly' (Kathleen). Several nurses remarked on how tricky it was to assemble the hat:

> You needed an A-level to make your hat, it was a square like that, and the girls showed me to wrap it around my knee and pull it and you had to bring the corners up, you really did. (Bridget).

Colette vividly recalled that one of her colleagues was very skilled at making the hat and all the others relied on her to help them: 'they were very strict on the hat and there was one girl from Donegal, "S", she used to do all our hats for us, she was very good at it, they had pleats down the back'.

Having assembled the hat, Helen, who had a particularly good crop of hair, then recalled the struggle to tuck it all into the hat: 'you had to fold up however much hair you had at the time'.

While Aileen was somewhat critical of how the uniform had changed in recent years, as we will hear in Chapter 9, she was glad that the hat was no longer a requirement: 'I'm glad they got rid of the hats, they were a bit of a pain.'

While many nurses were very fond of their uniform, some, particularly those who trained in the 1970s, were less keen. Sinead, for example, had no particular attachment to the uniform she wore in the hospital setting: 'Just a blue and white, like a "J Cloth"[2] really, you know blue and white check, never really thought much about it.' Another nurse vehemently disliked her uniform:

> It was dreadful, it was awful, it was the worst. I hated it, it was a purple dress with a stiff white collar with a stud, a paper hat ... and in the third year you had a bright yellow golden coloured belt which, if you were at all plump, which I wasn't in those days, but I always felt sorry for girls who had wide waists, they looked awful! (Orla)

Growing up in Ireland in the late 1960s and early 1970s, Orla was more familiar with American TV programmes which often featured the all-white uniform of US hospital nurses: 'I sort of thought that it would be a white uniform like American nurses'. Mairead had similarly expected to wear a white

---

2 J Cloth is the brand name for a popular type of thin, water absorbent, cleaning cloth.

uniform and she had bought a new pair of white shoes only to find that she had to wear black shoes and stockings.

As will be discussed in more detail in Chapter 9, the changing nurses' uniform was often used to symbolize how much the NHS has changed over time. Instead of dresses, hats, aprons, belts and black shoes, nurses now wear scrubs and trainers.

Overall, while most participants said they enjoyed their nurse training, as we will hear in the next section, they also referred to the pressure to pass exams.

'I WORKED REALLY, REALLY HARD': THE PRESSURES OF EXAMS AND FEAR OF FAILURE

> We had to do practical exams and we had to do written exams and we had to do multiple choice exams and if you failed them ... If you failed two or three of those exams you were out. (Sinead)

Aisling who trained in the early 1950s remembered all her exams:

> We went into the preliminary training school to begin with for three months and we sat an exam at the end of that time and if you didn't pass that exam you weren't kept on the training if they didn't feel you were able to cope. But, of course, I passed that and then three months training then went on the wards and you were assigned to different wards for various experience every three months. At the end of the first year you did your preliminary examinations which I must say I passed them as well.

Aisling went through her training without any setbacks but that meant she was too young to complete the SRN[3] qualification and had to wait for a few months:

> I completed the three years training but, because I started when I was 17 and a half, I couldn't sit my SRN examinations till I was 21 so I had to wait another six months after the training was finished to sit my exam which I sat in June 1954. (Aisling)

The different levels of nursing qualifications are worthy of some explanation here. As Eilish succinctly explained: 'at that time they had two levels of training. They had the SRN, which was the state registered nurse, and then there was

---

3 SRN – state registered nursing qualification.

SEN, which was the state enrolled nurse'. SEN was a two-year programme, while SRN was three years and widely regarded as a more prestigious and desirable qualification.[4] However, new recruits were sometimes not sure of the differences between the two training routes: 'That was back in the days of the SRN and SEN ... Neither of us really knew much about what it entailed but we just sort of thought we'd take a pot-shot and go for SRN.' (Maeve)

Indeed, it has been noted elsewhere in the literature that migrant nurses who were unfamiliar with the system could find themselves steered towards SEN, the lower qualification (Ryan, 2008). Hence, as will be discussed in Chapter 8, it was not unusual to find migrant and ethnic minority nurses clustered on the lower grades (Bheenuck, 2010).[5] During her student years, Orla had noticed: 'most of the West Indian nurses actually were doing the SEN programme'.

At least one nurse mentioned that she had to insist upon doing SRN training:

> I can remember that there were about three or four other Irish nurses there, and I think myself and another one, we were the only two that were selected for the SRN training. And I can remember this panel saying to me – 'Well if you weren't offered a position for the SRN training how would you feel?' And I said, 'Well I wouldn't be prepared to accept anything other than getting onto the SRN.' I still remember that day and I was clear in my mind I wanted entry onto the SRN training. (Bronagh)

For some of our participants, especially those who had only completed National School education in Ireland, the exams could be particularly daunting. One participant,[6] had grown up in the care system in Ireland, and been in foster care off and on throughout her childhood who had only completed primary (national) schooling in Ireland. This background impacted on her self-confidence. Initially, she worked as an auxiliary nurse.

As we will discuss in Chapter 7, while this book celebrates the enormous contribution of Irish nurses to the NHS, it is important to note that many Irish people worked in other roles across the health care services, including as auxiliaries (or nursing assistants), and their contribution is just as worthy of celebration. For example, two of our participants, Deborah and Helen, enjoyed long careers as auxiliaries.

---

[4] Those with an SRN qualification were able to perform a wider range of roles and take on more responsibility than those with an SEN qualification.   [5] For a discussion about experiences of racism in nurse training see Markey & Tilki, 2007.   [6] We will not name this nurse here to protect further her confidentiality.

Others, having started out as auxiliaries, later made the transition to nursing qualifications. For example, after initially becoming an auxiliary, Kitty grew more confident and decided to undertake the nurse training course. She worked very hard to pass her exams:

> I thought I don't want to be the first but I certainly don't want to be the last with my exams so I studied what I could, really. Our school was just a national school really. We did learn but because of our upbringing we weren't confident … I did exams and got through first time. (Kitty)

Kitty remembers her nurse training as 'a lovely time' and she particularly appreciated the feeling of making progress and developing over time: 'you were moving up the stairs, type of thing as well. It was exciting.'

Niamh, in Yorkshire, also found some subjects unfamiliar and had to work hard to pass her exams:

> I had no knowledge of sciences whatsoever, but I was determined. I worked really, really hard. We stayed there for three months and then at the end of the three months we had an examination. Luckily, I did pass the examination. (Niamh)

Her experience contrasts markedly with Orla who had studied sciences for her Leaving Certificate in Ireland and found the academic element of her nurse training 'very shallow'. She recalled: 'I'd studied maths and physics and chemistry, and I was thinking we'd be doing stuff like biochemistry and stuff and it was all very basic.'

Our interviewees are quite varied, not just by decade of arrival, but also by their backgrounds, including their schooling in Ireland. As noted in Chapter 3, secondary education only became free in the Irish Republic in the late 1960s. While those who arrived in the early 1970s, like Orla, had secondary education, several of the earlier arrivals, like Kitty, had finished education at 'national school'.

For some of these nurses, learning and exams came quite easily and they did very well. For example, Bronagh, who trained in the 1960s, received a medal for her exam results: 'I've still got my silver, I was a silver medallist.' However, we heard about some who had failed the exams. Claire told us that she 'messed up' and failed her final exams. She reflected that she was 'too giddy' and if she had her time over again, she 'would have studied very hard'. However, as discussed in Chapter 7, years later, after marrying and having her children, she went back to retake her SRN qualifications: 'when I did the conversion,[7] I sort of flew through it because I was more focused'.

Eilish, as noted in Chapter 3, had been very disappointed in her Leaving Cert results and did not achieve sufficient grades to do the SRN course. Therefore, she had done the two-year SEN course in Leeds.

> I did get in to do the state enrolled nurse, which was a two-year course. And then when I finished that, I thought at some date I will do my SRN training, and I did do, but I waited till 1990 after my children were all at school and doing their own exams and things like that before I went back to university and did a year just to upgrade to a state registered nurse. (Eilish)

Thus, like Claire in London, Eilish in Leeds did eventually achieve her dreams and gain her full SRN qualification. As will be discussed in Chapter 7, it was not unusual for our participants to undertake various courses and programmes of study throughout their working lives and indeed several achieved advanced qualifications including Masters and Doctoral degrees.

After completing their initial classroom-based training (PTS), the students went on to the wards to apply their learning with actual patients.

'VERY REGIMENTED': GOING ON THE WARDS

Although our participants had spent blocks of time in the classroom as discussed above, their most vivid memories and interesting anecdotes related to being on the wards: 'all my memory is of being on the wards' (Bronagh).

While school and classrooms were familiar to these Irish teenagers, the NHS hospital ward was often a completely new and unfamiliar experience. As Una remarked: 'when I first went on the wards, the very first day, I'd never been in a hospital, never been on a ward, knew nothing about it'.

Participants described the wards as big and long with large numbers of beds arranged down each side in the old Nightingale style.[8] Gretta, who arrived in 1948, remembered the ward being huge and some wards having up to 50 beds. Anita remembered 'big, long wards … 40-bedded wards, some of them'. Bridget who trained in the early 1950s recalled: 'In the ward we had about 34 patients in a great big ward with a wooden floor.' Aileen, who trained in the early 1970s, vividly recalled standing 'at the top of a Nightingale ward, 15 beds down,

---

7 From SEN to SRN.   8 This refers to long wards with beds lined up against the walls on both sides.

15 beds (up).' Thus, during those decades, from the 1940s through to the 1970s, it appears that the overall layout of the hospital ward had not changed much from the original Nightingale format.

In describing their nurse training, especially their initiation to working on the wards, one word continually re-occurred in the interviews – 'strict': 'it was strict' (Trish); 'very strict' (Claire); 'extremely strict' (Colette).

On the wards, relations between colleagues followed a rigid hierarchy and clear status, as explained by Una who trained in Liverpool in the 1960s:

> The wards were regimented then because there was a domestic and then there was an orderly ... everybody had status. Then there were the very junior nurses and the more senior second-year nurses and third-year nurses, you wouldn't really talk to them if you were a junior and then qualified nurses and then the sisters and then the matron, it was that sort of system. When the doctors came around on the rounds, things were very different ... everything had to be perfect, you had to be silent on the ward, nobody could make any noise. (Una)

Maeve who trained in London in the early 1970s made a very similar observation: 'Oh, it was very regimented in every way'. The hierarchy and regimented formality on the wards were reflected in how staff addressed each other:

> You wouldn't dare call the ward sister by her Christian name. It was Sister X, Sister Y, Sister whoever ... Even the staff nurse it was 'Nurse'. Anyone who was qualified there was a very definite respect for them and you never referred to them by their Christian names. (Maeve)

Caitriona, who trained in Manchester in the 1960s, described the particular role of the ward sister:

> the ward sisters were very powerful people in those days, they were very powerful people because they ruled the roost, they were very powerful people and you had to do what they said and you just were under their control. I never got a bad report, thank God, but (some) people did and you know, it was very difficult. (Caitriona)

This point about the ward sister 'ruling the roost' was echoed by Maeve: 'then, the ward sister owned the ward. They said who came, what your business was. They actually ran the ward and they knew exactly what was happening'.

Student nurses were expected to follow orders without question. Kitty emphasized that 'answering back' was not allowed: 'you knew your place and the discipline, you just took everything in correctly as well. You didn't answer back'. This point was reiterated by others: 'don't give backchat because you won't win in your backchat' (Maeve). However, in her hospital in south London, Maeve recounted an incident where a student did 'answer back', gave 'backchat', and defied the ward sister:

> I remember her nearly eating a student nurse … I heard this absolute raging roar and I thought, 'Oh my god, what's happening?' So, I went down and this student came out and she was all in a fluster and she was crying.

Nonetheless, despite the strictness and rigid hierarchy, Maeve appreciated the regimental style of her training.

> it was incredibly regimental but in a weird sort of way … it kind of stood you in good stead if you could handle the regimental … because it taught me everything I needed to know. (Maeve)

Similarly, Bridget, reflecting back on her training in the 1950s, especially appreciated and respected the matron who ruled over the hospital: 'matron was a lady but a dragon underneath'.

However, sometimes the strictness seemed excessive. Sinead singled out one difficult character: 'this sister was a bully and was allowed to get away with it … it was horrendous.' This incident was far from unique. Colette referred to another sister who 'really ridiculed us, we couldn't even whisper and we were told off'. Interestingly, Niamh trained under an Irish staff nurse whom she described as 'horrible':

> She wasn't a bit nice to me. She would ask me, 'Can you go and fetch so and so?' Well, I wouldn't have a clue what she was asking me for so I'd come back and say, 'I can't find it,' and then she'd say, 'Well you don't even know what it is, do you?' That sort of attitude. I never forgot her. I don't know why she was like that, but I suppose you always find one, don't you? (Niamh)

Although our interviewees often mentioned that, during their training, other Irish nurses had been helpful and encouraging, Niamh's experience is interesting because it suggests that senior Irish staff were not necessarily supportive of Irish students.

While everyone mentioned the strictness and hard work associated with nurse training, many also spoke about being nurtured. Niamh had a very kind and supportive tutor: 'He was a gentleman.' Sinead referred to the support she received from a ward sister: 'my first ward was a female surgical ward, the sister was absolutely lovely and she did nurture us and look after us.'

In addition, many nurses emphasized how their fellow students looked after them and provided much needed encouragement and support: 'we were all in together and the third-years were looking after the first-years and the first-years were looking up to the third-years' (Maeve).

'VERY LONG HOURS': FROM POLISHING BEDPANS TO RUNNING WARDS

Their introduction to the wards involved the practical application of what they had learned in the classroom. As mentioned in the opening quote of this chapter, many participants talked about learning to make beds and the precision required to achieve envelope corners. One nurse explained that the exactness required on the wards even extended to the wheels on the beds all facing the same direction.

> all the wheels of the beds had to be turned in and all in a straight line and there'd be some kind of lines on the floor where they all had to be and then you'd fold all the bed linen back … and it was all blankets and sheet then and those counterpanes, the green counterpanes. (Aoife)

Another task the student nurses had to learn was how to clean and polish bedpans. As Jane in Liverpool explained: 'you were in the sluice washing bedpans'. Bridget also mentioned being in the sluice polishing bedpans. Una put it succinctly: 'a lot of my first time in the hospital was polishing bedpans!'

Aisling summarized her student experiences on the wards in the 1950s:

> we worked very long hours because we started at 7 o'clock in the morning, you got called at 6 in the morning, and the day shift went on until quarter past 8 at night and during the day you had off two hours in the afternoon … I think it was 48-hour week we worked then. It really was quite hard work. Then, you know, we did all the basic work we did dusting and doing the flowers, the beds and everything. We did have ward orderlies which helped, when you were a junior you got all the crappy jobs to do and then as you progressed it became somebody else's turn to do that. (Aisling)

Julia emphasized that student nurses were 'dogs bodies' which chimes with Aisling's statement that they got all the 'crappy jobs'.

As well as sheer hard work, being on the wards also held other surprises for these young students. Miriam recalled: 'I ended up in a male medical ward with a male nurse for my mentor. I had never seen a male unclothed in my life so it was a huge learning curve but exciting and embarrassing.' Likewise, Niamh noted: 'My first ward was a male, surgical ward. Now, can you imagine, this little girl from Ireland'.

The shock of not only seeing but also washing naked patients was elaborated by Una: 'Now I had never seen anybody naked ever before! I walked into this bathroom and this lady is there, I was so embarrassed! But she probably didn't even notice, she was a little thin old lady'.

While naked bodies could be surprising and embarrassing, dead bodies were an altogether more upsetting issue. Carmel can still vividly remember when she saw a dead patient for the first time:

> I remember the first ward, because I was the youngest in the group, I was put on the children's ward. But the first day I got a shock when a little girl had passed away, and they had the little girl dressed up like a doll. I can still see that child. I'd never seen a child dead before. (Carmel)

Fidelma also mentioned how working on a children's ward could be quite an emotional experience: 'There were sad times too when you came across things you had to face up to and look after, especially children. Paediatrics was tough.'

While their first months on the wards could involve a lot of bed-making and polishing bedpans, as time went on these students were given more and more responsibility. Indeed, many found themselves running entire wards while they were still students. Sheila recalled: 'At 19 years of age I'd be in charge of patients … It was terribly responsible and so yeah, you'd be in charge, in your second year, you'd be in charge.'

Having this level of responsibility meant familiarizing themselves with the names and details of all the patients, which, on a large ward, could be a real challenge:

> you knew what had to be done, who needed discharge papers, who was going, who was … and you knew Miss Smith has to go home, he has to go to X-ray, … who'll be on duty, who'd be coming behind you, what time breakfast will be out – it was like this thing going on in your head. (Aileen)

Many nurses vividly recounted how nerve-wracking it was being quizzed about particular patients and their diagnoses by the ward sisters:

> they would pick whoever and you'd just think, 'I hope it's not me tonight because I don't know if I know enough about the patients.' They would take you round the ward and say, 'Right, so who is this?' You'd have to give the name, age, the diagnosis and the care plan. (Maeve)

Indeed, some felt that student nurses were given too much responsibility in the past.

> So, you would maybe have even a third-year student in charge. Sometimes a second-year student in charge. Sometimes it would just be all student nurses who were running this ward and maybe health care assistants, auxiliary nurses, at the time. (Sinead)

According to Sinead this practice was stopped in the early 1980s:

> That changed when the new nursing officer came and I had qualified ... Student nurses were not allowed, by 1982 students were not allowed to be in charge. But when I did my training, you would have a third-year student, second-year student, first-year students actually running the wards.

Sinead expressed the view that student nurses were sometimes 'thrown to the wolves' in terms of being put into very difficult and demanding situations. She recalled one incident that occurred during her student days.

> I did psychiatry then, it was my third placement in first year ... I remember one day this woman came at me with a, it was like a long nail file, she went like screaming at me with this. I mean, I got such a fright and I remember then the nurses grabbing her and putting her on the ground and giving her an injection. I just thought, 'Oh my god!' It was quite scary and I was 18/19 years old. (Sinead)

Many nurses spoke about being exposed to risks during their student days. Bronagh trained in Kent in the mid-1960s. She spent time on the infectious diseases ward: 'infectious disease was a big, big thing then in the 60s'.

> I can remember ... Mrs K, who had rabies and had came off the boat from India, and I nursed her. So, we had a big isolation ward ... So, I was

> a student nurse and that was Mrs K, who came into the country, and I mean obviously she was in a very poor state when she arrived in the isolation unit in Kent. (Bronagh)

Bronagh later wrote a piece in a nursing magazine about her experience of nursing someone with rabies. She also encountered many TB patients, particularly among poor families from the East End of London who were moved out to Kent for treatment.

> So, there was that speciality that they would have catered for. So, we had the East Enders ... I'd no idea that the East End way of speaking was so different from rural Ireland. Couldn't understand a word they said ... some of the many culture shocks that this young naïve Irish woman experienced. (Bronagh)

Gretta, who arrived in 1948 at the very start of the NHS, trained in London and was assigned to a TB ward. First, she had a Mantoux test to see how resilient she might be to TB, and when they found she had a higher resistance, she was put on wards.

Anita, who arrived in London in 1963, was also assigned to a TB ward:

> I worked on the TB ward, and I did that for nearly eight months I think it was and I found that very hard, the TB ward with wearing the masks and the gowns and all that kind of thing ... So, I felt very sad because some of the people were young people, you know. And I used to worry about my health, if I picked something up off of them but thankfully, we never did seem to pick up anything. (Anita)

The fact that participants from the 1940s through to the 1960s were still being assigned to TB wards shows the enormous prevalence and endurance of that disease.

Another risky practice, raised by several nurses, was lifting patients. Delia spoke about a back injury she had sustained from lifting patients – which she described as a typical 'nurses' problem' – and which ultimately cut short her nursing career (see Ryan and Doshi, 2024 and Chapter 7). Another nurse explained how student nurses were expected to lift patients:

> I was put on a female orthopaedic ward and in those days most of them were on traction and Thomas splints and in bed for three months with fractures, pelvis, fractured hips and things and I remember as these people

were getting more mobile, lifting them myself on my own from the bed on to the armchair. (Una)

Many nurses mentioned that the whole approach to patient care had changed enormously. For example, in the 1950s–60s, patients tended to stay in hospital for considerably longer periods of time than is common practice today:

> a lot of the patients were confined to bed, they weren't mobile, they weren't up and about ... It was orthopaedic so they were having fractures and fractured hips, pelvis etc. and they would be in bed for at least three months at that time, at least three months. Some of them had cancers and things, they were confined to bed and treatments were very, very different in those days. (Una)

Indeed, Ruth, who trained in Hampshire in the 1960s, mentioned that patients were in hospital for so long that a barber was brought in specifically to cut their hair. However, the barber seemed to have quite basic hairdressing skills and all the men got the same haircut:

> The one funny thing that sticks out in my mind is on the wards, they used to have somebody in to shave the men and cut their hair and do all that. We had a guy and he didn't know how to cut anybody's hair. Everybody used to end up looking like Ken Dodd,[9] because he gave everybody the same haircut. You could always tell when he'd been around ... I'd think, 'oh God, not him again'. All these men would be sitting up in bed like this, and they've all got the same haircut. (Ruth)

Long stays in hospital meant that the nurses got to know patients and tended to remember particular patients quite well even after the passage of decades.

In the 1950s, Carmel trained in a London hospital, close to a prison, and vividly recalled when a prisoner spent time on her ward:

> I recall on one occasion we had a young man on the male ward being treated for whatever. He was a prisoner, and there was a policeman sat with him day and night. And in those days the trolley with the food came onto the ward, and the sister dished up the food and we all stood by with our trays bringing it to so and so. We all used to be queuing up hoping we were going to get the tray of food for the prisoner so we could talk to the policeman. (Carmel)

---

9 A popular British comedian in the 1960s–70s.

As will be discussed in Chapter 6, there was often an attraction between nurses and police officers. They often encountered each other socially and professionally and several nurses mentioned dating or marrying police officers.

'YOU USED TO BE SO TIRED': NIGHT DUTY

One of the most powerful memories of nurse training was doing night duty: 'I remember the shock of going on night duty as an 18-year-old and trying to have to stay awake all night. It was crazy but we did it' (Fiona). Many recalled how exhausting a stint of night shifts could be: 'when we went on night duty we were ten nights on and three off. Mind you the first night and the next day was nearly always spent in bed, you used to be so tired' (Carmel).

Sinead vividly recalled her first ever experience of night duty as an 18-year-old student:

> my very first night ever, there was me and an agency nurse who'd never worked on the ward before and that was it and a night sister coming around and I was supposed to be in charge of this ward. I mean and then the next morning it was chaos, we hadn't done what we were supposed to do and I remember the sister shouting at me and she wouldn't allow me to go home until I had finished something and all the rest of it and it was awful. (Sinead)

Bridget, related a story about struggling to stay awake on night duty.

> I was always falling asleep, especially at 12 o'clock. We had a night sister, we called her 'the beetle' because she crept around all night catching you doing whatever you shouldn't be doing, and 'R' actually put sugar in the corridor so that her feet would make a noise.

Despite their best efforts, Bridget and her friend 'R' were caught by the 'beetle' and summoned to the matron next morning.

> Matron's office was in the main corridor and you had to have a clean apron before you went in there. And you went in, and she's sat behind her big desk, she looks just like Florence Nightingale with her little bonnet on and she said 'Nurse, I want an explanation about your behaviour ...' (Bridget)

In this case, Bridget and her friend were let off lightly but, as noted earlier, the discipline could be quite harsh and being told off, shouted at and even humiliated by senior staff was not uncommon.

A nurse who trained in the early 1970s related an anecdote about rule breaking:

> I remember one night I was on the wards then, we were on night duty, I had (another student) and she went to have tea and the sister was coming up and she said, 'Hide the tea.' Well, she came in, so walked straight up to me and she was so awful to me, because you weren't meant to be having tea on the ward. Of course, she saw me hiding it ... She really tore strips off me. But you took it all then, you did take it, you had no choice really. (Angela)

As mentioned earlier, while working on the wards, these young students often encountered entirely new situations. As discussed below, this could result in embarrassment and confusion.

HOSPITAL WARDS AS PLACES OF ENCOUNTER

Hospital wards were 'places of encounter' where young Irish students had new experiences and met new people, from different cultures and backgrounds, for the first time. As noted above, Bronagh, while training in Kent, met many TB patients from the East End of London and found their Cockney accents hard to understand. As she mentioned, she had not realized that people could speak the English language so differently. Several nurses spoke about the challenges of understanding unfamiliar accents.

In Yorkshire, Nessa related an anecdote about accents and colloquial expressions.

> There was a lot of different — both sides, both understanding what they were saying and ... I remember going onto a ward once and a sister saying to me, 'Can you make a pot of char and put it into my office?', and I came out and in those days, you didn't question what the sister was saying, so I came out and I had to ask somebody else what it was she wanted and all she wanted was a cup of tea but [laughs] I hadn't a clue what a cup of char was or a pot of char was. (Nessa)

As mentioned in Chapter 3, Joseph initially struggled to understand the Liverpudlian accent and to have his own strong Dublin accent understood. As also noted in Chapter 3, some new arrivals were shocked by the levels of deprivation they encountered. For example, Jacky went to Scotland to study midwifery and recounted the poverty she observed among her patients:

> my first placement was labour ward and then it really was, you had another student of the same age with you. You had somebody to share the drama and the trauma at times with … It had its ups and downs but just because you were young … you didn't really dwell on … it's only now when you look back at the poverty. Yes there was indeed. There was poverty. (Jacky)

Another shocking issue for many of our participants was abortion which was illegal and completely taboo in Ireland at that time. As one nurse stated:

> I found it hard to relate to some English people, how would I say it? Not so much to do with morals, but to do with sort of a different lifestyle … for instance people coming in for abortions. (Veronica)

In some cases, student nurses could be exempted from dealing with terminations, if they chose to do so, on religious grounds. For example, Julia trained under an Irish Catholic sister who discouraged the students from engaging with patients having terminations:

> they used to do abortions in a small hospital across the road which was part of our hospital, and our nurses used to be sent over there to scrub, and she wouldn't allow any of us to go over there. That did cause turmoil because they said we should have been taught that. But she was trying to protect us. (Julia)

Fiona mentioned that 'a couple of Polish doctors' in her hospital also refused to deal with any abortion cases. Fiona vividly recalled her first encounter with an abortion: 'I remember my first (operating) theatre was a little girl who had had a termination.' Fiona was shocked by the callous attitude of many of the medical staff: 'Some of the consultants, one of them who used to perform the terminations, was so horrible to the girls that you just thought, "This is awful. Absolutely awful."' Even as a young student, Fiona felt a strong sense of indignation and injustice about how the patient was being treated: 'How can they just leave her? It's not her fault whatever happened to her.' The powerful memory of that first experience had a profound impact on Fiona and, as we will hear in Chapter 7, actually shaped her future career: 'I think that marked the

'On the wards': nurse training begins

rest of my career, basically, so I really wanted to work in family planning and sexual health'.

Bridget, who had trained twenty years earlier, in the 1950s, before abortions were legal in Britain, also referred to the very callous attitudes of some hospital staff towards women who had 'back street' or home induced terminations. Her account of what occurred was highly graphic and deeply upsetting (*warning: probably not for the faint hearted*).

> Because abortion in those days was illegal and these poor women had abortions and they all suffered terribly. Sister was a dragon, she was Irish, she hated them because they'd committed 'sin'. These poor women bleeding to death, and we had to save their bedpans in the sluice because the abortions were incomplete and you might find a little – in the bedpans, they were metal bedpans in those days, and we had a big sluice with a big draining board, and they were all laid out there. And the doctor had to come and examine them. So, we had to save all those metal bedpans and the doctor had to come and examine them and sometimes there was particles of babies in there. (Bridget)

Like Fiona, two decades later, Bridget also expressed a deep sense of sympathy for these women: 'I felt so sorry for them because they were desperate.'

Although issues like unwanted pregnancy were taboo in Ireland, that is not to suggest that such things did not occur on a regular basis. Having a baby out of wedlock was considered a social disgrace, as well as a sin and some young women went to great lengths to conceal unwanted pregnancies (Ryan, 2003b). One option, for those who could afford it, was to travel to England and have babies given up for adoption (Garnett, 2000). Secrecy was paramount in such cases and every possible effort was made to prevent neighbours and relatives from finding out. Thus, one can only imagine the shock when a woman planning an adoption discovers that the nurse on her hospital ward in London is actually a neighbour from back home in Ireland. Exactly such an incident was recounted by one of our nurses. To ensure complete confidentiality we will not mention which nurse.

> I remember my second year being on midwifery and obstetrics. Pushing the breakfast trolley onto the ward and looking over to my left and I thought, 'Oh no, there's a girl from home in the bed.' Having delivered her baby. I nearly dropped the whole trays and everything. I thought, 'Goodness me'.

I went to school with them. Very, very posh family ... she was from a very well-to-do family and the baby was being put up for adoption. So, she spotted me and recognized me. You can imagine in the middle of the ward ... worst nightmare. We were only young ourselves.

She said, 'Oh, no.' She started crying and I thought, 'God, how am I going to handle this?' She called me up and she said, 'Look, my mum is due in, I'm begging you, don't let on you know me because I'm shipped out of Ireland to do this and this would just ruin everything for her.' ... 'My mother will just go off her head if she knows there's somebody from home looking after me here so I'm begging you.' I thought 'just get out of here'. I told the sister on the ward. I said, 'I've got to go.'

So that really shook me. Really, really shook me. The poor girl. I think I saw her once when I went home and I just thought she must be thinking, 'Oh my god, if ...' but obviously we're bound by confidentiality.

So far, the focus has been on some of the challenges and difficulties that student nurses experienced, but it would be misleading to suggest that it was all hard work and no fun. As we will hear in the next chapter, many student nurses worked hard and also played hard. Moreover, several nurses spoke about the special efforts made to ensure that Christmas was an enjoyable time on the wards.

'REALLY NICE': THE JOY OF CHRISTMAS ON THE WARDS

Carmel recalled her first Christmas in the hospital:

> on Christmas Day we were all on duty ... The sister did give us a few hours off, but we were all on duty because that was a day for the patients and their relatives. Everything revolved around them. They had their dinner, we had a dinner.

Having enjoyed a Christmas dinner at the hospital, Carmel was then given some hours off to visit her aunt and uncle who lived close by. She discovered that they had kept another Christmas dinner especially for her and so she ended up eating two dinners that day.

Several nurses recounted the special preparations for Christmas on the wards.

> We used to sell teas and coffees to relatives to get money to buy Christmas decorations for the wards. That was one of your jobs was to sell these teas and coffee but it would only be from October until Christmas. (Aoife)

Niamh spent her first Christmas away from home working on the children's ward, however, she did have an embarrassing experience:

> I remember Christmas Day, Matron came to tea. Somebody passed round some liqueur chocolates. Well, I'd never had a liqueur chocolate before so I didn't realize when you take a bite and all this liquid went all down my lovely white apron, so that was a bit embarrassing.

CONCLUSION

In this chapter, we focused on the nurses' stories of their training; from the pressure of exams to the practical application of their new knowledge on busy wards. There were recurring themes of strictness, discipline and respect for authority. From the precision of making beds to the exactness of their uniform, their student days were defined by following rules or facing harsh criticism and chastisement.

Despite hard work and strict discipline, most of these nurses expressed the view that their training was excellent and equipped them well for their future careers in health care. We will hear more about how their careers developed in a later chapter, but first, in the next chapter, we turn to their social life. We will hear about the fun they experienced, as student nurses, and how they made the most of the entertainment opportunities in their new environment.

CHAPTER 6

'Let free for the first time': the social lives of student nurses

> it was the first time I'd ever left home. In those days, at home, you weren't really allowed out anyway, but then all of a sudden, wow, you're out in the great big world. (Fidelma, began nurse training in Bedfordshire in 1966)

In the previous chapter we heard about the rigour of nurse training as our participants combined study and exams with demanding shift work on the wards. These teenage students often held responsible and stressful roles on large wards, despite their relative inexperience. In this chapter, we shift the focus to their social life and hear about what they got up to during their leisure time. As observed in the opening quote above, most of these young nurses were away from home for the first time and so could enjoy themselves without the supervision of parents.

Moreover, as students, living in Nurses' Homes, they also had access to a ready-made circle of new friends. Together, these young people could explore new places. However, as we will hear, geographical location mattered and some areas were more exciting and entertaining than others.

While overall, this chapter focuses on fun and enjoyment, we also hear about some of the risks and challenges faced by young people, especially women, who were encountering new people in unfamiliar contexts.

'YOUNG AND FREE': NAVIGATING NEW PLACES WITH FRIENDS

For most of these young Irish nurses, arriving in the 1950s–70s, cities like London were a new world:

> London was vibrant, West End. Even in those days, Covent Garden wasn't like it is now, but it was still big shops, and the buzz of it all. We went up there New Year's Eve, just on the cusp of '72. We said, 'Must go up to Trafalgar Square,' you can imagine the crowds there. I mean that was just phenomenal. (Finnuala)

'Let free for the first time': the social lives of student nurses

The word 'buzz' was also used by Mairead who had previously lived in Dublin, where she had done her initial nurse training before moving to London in 1973. She compared London to Dublin: 'It was the buzz I think more than everything. Now the buzz is in Dublin but it's a smaller buzz'.

As noted in Chapter 2, Irish society in the mid-twentieth century was a conservative and often quite controlling environment, especially for women. Arriving in British cities, away from parental control, could be a liberating experience. Echoing the sentiment expressed by Fidelma in the opening quote, Claire stated: 'we felt ourselves young and free and off we went'.

Encountering such freedom could present temptations that were hard to resist. Finnuala recalled: 'we did go a bit mad'. A similar point was made by Trisha: 'we were lunatics, and that's the only way to describe it. We went dancing I'd say five nights a week, the whole gang of us'.

While migration can be a lonely experience, the big advantage for these student nurses was the ready access to a friendship group of other young people. Many participants emphasized that they had made enduring friendships in Nurses' Homes:

> I lived in the Nurses' Home and that's how we made friends. Basically, so I'm still friends with some of the girls that we made friends with – you know, 'A' and myself are still best of buddies ... And because we were all in the Nurses' Home together, different groups you know, we used to have little parties and music sessions. (Claire)

Similarly, in Liverpool, another nurse highlighted the importance of her fellow student nurses as a source of companionship and socializing:

> We used to have great fun together and you'd meet in somebody's room and because there were no televisions, no phones and things, you would just meet in one of the girls' rooms. I don't know what we did really, we'd just chat and talk and play music if Radio Luxemburg or one of those radios would be on, we'd play pop music. That was our recreation. (Una)

Kathleen put it succinctly when she described the importance of her new student friends: 'I had a support group around me, my peer group and we went out together socializing.' Similarly, Aisling stated: 'you made a lot of friends with the other girls in the hospital and your social life revolved around them'.

As noted in Chapter 3, Aisling moved to Middlesbrough in the early 1950s to join her aunt and uncle. She did not know anyone else in the city. Thus, living in the Nurses' Home and making friends with other student nurses enabled her to safely and confidently navigate her new environment.

> The girls … were very friendly, with the living-in you make your own friends, so that was it. The main entertainment – dance halls – which we went regularly to and it was so easy to walk around Middlesbrough at that time, I mean you were never frightened of being attacked or anything like that. We used to get a bus which was quite close to the hospital but you know we could walk home at 12 o'clock at night, two or three of us together. (Aisling)

As Aisling explained, socializing in groups enabled these young women to feel safe, even quite late at night. It gave them the confidence to go out and enjoy socializing in the knowledge that they would all travel back home together. This point was repeated by many interviewees. For example, Trisha emphasized the importance of friends as she explored new places in London: 'We were always in a group, we were never separate, which was nice, and it felt comfortable, there was a few of us together.'

These student friendship groups looked out for each other:

> we were a group of 18-year-olds let free for the first time. We had absolutely common sense by the bucketful. We were very sensible, all of us. The group of us, we locked on to the girls who were second-year Irish girls and third-year Irish girls and they were very accommodating. They would invite us to places that they were going or they'd say, 'We're going to so and so, would you like to come along?' (Miriam)

In Glasgow, Jacky also noted how she felt safe and secure socializing around the city: 'It was exciting, it was a city, a big city. We always felt very safe but of course we had a group, we were always together'.

It is important to note that not all our participants had been party animals; some enjoyed quiet, relaxing leisure pursuits. For example, Aine in Liverpool stated: 'I didn't go out clubbing or anything really, no'. Instead, she preferred to stay in the Nurses' Home and 'read or do crosswords and stuff like that, and I used to do a lot of knitting.'

Indeed, some hospitals provided entertainment for the staff. Aisling mentioned that her hospital, in Middlesbrough, had a badminton court for staff. Deborah who trained in Hertfordshire talked about a social club for the staff at her hospital. Bronagh, who was based in Kent, recalled that her hospital had an outdoor swimming pool:

> In the summer the swimming pool was a very popular venue. We loved our swimming pool … I didn't know how to swim, but I mean that didn't stop me [laughter]. You were fearless then, weren't you? (Bronagh)

Among our interviewees, it seemed that hospitals outside London, perhaps because they had more space or because there was less local entertainment, tended to provide these kinds of social amenities for staff and students.

We interviewed nurses across Britain, and it is apparent that geographical location impacted on their opportunities for socializing. Apart from the swimming pool, Bronagh recalled that her social life in Kent was rather limited. For instance, the lack of public transportation severely curtailed her ability to explore new places: 'There was a couple of buses, they didn't go very regularly, and then there was a train to London. But the transport was very limited.' As a result, an occasional trip to London 'was a great outing'. Overall, Bronagh concluded: 'we didn't have a great deal of social life. That's how I recall it.'

Similarly, Nessa, who trained in a small Yorkshire town, stated that there was little entertainment available locally. Therefore, she and her fellow students had to travel miles by bus to go to a dance: 'We used to go to Skipton, which is maybe ten miles away from us. We used to go to the dances there or we would go into Bradford for dancing.'

For nurses based in London, the sheer scale of the city could be somewhat off-putting. Fiona described London as 'huge', so, she and her friends focused on getting to know the local area around the hospital: 'I think we were predominately south-east. We stayed a lot in the area we worked in.'

Indeed, for some of these young student nurses, the social scene in suburban London could come as a disappointment. Orla came originally from Cork city and had worked in an office there for a few years before deciding to train as a nurse in London. Thus, unlike many other student nurses who left Ireland as teenagers straight from school, Orla was a few years older and had worked and earned money before migrating. Furthermore, she came from a middle-class family and had enjoyed leisure pursuits such as playing tennis and boating on the river Lee. In contrast to her busy social life in Cork, she initially found south-east London rather dull and disappointing: 'I had a great time in Cork … The social life in London was very different and I think at the beginning it felt like a let-down but then I figured it out'. Once she made new friends and started to explore the London social scene, Orla began to enjoy herself.

As mentioned above, one of the main sources of entertainment for these student nurses was dancing and, as we will hear in the next section, many showed tremendous commitment to pursuing this activity, even if it meant bending some of the strict rules of the Nurses' Home.

'WE WORKED HARD AND PLAYED HARD': THE DANCE HALL DAYS OF STUDENT NURSES

Deborah was based in Hertfordshire. She mainly socialized locally and in the hospital where, as noted earlier, there was a social club for staff. But on Sunday evenings she and her friends would go to Cricklewood, in north London, for a dance, and then travel back to Hertfordshire late at night.

> We used to go up to the Galtymore on a Sunday. You'd go to Mass at 7 o'clock and leave at Holy Communion time, run out, get the bus into Watford, and get the bus up to Cricklewood … and try to run out before the national anthem.[1] (Deborah)

The repeated references to running and rushing indicate the difficulties of getting to and from the hospital in Hertfordshire on a Sunday evening. But clearly Deborah and her friends felt it was worth the effort.

Many participants described going to Irish dances and some dance halls, like the Galtymore,[2] were mentioned repeatedly by different nurses:

> We went out to places like the Galtymore in Cricklewood … It's not there anymore. There was a place on Holloway Road, I can't think what it was called. I think it was the Gresham. There was a place I think in Shepherd's Bush as well … We used to actually go to a lot of dances, a lot of parties, a lot of Irish social things with all the Irish music and stuff. We went more towards the Irish scene when we got to London. (Ruth)

Our participants in Liverpool also described going to Irish dance venues. For example, Aoife used to go to the Irish Centre in Liverpool every week where she enjoyed traditional Irish dances: 'you'd be dancing all night and it would be the Irish dances'. Aoife fondly recalled particular step-dances like four- and six-hand reels and the intricate patterns of céilí dances 'like the Siege of Ennis and them kind of things … and somebody would teach you how to do it'. These venues also had other kinds of dances: 'and there'd be waltzes' (Aoife).

Interestingly, some Irish venues made a special effort to attract nurses. In south London, an Irish club was so keen to attract more women that it provided free transportation:

---

1 It was traditional in those days for the national anthem to be played at the end of social events such as dances.   2 For more information about Irish dance halls in London see Finbarr Whooley (1997), *Irish Londoners*, Grange Museum. A lovely ethnographic account of Irish dancing can be found in Maev McDaid (2021), Older Irish people living in east London and their stories of migration and dance (PhD thesis).

the Irish club in New Cross Gate gave a free coach right back to the door of the hospital … They wanted more girls to come because there were a huge amount of Irish guys working in the construction industry and other industries around London and they would guarantee that they would have plenty of girls at their dances, in those days. (Miriam)

But it was not only Irish venues that tried to attract nurses in an effort to boost the numbers of women. A male nurse in Yorkshire explained how this special offer was based on the assumption that all nurses were women. He and his fellow male psychiatric nurses took advantage of this discount:

one of the nightclubs in Huddersfield … they decided that it would be a good idea to allow nurses in on a Monday night for free and the reason they did that was because they perceived nurses all to be female. They were shocked when we all turned up on the Monday! (Sean)

Across our interviews, we heard many stories of nurses being sought out for a range of different dances. For example, Ruth also mentioned that student nurses were invited to special events when there was a lack of female dancing partners. The hospital where she trained in Hampshire was located near an RAF[3] base and student nurses were invited to parties on the base:

These guys used to send a coach for us, and we used to go to their dances … They would actually pay for a bus, because there were so many men, it was amazing. Because that's where I met my husband, he was in the Air Force. (Ruth)

This was not a unique arrangement. Another nurse told us how she and her fellow students were invited to a party at the local fire station:

the firemen had their fire station … down the road from the hospital … and they put a letter through to say we were invited to the party on Christmas Eve at the fire station. We were going down the pole … they were so lovely. I mean obviously then they were all men, but there was no problem, they just wanted to party, there was nothing at all, we weren't pestered by them, they were just having fun, just wanted company. We just stayed a couple of hours, and we came home, but you just felt comfortable. (Angela)

---

3 Royal Air Force.

There were also reciprocal agreements between hospitals and local police stations:

> We used to dress up for this ball at Christmastime, and because most of the nurses then were girls anyhow, they always invited some policemen from the local police station to come to our ball. And vice versa, when they had theirs they invited nurses to come to them. So, I dated a police officer, for a short time, before I met my husband. (Carmel)

This reference to romance was not unusual and several nurses mentioned meeting future partners at dances and parties, as discussed in a later section below. Policemen seemed to have a particular appeal for nurses perhaps because, as noted in Chapter 5, they encountered each other socially and professionally. Bridget mentioned that policemen used to look out for nurses and sometimes escort them home.

> We'd be standing on Putney Bridge waiting for the bus and the police cars used to come along, the old Wolseleys[4] ... They got to know us, in those days ... they used to drop us round the corner from the hospital ... they all knew we were nurses ... and two of my friends married coppers from the police cars. (Bridget)

Of course, as discussed in Chapter 5, these teenagers were not simply students but as student nurses they had responsible and demanding jobs. Somehow, they managed to combine their busy work-life, including long shifts and night work, with energetic social lives. As Ruth fondly reminisced: 'we worked hard and played hard'. In some cases, this meant they 'burned the candle at both ends' (Fiona) and were out dancing into the early hours of the morning and going on the wards next morning with little or no sleep. This frenetic schedule was vividly described by Carmel, who trained in London in the 1950s.

> we loved dancing, and there used to be afternoon dancing up in the Blarney in Tottenham Court Road. Strangely enough years later that's where I met my late husband, the Blarney in Tottenham Court Road. Afternoon dancing.
> We'd come off duty at 8 o'clock. I suppose we had our food. We lived across then in houses belonging to the hospital, across the road. And we were supposed to be in bed probably around 11 o'clock in the morning,

---

4 Large model of cars frequently used as police vehicles in the 1950s.

but very often some of us would decide that we'd go to the Blarney this afternoon. So, we'd be dressed in our skirts or nice dresses underneath the blankets. It was no duvets then, it was all blankets and sheets.

There was matron, the assistant matron, and then there was a home sister who was very much into looking after our wellbeing, and she had to do a round about 11.00 a.m. or 11.30 a.m. in the morning to make sure we were all in bed. You'd hear her gently opening the door to see if we were in bed. And, of course, we're in bed, with the dresses on, waiting for her to go. And as soon as she's gone, we could see her going back into the hospital, we're out of bed and away down Clapham Junction to get the bus up to the Blarney in Tottenham Court Road, dancing for a few hours.

Back to the hospital, back into our uniforms, down for our meal and for the roll call going on duty again and we hadn't slept at all. And we were busy at night, it wasn't as if we could have a sleep. Maybe we had an hour or two off, but we loved our dancing. (Carmel)

This account of pretending to be asleep when the home sister did her rounds is suggestive of school children in a boarding school rather than professional young women. Indeed, the Nurses' Home did resemble a boarding school in many ways, for example, there were curfews, and the front door was locked at 10.00 p.m. Hence, although they had 'freedom', they also had to conform to set rules within the Nurses' Home. Student nurses usually got one 'late pass' but that was rarely enough for these lively and adventurous teenagers. As Aisling explained: 'you got a dance pass once a month which was till midnight; we found ways around that of course – we always found someone to let us in the window, you see'.

One nurse even mentioned that her Nurses' Home in Leeds was patrolled at night by a security guard: 'And they had a lovely security man … walking round with two big Alsatian dogs each night' (Eilish). Initially the security guard used to chase away her boyfriend when he accompanied Eilish back home after evenings out. But over time, the security guard came to know her regular boyfriend (and future husband).

So he eventually got to know my husband, so he stopped chasing him out of the grounds at 1 or 2 o'clock in the morning, and they did become more relaxed then, when they got to know that you were going out with, say, somebody for a number of months or whatever; that they weren't just somebody that was coming in, and coming and going. (Eilish)

While noting that some nurses felt that the Nurses' Homes were overly restrictive, Eilish did not mind what she perceived as security and protection: 'you were much more protected in them days'.

Despite the restrictions, students found inventive ways of getting around the rules and regulations. We heard many stories of student nurses sneaking in through windows after late nights of dancing. Ruth recalled: 'I had a colleague that actually slept on the ground floor … and we used to bang on her window. We used to crawl through her window at 2.00 a.m., and just knock all her stuff on the floor. And she'd say, "I'm not letting you in tomorrow, you're not coming through my window".'

Bridget, who was a student nurse in London in the early 1950s, described how she and her friends managed to defy the curfew:

> we had to be in at 10 o'clock every night … The night sister locked the door at 10 o'clock every night, well we had one lovely girl, 'J', older than us, she was well in her late 20s and she never went out. It was a big Nurses' Home where sisters lived on the ground floor and the first-year nurses, second and third-year nurses – that was us – we were on the top. So, we used to bribe 'J' with the Woodbines,[5] she'd do anything for a Woodbine in those days, if we threw stones up … she'd come down and open the door and we'd all troop in. (Bridget)

Of course, interviewing older participants about their youth involves processes of memory and retelling stories. As noted by oral history researchers, memories of the past are often framed by nostalgia for the 'good old days' (Gardner, 2002; Thomson, 1998b). Youth is usually remembered as a time of freedom and fun before the responsibilities of adult life (Ryan, 2006). However, while our participants told many stories about the joy and amusement they experienced during their student days, some also mentioned the darker side of life during those years, as discussed in the next section.

'A CATTLE MART': ALCOHOL AND HARASSMENT AT DANCE VENUES

Many of our older participants mentioned that they did not drink or go to pubs, as Bridget noted in the 1950s: 'of course, women didn't go to the bar' so when they went out dancing they 'had a lemonade'. This point was echoed by Miriam, who arrived a decade later:

---

5 A brand of cigarettes.

> We weren't drinkers. The group of us that were student nurses most of us came from Ireland and most of us had never touched alcohol so when we went out it was soft drinks. We didn't go to pubs ... so girls just did not go into pubs in the late 60s, even in England. (Miriam)

Aoife, who trained in Liverpool in the 1960s, also mentioned that there was no alcohol at Irish dance venues: 'of course it was all minerals, there was no drinking, there was no alcohol.'

Julia was shocked by the central role that alcohol seemed to play in socializing in Glasgow: 'here everything surrounded drink. Everything.'

> I was a Pioneer[6] ... I found that the alcohol side of it in Scotland was awful ... My mother was a Pioneer, my father didn't drink. I never was used to it. I always have been the life and soul of the party, I've always enjoyed company, I love people. (Julia)

However, it was not only in Scotland that alcohol was a potential problem and an issue to manage on a night out. Although alcohol was not served on the premises, it was not unusual for some young men to have several drinks[7] before they arrived at a particular Irish dance hall in London:

> (it) was like a bit of a cattle market, you know ... all the girls would stand on one side and all the lads there, and of course even though they didn't serve alcohol, you don't blame the lads for getting drunk before they came in ... I would hide or go to the toilet if I saw them coming down kind of staggering. I used to hate to say no to them because I felt sorry for them ... because I still understand why they would come in drunk, because it was so difficult for them to ask a girl to dance and then to be turned down. (Linda)

Miriam also observed that some dance halls could be intimidating: 'They (men) stayed one end and the girls were the other end and it was never the two shall meet. It was quite intimidating.' Bridget remembered that some dances could become rough or even violent: 'There was always a fight ... and the next thing there was a punch up and they were all on the floor and we were all running for the bus'.

---

6 This is a reference to someone who does not drink alcoholic beverages and may be a member of the Pioneer Total Abstinence Association which was common in Ireland in the twentieth century.   7 For a discussion about drinking and the role of alcohol among Irish male migrants see Mary Tilki, 2006.

Indeed, some dance halls had a bad reputation. For example, in Liverpool, the Shamrock was regarded by some as quite a rough venue:

> and, of course, the Irish men used to come in at the last minute and then they tried to pick up a woman or a girl ... They didn't waste any time, you know. I mean I was only starting so I hadn't a clue and I was all innocent ... It was a real eye-opener. (Kitty)

Such were the concerns about the Shamrock that some student nurses were strongly discouraged from attending. Jane was training in a hospital run by nuns, and they strongly disapproved of the local Shamrock Irish club:

> We went to a place called the Shamrock and it was all Irish there and it was stone steps up in to it and all that, but once the nuns found out ... so once they found out we were going out, that finished, we were stopped straight away from going there. (Jane)

This was not a unique incident. In Essex, Colette and her friends frequented the Shandon Dance Hall.

> Miss H (matron) said we were not to go there. If you had a late pass, but if you said you were going to The Shandon you would not be awarded it ... because it obviously had a bad name ... when I think of it, it was a bit rough I suppose ... in The Shandon, you just got glasses of lemonade or something, and the boys would come in half drunk. We were told to be aware of them, so probably she had good ideas of what The Shandon was like. But she was very good, she was, you know, it was for our own good. (Colette)

For many students who came from small towns and villages in rural Ireland, a big difference when going dancing in large British cities like London or Liverpool was not knowing any of the men. As Sorcha, originally from Co. Clare, put it: 'it was very strange because you didn't know who you were meeting. Coming from (Clare) ... where you knew everybody, it was very different'. An identical observation was made by Miriam: 'from a country dance hall in Ireland where you knew everybody to a sea of male faces that you didn't know anybody'.

Not knowing anything about the men they met came with some risks. Bridget related a story about meeting a particularly attractive English man: 'I met this gorgeous looking man, and it was wonderful, and I went out with him a few times'. However, much to her surprise, she found out he was a married man with three young children. She quickly ended the romance.

As Kitty stated above, these were 'innocent' teenagers with little experience of life and as noted by Fidelma, many had not socialized much in Ireland, outside their trusted circle of family and friends.

One nurse[8] mentioned that several students became pregnant, including herself: 'I didn't finish my training …' She explained that the 'girls were all going dancing and had boyfriends and all that … We all got pregnant'. Echoing points made by several other nurses, above, she observed that 'England's so different to Ireland'. This reflected the theme that young Irish students were socializing in different spaces and encountering men they did not know. While this could be liberating, particularly from the conservative and traditional constraints in rural Ireland, it also carried some risks. After discovering she was pregnant, this particular nurse quickly married the father of the baby but, as will be discussed in a later chapter, the marriage was not a success. He turned out to be an abusive husband and, after years of unhappiness, the marriage eventually ended.

Of course, although many of the nurses frequented Irish venues, it would be misleading to suggest that they only socialized with Irish people. As mentioned in Chapter 4, hospitals and Nurses' Homes were often ethnically diverse places with opportunities to get to know people from different cultures. In the next section, we discuss encounters with diversity.

'A DIFFERENT PERSPECTIVE ON LIFE': ENCOUNTERING DIVERSITY

The geographical location of their hospitals shaped these young students' opportunities for meeting particular kinds of people. Veronica, who would later move to London, originally trained in a hospital located in a small city in the English Midlands, during the 1960s. Looking back now, she is glad that she had the opportunity to live in a different part of England and to get to know English people.

> I got a different perspective on life in the UK by being in (Midlands), which I think was interesting. Whereas if I'd have gone to London, I think there were so many temptations for the Irish in London, you'd really only be mixing with the Irish, you'd be at the Galtymore, all that kind of thing. Whereas in (Midlands) there was none of that. My main entertainment was going for afternoon tea at patients' houses. (Veronica)

---

8 Not named here for reasons of confidentiality.

Nurses outside of London, especially in towns and cities with fewer Irish residents, seemed to socialize more with English nurses and visit the homes of English families. A similar experience was described by Nessa who went to a small town in Yorkshire in 1957. On her days off, she was often invited to the homes of local student nurses from surrounding towns: 'They always made us feel welcome and as I say, the nurses that were going to their own homes, they always took us, invite us for tea to their houses and things like that. We never felt out of place there.'

Of course, many British cities, especially in the period after the Second World War, were becoming more ethnically diverse. For example, Claire described a central London dance venue as 'like the United Nations' in terms of the many different cultures she encountered.

Moreover, because of NHS recruitment overseas, the staff became increasingly ethnically diverse over time (see Chapter 2). Therefore, hospitals and Nurses' Homes brought these young Irish people into intimate social settings with nurses from around the world. Finnuala commented that there were Chinese, Irish and black nurses 'running that hospital'. Similarly, in a large north London hospital, Trisha remarked: 'There were mostly West Indian and African girls, and the Irish.'

Several of our participants mentioned socializing with students from other countries:

> The West Indian girls had lots of friends, and they used to have garage parties and bottle parties. It was crazy really, because we never drank or anything before we left home. By the time we left (hospital) we were definitely used to going to a party and bringing your own bottle. It was quite fun. (Ruth)

Bridget recalled bringing her friends to Irish dances: 'There were the Jewish girls, Dutch girls, German girls, all of us and I used to take them to an Irish dance hall in Hammersmith ... And we were all doing Irish jigs and Irish dancing'.

This socializing could lead to enduring friendships. Bridget went on to recount how one of the Jewish nurses became her close friend: 'R' my Jewish friend ... her uncle ran the London school of hairdressing in Piccadilly, and we used to have our hair done for half a crown,[9] two and six.' This friend later moved to the US. During our interview in her home, Bridget proudly showed us a photo of the two old friends together, during a holiday visit, still friends after 50 years.

---

9 Half a crown and two and six are references to old, pre-decimalization money.

Linda recalled: 'my main best friend for most of the time was a Jamaican girl, 'R', she was the most beautiful, tall, she was like a model, but she was lovely'. As noted below, Fidelma brought some student nurses from Malaysia back to Ireland for holidays.

While several nurses formed close friendships with nurses from other countries, overall, across the interviews, we observed that the ethnic composition of friendship networks was related to geographical location and the ethnic make-up of the hospital staff. For example, Jacky trained in midwifery in Glasgow and observed that most of the students she met were Scottish. The ways in which location shaped friendship and socializing is clearly illustrated by Ruth. As noted above, when she trained in Hampshire, she socialized with nurses from diverse backgrounds, including going to 'West Indian' parties. However, after moving to a hospital in London, Ruth tended to socialize more in Irish venues: 'We gravitated more towards the Irish scene, because they seemed to have much more going on, or so we thought anyway'. This chimes with the earlier observation by Veronica, who trained in the Midlands, that Irish nurses outside London tended to mix more, while nurses in London tended to socialize in Irish circles.

Liverpool was another city which provided plenty of opportunities to socialize in Irish cultural venues. Joseph spoke about his largely Irish social circle: 'I might as well have been in Ireland because my company was mainly Irish'.

However, that is not to imply that all Liverpool-based nurses chose to gravitate towards Irish venues and Irish friendship groups. The experience of two sisters, Aoife and Una, interviewed together in Liverpool, reveals how hospitals, even in the same city, could vary enormously. The sisters trained at different hospitals and, as a result, tended to socialize in different circles. Aoife worked in a hospital which recruited largely from Ireland and hence had large numbers of Irish student nurses. As mentioned earlier, Aoife and her fellow students tended to socialize mainly in Irish clubs and enjoyed céilí dancing. Meanwhile her sister Una trained in a different hospital where there were very few Irish students and thus, she tended to socialize with a more diverse group of people. As a result, Una rarely went to Irish dances in Liverpool.

So far, we have focused on social life and entertainment, especially going to dance halls. But that is not to imply that these young students had plenty of money to spend. Indeed, as discussed below, their finances were usually rather limited.

'WE NEVER HAD ANY MONEY': ENJOYING THEMSELVES ON A SMALL BUDGET

Most of the nurses remembered their student years as a time when they socialized a lot and had fun but within very limited financial means. As students they were paid while they trained but wages were small. Bronagh recalled that 'money was limited', while Carmel stated that 'money was very small' and Trisha stated emphatically 'we never had any money'.

Most recalled that their monthly salary was meagre. Three 1950s migrants recalled their salaries. In Leeds, Nessa remembered receiving £12 per month, while Carmel in London stated that she received between £12 and £15 per month and Aisling, in Middlesbrough, recalled that her monthly pay packet was between £10 and £12.[10]

As students, most participants stated that their accommodation was 'free'. As Nessa stated: 'we had free board and free food'. Similarly, Bronagh recalled: 'we had free accommodation, food, we were well fed, too well-fed, sometimes'. Moreover, their laundry was also provided. As Aoife explained: 'they did your laundry, the hospital did your laundry ... you could just take your laundry off, your uniform off and somehow it got returned to you'.

However, while these services were described as 'free', other participants explained that the costs of all these services were deducted from their wages at source: 'they took your accommodation costs and food and everything out of your wage' (Sean). Similarly, Aisling explained: 'When I lived-in as a student and of course ... your board and lodging was taken off.'

Nonetheless, most live-in students acknowledged that they had very few living expenses except for buying their black stockings and shoes. However, as young people they spent most of their limited wages on going out and socializing.

Eilish described going out several nights per week, sometimes four nights, mostly to the Irish Centre in Leeds: 'It probably wouldn't have cost us much to get in, but it was always the place to meet, and they had like Big Tom, Philomena Begley,[11] all of them would have been in the Irish Centre'.

A busy social life on a small salary meant that some young students were running out of money by the end of the month: 'I was kind of always overspending with my finances' (Mairead) and 'of course we ran out of money, because we were going out and spending it!' (Finnuala).

---

10 this is the equivalent of around £300 per month in 2024 – https://www.inflationtool.com/british-pound/1956-to-present-value?amount=12&year2=2024&frequency=yearly.
11 Popular Irish entertainers in the 1960s–70s.

They had to find ways to reduce their costs. Trisha recalled walking to venues instead of taking public transport to save money but also getting occasional free bus rides:

> We'd walk ... down to Manor House, because we never had any money as usual. But the bus drivers, the clippies[12] on the bus, they were always Irish and they'd see us come. 'Come on girls'. They'd let us on for free. We really, really enjoyed life, absolutely, even though we didn't have a lot of money but we got by. We thoroughly enjoyed it. (Trisha)

Other interviewees also mentioned getting free bus rides. For example, a nurse in Liverpool recalled:

> The drivers always let you on the bus for free. They wouldn't do it now ... Because they knew where you were going and you had your uniform on sometimes, you see, and they'd let you on, 'Go on.' It was a bonus really, wasn't it. (Aine)

Trisha also mentioned how students used to save money on fashion: 'we shared our clothes as well. If my item fitted somebody she'd wear it, so we got by, it was lovely.'

But not all these students spent their money on going out and socializing. Some were more careful with their limited funds. 'I was always a bit of a saver. I used to save up for my holidays, and then I would go to Ireland' (Bronagh). We will hear more about holidays to Ireland in a later section.

Carmel described how her uncle in London helped her to open a savings account and encouraged her to manage her finances.

> My uncle, God rest him, took me to the Post Office before I even started my nursing to open an account, a little savings account. And he made sure every month I put a few pounds away towards my holiday. (Carmel)

While those nurses who remained in the Nurses' Home could save or at least manage their money, those who 'lived out' in flats had to budget much more carefully.

---

12 Old name for bus conductors who issued tickets on buses.

'LIVING OUT': MOVING INTO FLATS

Although of adult age, these students were not allowed simply to move out of the Nurses' Home: 'Then you had to get a letter from your parents to say that you had permission to move out.' (Miriam)

However, as Colette explained, obtaining such letters could involve a bit of subterfuge: 'if you wanted to live out, you had to have a letter from your parents. But of course, we all wrote our own, we always wrote letters pretending'.

Miriam moved to a flat in south London in her final year, along with two other Irish students:

> We found a two-bedroom flat over a furniture shop and three of us ... it was two single beds in one room and a one bed in the other room. Tiny little room. You went up two steps to the bathroom and down two steps to the sitting room and kitchen and we thought we had landed. It was lovely. It was the freedom. We had a television that we used to have to bang on the top to get a proper picture. We bought cheap saucepans in the market. We bought cheap food in the market ... We used to come up to Tooting Market to buy clothes because it was cheap and it was wonderful. (Miriam)

While several student nurses chose to live out and enjoyed the 'freedom', in one case a student was given no choice but to leave the Nurses' Home.

As noted earlier in this chapter, many nurses managed to circumvent the strict rules at the Nurses' Home. However, only one nurse stated that she had breached the rules so much that she was asked to leave. Linda stated quite frankly: 'I was chucked out of the Nurses' Home'. During her nurse training, Linda had to return to Ireland suddenly following an unexpected family bereavement. Her sister, who was a nurse in the US, also returned to Ireland for the funeral. The sister was reluctant to return to the US and so decided to join Linda in London and get some work with a nursing agency. Linda invited her sister to move into the Nurses' Home, temporarily, while she sought accommodation.

> She came over and stayed with me in the Nurses' Home. So, of course, that wasn't allowed, so anyway, she came and stayed and was there for only about a week. We managed to hide her in there. But I think one of the cleaners found out and squealed on us. (Linda)

Having been discovered, both Linda and her sister were given notice to vacate the Nurses' Home.

Living-out, as it was called, meant not only leaving the security of the residential accommodation but also having to manage money in a different way; to pay rent, deal with utility bills and buy food. In Liverpool Una recalls moving into a shared flat with four other students:

> Most of the other girls I was with, because I was with English girls and Welsh girls, they went off home on their days off but I would be there, so I would be the one that would have to do this coal fire and go and get coal from outside in the coal shed or something and try and light it and deal with it.
>
> We would have no money for the electric meter and in the mornings we would get up and mostly wash our hair in absolutely cold water and shower yourself in absolute cold water and then run like anything to get the bus and nothing, no breakfast, nothing to eat. (Una)

Ruth moved into a flat with a friend in west London:

> It's a whole new way of life, because when you live in the Nurses' Home and you're close to the hospital your life is very structured. You get up in the morning, you get dressed and have your breakfast, and you just walk ... The Nurses' Home was there and the hospital was there, so it was just very convenient. A bit spoiled really, I suppose. (Ruth)

However, living in a flat meant being more organized: 'You had to travel. You had to get up in time and get a bus in the mornings, and the evenings for night shifts and things like that' (Ruth).

Another nurse recalled that at the end of each month, she and her fellow nurse flat mates would have to pool resources to buy food.

> I remember at the end of the month we were all getting together, there were five of us, we had no money for food, and we all had to get together to see how much each person had. I had about 20p left, this was for dinner that night. This one girl, you'll never guess, she had a pound, we were all thrilled, she had a pound, the rest of us had pence, but we managed to get together and we could afford something to eat, you know, crazy. (Angela)

In the Midlands, Veronica and her friends moved out of the Nurses' Home but quickly realized they had made a mistake and were keen to return to the security and comfort of the Home:

> I remember we went to live with an Italian family, and it was hell. We were trying to get back into the Nurses' Home, believe it or not, after about two months because it was ... it wasn't good. We wanted to get back in, we were frozen, and we were starving, to get back into the Nurses' Home because we would have a staff nurses' sitting room, with an open fire, and better treatment as a staff nurse. But we had made the foolish decision to move out. (Veronica)

Given their limited funds, it is no surprise that student nurses could not afford foreign holidays. In any case, for the vast majority of these young people, they wanted to spend their annual holiday in Ireland. But, as we will hear below, this could also be an emotional experience.

'THE EXCITEMENT OF BEING BACK HOME': HOLIDAYS IN IRELAND

For most of our participants, their annual holiday meant a trip back to Ireland to see family and friends. As Miriam recalled: 'We honestly never went anywhere else but to Ireland.'

As students and then as newly qualified nurses, they could not afford foreign holidays: 'then of course we never could afford holidays anywhere so we always went back to Ireland on our holidays ... foreign holidays were just a no, no' (Aisling).

But even going to Ireland was not necessarily a cheap holiday:

> I would save up and that was where my money was spent, and it wasn't cheap then. We didn't have the EasyJets and you didn't have some of the low-cost airlines. It was flying with British Airways from Belfast to Heathrow, so it wasn't cheap. But that was where I saved up my money and I went home, and I had a good time there, and I used to share stories with my sisters obviously about nursing, and tell them all the stories, which they all seemed to enjoy hearing about my life. We used to write as well. I'd write a lot to them. (Bronagh)

Carmel also remembered saving up her holidays to go to Ireland once a year: 'we couldn't afford to go to Ireland twice on that sort of money. I used to go always in September, I love September in Donegal.'

1. Mary Hazard, in nurse uniform 1952

2. Nora and Tony Hayward, wedding day 1954

3. Teresa Doherty, in uniform 1955

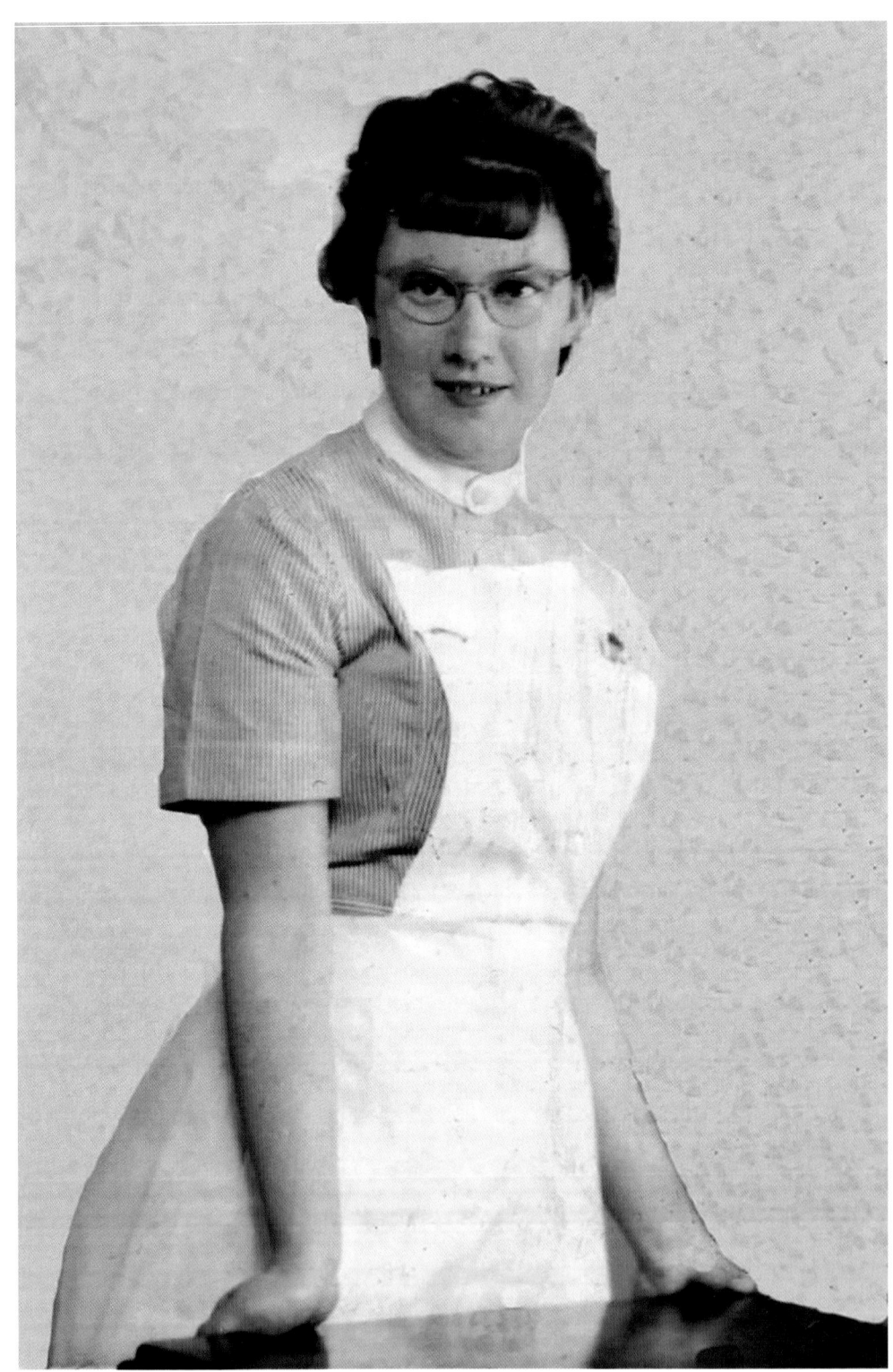
4. Josie Caulfield, in uniform 1959

5. Noreen Schierz and nursing cohort, 1961

6. Dee Cokeley, in uniform 1965/6

7. Bernie Naughton and nursing students, 1966

8. Ethel Corduff, outside hospital building 1966

9. Lorna Keating, in uniform 1972

10. Maureen Ryan, on the picket line 1974

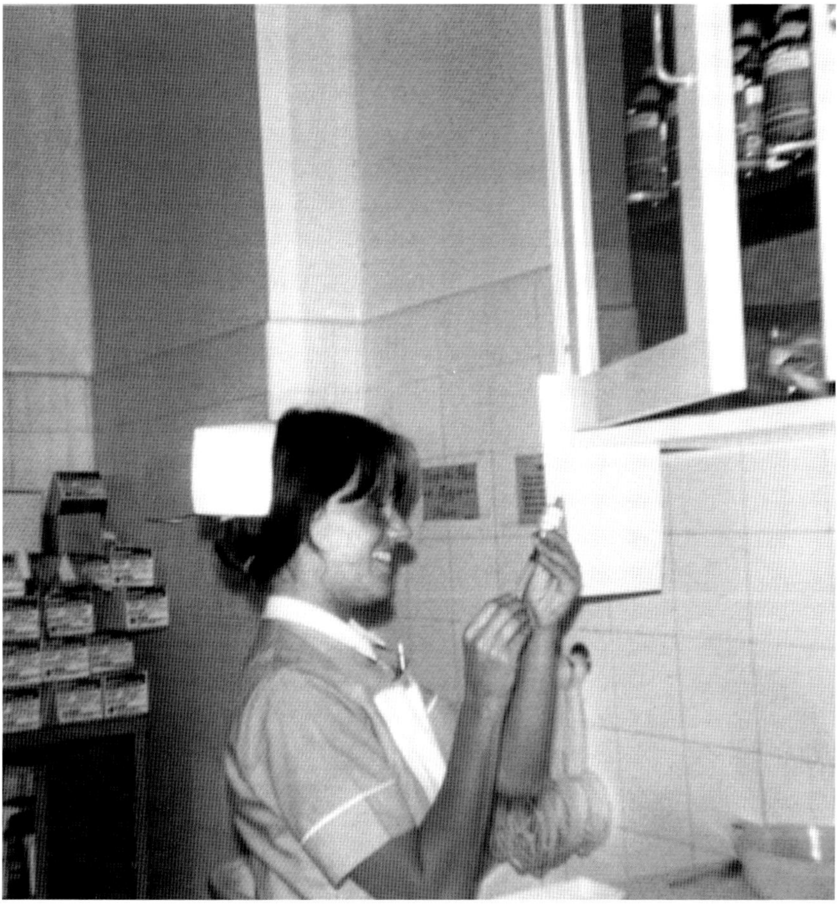

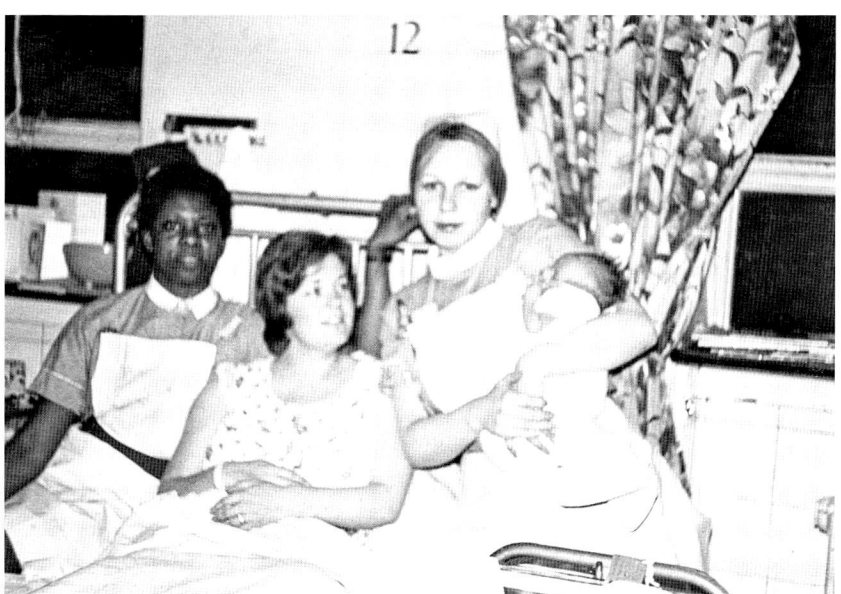

11. Phil Ellen Donovan, on the wards, *c.*1975

12. Geraldine Hilder, on the wards, 1970s

13. Betty Graham, district nursing 1986

14. Betty Halfpenny, in uniform 1990s

15. Eddie Mulligan, graduation 1994

16. Group photo of Irish nurses outside Lewisham Hospital, 2022: (*left to right*) Anne Ranshaw, Anne Scriven, Marian Davies, Olive McKeown, Maria Rankin *and on the far right is* Phil Ellen-Donovan (photo by Fiona Freund)

17. Group photo, Luton Irish Forum St Brigid's Day event, 28 January 2023: (*left to right*) Rosanna Anderson, Rosaleen Burke, Betty Halfpenny, Louise Ryan, Gráinne McPolin

18. John Redmond, 2023

19. Group photo at Liverpool Institute of Irish Studies, June 2023: *(back row, left to right)* Carmel Mohan, Louise Ryan, Neha Doshi, Gráinne McPolin; *(front row, left to right)* Mary Dowling, Margaret Robson, Eileen Walsh, Mary Cook, Dame Lorna Muir.

20. Group photo at Irish Embassy, London, film premiere, February 2024: (*back row, left to right*) Gráinne McPolin, Mohamed Ali Elota, Ethel Corduff, H.E. Ambassador Martin Fraser, Tom McGorrian, Olive McKeown, Neha Doshi; (*front row, right to left*) Louise Ryan, Rosemary McLoughlin, Mary Hazard, Bernie Naughton, Lorna Keating, Madeline Brett-Richards

A fortnight's holiday in Ireland had to be negotiated around working commitments: 'I used to go home about once a year. I didn't go home for Christmas because you couldn't get Christmas off, everybody had to be there at Christmas ... I think we only got two weeks holidays' (Yvonne).

For most participants, the annual trips to Ireland usually continued throughout their lives (see also Ryan and Doshi, 2024), particularly whilst their parents were still living: 'Probably once a year at least, while my mum certainly was still alive, I would have gone back once a year.' (Pauline)

Some nurses brought friends back to Ireland with them, for example Fidelma used to bring fellow students for a holiday: 'even the Malayan girls, we brought them to Roscommon for a holiday, which was really nice'.

Niamh vividly described her joy on arriving back in her hometown: 'I can remember the excitement of the train pulling into the station ... the excitement of being back home again was just unbelievable.' However, after the fortnight, leaving home at the end of the holiday was 'really sad'.

Eilish explained that the departure felt even sadder because of the limited communication between visits:

> Oh, it was horrible because in those days, there was only, you'd write a letter and you waited a week for that letter to come. Nobody had mobile phones that you could ring home every couple of hours or anything like that. It was, you felt as though, you were leaving for a long time. (Eilish)

But although they felt sad leaving home, most of them quickly settled back into the routine at work: 'It was heart-breaking, I used to cry my eyes out. It was quite hard ... then once you got back to work, and you got back to a routine again you were absolutely fine, until the next time' (Ruth).

Of course, it is important to note that some participants were not on good terms with their families and did not visit regularly. For those who grew up in the care system, and did not have a family home to visit, the extent to which they had holidays in Ireland depended on connections with friends or former foster carers: 'I always went to the foster people that I knew in my younger years'. Another nurse who also grew up in the care system had been desperate to leave Ireland and vowed never to return and indeed 'it was a few years before I went back' but eventually she did start to visit a good friend and began to enjoy holidays in Ireland.

Some other participants had strained relationships with their families. Bridget did not get along with her mother and did not visit Ireland very often, until later years. Sheila was estranged from her parents after a family dispute and did not visit Ireland for many years: 'It was very hard and it was just the way it was.' In some cases, these family disputes related to the choice of partners. As discussed in the next section, most of our nurses met their spouses in Britain, frequently at dance halls.

'I WAS MADLY IN LOVE': MEETING FUTURE PARTNERS

Two of our interviewees were joined by boyfriends from Ireland – Jane's boyfriend joined her in Liverpool, while Niamh's long-term boyfriend followed her over to Leeds. But the vast majority met their partners in Britain. Usually when they were very young and mostly while still students. Typical among these was Anita who stated that, when she started dating her future husband: 'he was 19 and I was 20'.

Some met their partners through blind dates arranged by friends. Trisha vividly described meeting her future husband on a blind date organized by a mutual friend: 'She was a friend of mine and she invited me for dinner one day … and when I went in who was there but 'T' sitting there. He'd asked her to invite me, and that's how I met him.' Prior to this, Trisha had seen 'T' a few times in the local pub where he played music:

> I had seen him and I admired him because he never swore. Because all the Irish used to swear like a trooper. Now he's of Irish descent … I thought, 'He's a nice fella'. And a good sense of humour and everything … I'd see him in the pub. He was a great singer, played the guitar, full of jokes and a happy chap. (Trisha)

Given that dancing was one of the main leisure activities of our participants, it is hardly surprising that most met their partners at dances. Interestingly, the type of dances changed over time. In the 1970s the dances were more likely to be discos. For instance, Claire met her future husband on a disco boat on the river Thames. Fiona was at a reggae dance when she met her future husband. But in the 1950s and 1960s, it was more likely to be ballroom dances:

> I got married in 66. A chap from Liverpool. It was very good. We met at ballroom dancing lessons at the Odeon Cinema in Liverpool. They had a room upstairs … you could go down to Liverpool, get the bus, and it was safe. So that's what I did … My hubby was my partner and continued to be my partner. It was a long romance. Nowadays everything is so quick; they all go to bed now … We learnt together and of course it was ideal for the rest of our lives to dance. (Kitty)

Indeed, Kitty and her husband became well-known for their love of ballroom dancing: 'proper ballroom dancing ... It is graceful, very graceful. They used to call us Fred Astaire and Ginger Rogers'.[13]

Kathleen also met her husband at a dance in Liverpool but, unlike Kitty, dancing did not become their main hobby:

> he could dance, he had a gold medal in dancing ballroom and stuff and I just had Irish ballroom, so we couldn't really dance together but we loved walking and we loved the theatre and the cinema, all those things in common, so mostly that's what we did. We didn't do a lot of dancing but we did go out for days out, we loved going to the seaside. (Kathleen)

Deborah met the man she would later marry at a dance hall close to the hospital where she worked:

> the Wesley Hall belonged to the Wesley Church. They didn't sell alcohol, so you could go to the kitchen and get minerals, so I went out, got a mineral, come back in, and that's when he come and asked me to dance. (Deborah)

Gretta, our oldest participant, arrived in London to train as a nurse in 1948. We interviewed her at home accompanied by her husband and daughter. Throughout the interview, her English husband, aged in his 90s, appeared to be asleep in a chair. However, when we asked Gretta where she met him, her husband suddenly entered the conversation. When Gretta said 'I met him at a dance I think' he supplied the name of the venue: 'St Joseph's' – a Catholic social club: 'yeah, I met her in there and that was it, yeah'. In this brief but lovely moment, the couple remembered the first meeting that led to their marriage of over sixty years.[14]

Like Gretta, it is noteworthy that more than one third of our interviewees married British partners – mostly English, but some Welsh and Scottish. Those who married British men tended to meet them at hospital events or through volunteering. For example, both Mairead and Sheila met their English husbands through charity volunteering activities. Others, such as Sorcha and Orla, met their British partners through mutual friends.

Angela, in south London, noted that she and most of her Irish nursing friends married English men. Mairead, in north London, jokingly remarked that

---

13 Stars of many Hollywood musical films and internationally renowned for their great dancing partnership.   14 We were sad to hear that both Gretta and her husband passed away during the last year after a very long and happy marriage together.

there were advantages to marrying a 'native': 'He is a local man, I think it's prudent to marry a local man, they have local knowledge.'

Finnuala, also in London, described her mother's reaction to the news that she was about to marry an English man:

> well my mother said to me, 'Couldn't you find an Irish fella?' and I went, 'What do you mean, find an Irish fella? Well, I didn't go out searching.' But he was nice, a nice guy, so my mother used to come over. (Finnuala)

But families did not always react so well: 'my mother was shocked when I married a Protestant' (Sheila). Another participant was so concerned about her parents' reaction that she did not inform them until after the marriage ceremony:

> I didn't tell her I got married because I knew she'd kill me marrying an Englishman, and my father, so I wrote afterwards. We got married in a registry office in Harrow, I was ... 21, 22. I'd just finished my training ... and he was my first boyfriend, I'd never had a boyfriend. So, of course, I was madly in love, wasn't I? (Bridget)

Marrying their first boyfriend at a young age was a common theme among our participants, as will be discussed below.

Angela said her family accepted her English husband but a neighbour, back in Ireland, made a curious remark:

> Yeah, they were fine with it because my older sister had married an English man, but my neighbour in Ireland said, 'Oh, I know now he's not a Catholic, but he's very nice and you're very lucky.' She said she won't hold it against him that he wasn't a Catholic. And actually he did become a Catholic afterwards, my husband became a convert. But yeah, there was no problem there really because I had older sisters that had, yeah. (Angela)

Claire also married an English man who got on well with her family in Ireland:

> my family thank goodness weren't politically, you know, they didn't have opinions. He's very good-humoured, so really, I suppose when he did go to Ireland ... So, he did fit in, I have to say – I mean obviously if he didn't, there would have been problems. (Claire)

For the majority of our nurses, who had married Irish men, they usually met at Irish dance halls. As a result of socializing in mainly Irish venues, it is hardly surprising that most of the men they met were Irish or second-generation Irish. Veronica explained how she met her husband at an Irish dance:

> there was a lot of work for Irish construction workers, so a lot of Irish men came ... including my husband. They started a dance there ... in the local primary school on a Sunday evening, so that's where I met my husband. (Veronica)

By coincidence, although a few years apart, two nurses had met their future husbands at the same dance hall. Carmel, as discussed earlier in the chapter, regularly attended afternoon tea dances in central London. At one of these dances 'I met my late husband, the Blarney in Tottenham Court Road. Afternoon dancing.'

Colette also had frequented The Blarney:

> I was at a dance in The Blarney in Tottenham Court Road and I was dancing with somebody and this other man said to me, 'Can you keep the next dance for me?' I said, 'Oh yes,' who turned out to be my husband eventually. I then arranged to meet him the following few weeks. (Colette)

As well as socializing in the same circles, one nurse explained that she was particularly attracted to her second-generation Irish husband because of shared cultural background:

> And it's a strange thing that you're drawn to people of the same culture ... there is a bit of a draw. Subconsciously, you're getting in the crowd and meeting up with somebody who's second-generation Irish. (Yvonne)

Helen married an Irish man who turned out to be a 'scoundrel' and they later divorced. She reflected that she had been young and a very 'innocent person.' As noted above, most of our participants married their first boyfriend at a very young age. Sheila married at 21, Aileen was 22 and her husband 23, Eilish was 23 and her husband was 22.

Niamh qualified in 1961, in Yorkshire, and married immediately: 'I got my final results in July 1961 and I got married in September 1961.' In London, Angela met her partner while still a student, started to plan their wedding and got married immediately after her qualification when she was aged 22: 'so I met him in the May in the second year and yeah, I think we just planned to get married when I'd finished my training ... we did the final in May and I got married in July'. Looking back, she does not know why they were all in such a hurry to get married young: 'I don't know why we all seemed to – yeah, we did all get married quite young'.

Another nurse, who also married immediately after qualifying, reflected that it was just the norm in those days to marry young:

> we all got married that year we qualified, all of my friends … we all got married within a few months of qualifying. I think psychologically if you weren't married by mid-20s there was something wrong. It's weird to say that, isn't it? (Orla)

Deborah was most unusual in that she married at the age of 30 and interestingly her husband was several years younger. On the day of interview, we met Deborah and her husband of over 40 years. Now in their 70s the age difference was not apparent but in previous years he had been considered her toyboy:

> he's three years younger than me. When the hospital, we were going to the doctors' ball and you could bring somebody, and I put down, 'Deborah and toyboy', and it stuck, they all call him the toyboy. (Deborah)

Remarkably by today's standards, Maeve, who married at 28, was considered an 'old' bride:

> My cousin used to joke and say, 'Oh, I don't think you'll ever get married,' but I wasn't in any hurry to get married. I was having quite a nice time. I was enjoying my career and I thought: 'I'm not getting married just to be married.' I was 28 when I got married. It was old.

As will be discussed in Chapter 7, Maeve credits her rapid career advancement to the fact that she did not marry early.

CONCLUDING THOUGHTS

As older people, looking back over fifty years, in some cases sixty or even seventy years, there may be an element of nostalgia in how the past is remembered. As teenagers and student nurses in cities like London, Liverpool, Leeds or Glasgow, they mainly recalled having fun, getting dressed up and going out socializing with friends.

Having left the conservative social atmosphere of mid-twentieth-century Ireland, and the watchful eye of parents, these young people enjoyed a new freedom in Britain. Nonetheless, while the overall tone of this chapter has been positive, there were also some hints at a more serious side of life. Dance halls, although great fun, could also be risky places where drunken men harassed inexperienced young women. Not knowing these men could result in some nasty surprises such as discovering a boyfriend was actually a married man.

Thus far, we have concentrated on the early life of these participants, especially their years of freedom as young, single student nurses. In the next chapter we now move on to discuss what happened after they qualified and how their careers developed over time.

CHAPTER 7

'The world is my oyster': developing and changing careers over time

> I mean, this career, I even say to this day, you can turn your hand to any side of it. (Fiona, began nurse training in London, 1974)

In Chapter 5, we discussed the nurses' training from the 1950s–70s. Interestingly, although they trained in different hospitals, across Britain, there appeared to be remarkable similarity in their training stories. In this chapter, we will hear how their careers developed over time. Henceforth, the stories become much more varied as their careers went in very different directions reflecting the enormous range of opportunities, within the NHS, to pursue different specialisms both within hospitals and across community settings.

Moreover, as discussed below, the career trajectories were rarely straightforward, linear progressions up the ranks of nursing. Following marriage and parenthood, many participants took time out or switched to part-time working, including night shifts, for many years. During the post-war era, as noted by Paula England (1992) in her analysis of women's employment, most mothers in Britain did not engage in paid work. So, nurses were quite unusual in being able to continue working within their chosen careers, albeit part-time, even when their children were young.

The extent to which so many of our interviewees managed to successfully develop their careers, after taking time out to have children, is testament to their own hard work and commitment but also the ways in which the NHS encouraged continuous professional development opportunities.

Given the range and variety of their career stories, in this chapter, keeping with the oral history approach, we follow their biographical narratives through key life transitions starting with qualification and their first posts.

'GOING UP THE LADDER': CAREER PROGRESSION POST-QUALIFICATION

After completing their training, several nurses took up responsible roles, while still at a young age. For example, Carmel, who qualified in 1957, got a staff nurse post at the age of 21:

> When I qualified I was the youngest nurse in the hospital, the youngest staff nurse in the hospital. I was just 21. I remember matron congratulating me. Then we were given a nice badge with the hospital name, and then we got the GNC[1] badge as well. I've got them both there somewhere. So, showing off where we trained. We always used to look at badges when other nurses came in. (Carmel)

Indeed, Carmel proudly showed us her badges when we visited her house to conduct the interview.

After completing her SRN training in 1971, Miriam applied for and, to her surprise, was successful in getting a 'Sister' post at a hospital in south London: 'I was the youngest sister they ever had appointed'. She relished the challenges of this new and demanding role and took advantage of all the training opportunities provided:

> It was a great experience. I loved every minute of it and I wouldn't change it. It was the best thing I ever did … There was in-house training. You went off and you could do management courses … and I did all that. (Miriam)

The early career progression of Carmel and Miriam reflect the experiences of several other participants. However, as noted in the previous chapter, most of our interviewees married young, usually in their early 20s, and had children soon after. This was also the case for both Carmel and Miriam and, as we will hear later on, both had to give up their responsible posts.

In contrast to many other participants, Maeve did not marry at an early age and, in her narrative, she drew a clear link between later marriage and being able to go 'up the ladder', in her 20s, with a specialty in the Intensive Therapy Unit (ITU).

> I was a staff nurse for two years and then I got a sister's post. I was the only staff nurse with the ITU course when I started there and I got a sister's post and then the nursing officer's post came up so I thought, 'Okay, let me have a go. Let me apply for it.' … I don't even know why I ever considered going up the ladder but I did and I got the nursing officer's post. (Maeve)

She went on to reflect: 'not having got married and had kids at that younger age did give me a better grasp of my career.'

1 General Nursing Council.

As noted in Chapter 3, nursing was often perceived as a ticket to international travel. Post qualification, as discussed below, a few participants moved abroad, but later returned to Britain.

'IF I HADN'T BEEN IN LOVE, I'D HAVE STILL BEEN IN CANADA': NURSING AND TRAVELLING

Caitriona, after completing her general nurse training in Manchester in 1965, headed off to Canada, on her own, for two years. She observed that there were many Irish people working in the hospital: 'there was a lot of Irish nurses there too and a lot of Irish doctors'. Although she found the Canadian system 'very different', overall, she described her time there as: 'very happy, a lovely Nurses' Home, very well paid and I travelled'. She embarked on a three-month tour of North America with four other nurses:

> a lot of Irish and English nurses would hire a mobile home and you'd travel all right through, before you came back, and we went right through, down through Mexico for three months, you got so very well paid, you could do that. (Caitriona)

But Caitriona had left behind a boyfriend in Manchester and ultimately decided to return to him: 'If I hadn't been in love, I'd have still been in Canada! That's life.'

Pauline was originally from Dublin and arrived in south-east England to do her nurse training in the early 1970s. However, she always enjoyed travel and was keen to go further afield. So, after completing her general training, she was attracted by advertisements to go nursing in the US. It is somewhat ironic that, having been lured to Britain by an active NHS advertising campaign, she was then lured away to the US by a similar campaign.

> I actually went to America on my own ... they were advertising for nurses in Arkansas of all places, so I applied for that and I was interviewed in London. They actually came over to recruit and I was interviewed so I went to Arkansas on my own then to nurse in intensive care for a year. (Pauline)

She emphasized the differences between nurse training in Britain and the US in the 1970s:

definitely there would have been more career opportunities. I mean all the nurses, even when I was there, were doing some form of degrees, trying to get higher up, they're very keen on educating themselves. (Pauline)

Nevertheless, despite these opportunities, and although she thoroughly enjoyed her time in the US, Pauline wanted to be closer to Ireland: 'I did like Arkansas and we had some good fun times and we did a lot of travelling but again it was very far from home really and very difficult to get back to Ireland if I wanted to'.

Pauline then got a place to study midwifery in Liverpool and planned to go travelling again after qualifying. However, she met her future husband and settled in Liverpool: 'he's very much a die-at-home Liverpool.'

For both Pauline and Caitriona, romance was a factor in returning to, or deciding to remain in, Britain.[2] Across our forty-five participants, all bar one had married, or were in long-term relationships, and became parents. In the next section, we explore in more detail how family life impacted on their careers.

'HOW DID WE DO IT?': JUGGLING FAMILY LIFE AND NIGHT SHIFTS

As noted earlier, our interviewees tended to marry and start their families at a young age. For example, Una was fairly typical: 'I got married when I was 22 so as soon as I qualified.' But, at that time, women were expected to give up nursing when they married and had children. In the late 1950s, Carmel, discussed in some detail earlier, got a staff nurse post at just 21 years of age. However, her career was halted when she married: 'once we got married and had children, they weren't too keen on having us nursing in case we were going to have too much time off, so they let quite a few of us go'.

Carmel's experiences were echoed by many participants, even into the 1960s and 1970s. For example, Fidelma migrated to Bedfordshire in 1966 and qualified in 1969. She met her future husband, while still a student, and they got married soon after her qualification. She described how marriage and motherhood impacted on her career:

> I got married and then obviously got pregnant, and then once you got pregnant in those days, you had to resign, which was awful. I was so excited about being pregnant, but I was devastated that I had to leave, because I

---

2 For a fuller discussion about long term migration decisions among nurses see Ryan and Doshi (2024).

hadn't planned it that way, but I wouldn't change that now. But yeah, that was the way it was and it was tough, whereas now everything is great, because you keep your job. (Fidelma)

As will be discussed below, Fidelma gave up her career in nursing and, as her children got older, she turned to a different line of work to fit around her childcare. However, the vast majority of our participants, after taking time off to rear their children, did return to nursing. In most cases, they returned to part-time nursing, especially on the night shift.

The story recounted by Aisling, in the Midlands, was fairly typical of the 1950s–60s generation of nurses:

> I became a ward sister and got married while I was still a ward sister. I had a break for about four or five years, oh longer than that actually, and by the time I had four children and then when my youngest was about six months old I got itchy feet again and decided that I didn't want to lose track of my nursing so I went back working just a couple of nights a week ... and got back into the swing of it again. (Aisling)

In London, Mairead qualified in the early 1970s, and 'always worked full-time'. In that respect she was very unusual among our interviewees. Her ability to combine nursing and motherhood was facilitated by a live-in au pair and later by childminders. But most of our participants did not have childminders and instead juggled childcare with their husbands or other relatives.

As Nessa explained: 'so my husband would look after them while I got some sleep at the weekend and that's what most nurses were doing in those days when you had a young family then you'd work nights and that was it.'

Linda also stated that this was the norm for many nurses: 'anyway, a lot of nurses did that'. However, she also noted that combining childcare and work was hard for both partners: 'So I think we worked pretty hard, to be honest'.

Sheila, who worked as a night sister for twelve years, emphasized a similar pattern of hard work: 'You just, you did what fitted in because your husband is there at night with the children, you'd go home in the morning, take them to school, you slept during the day.' However, she added that 'you were just like a robot really'.

Indeed, sleeping during the day with a small child was not easy:

> I had a lovely baby that was very good with his little toys, and (I'd) go up the stairs and I could have a sleep in the morning and get up. But then he started coming up the stairs and getting on the bed and bouncing me with

his head, singing, 'I'm the little white bull', that was the song at the time. (Helen)

As noted in a previous section, above, Miriam got a senior post at a young age. However, following her marriage, she encountered some negative attitudes. A male consultant made a hostile remark about her marital status: 'You're going to have a baby any day now and this charade will start all over again'. In fact, she had her first child three years later and then left the post. Like many other participants, she returned to work part-time for financial reasons: 'I was working because I wanted to go to Ireland in the summer ... We had a house, a mortgage. It was what we needed to do and I didn't give it a second thought'. However, now reflecting back, Miriam often wonders how she actually managed to combine long night shifts with rearing young children: 'looking back I think how on earth? We often talk about it actually as a group, friends, we always say, "How did we do it?"'

The need to obtain and pay a mortgage was mentioned by several nurses as motivation to return to work after having children.

> we were applying for our first mortgage at 22 (years of age) and my husband came from a council house and he had an ambition, I think the pair of us were a bit ambitious, he had an ambition he always wanted his own house. (Sheila)

Carmel's husband was a self-employed carpenter and it was difficult for them to get a mortgage in the 1960s. Thus, her job was a crucial source of income and security in obtaining the mortgage.

While some nurses enjoyed going back to work, for others it was a pragmatic, financial decision – a means to an end. Several interviewees prioritized family life. For example, Angela stated that 'once I had my daughter ... I knew I wanted to be a mother, really.' She added that her husband's career took priority: 'So my job was like secondary to my husband's really, he was in banking at the time'.

Several nurses from the 1950s, 60s and 70s generation made similar observations. In Yorkshire, Eilish stated that: 'to be honest, my husband and my family were as important, if not more important, than my career. I loved what I did work-wise, but it wasn't the be all and end all'.

This is an important point and worthy of some reflection. In this book, we are focusing on the participants as nurses. We are interested in their recruitment, training and work as professionals within the NHS. However, they are also people with complex and varied personal lives, including family responsibilities.

By emphasizing their working lives, we are not implying that their family lives were less interesting or unimportant. While many of our participants did go on to have long and distinguished careers, as discussed below, it is necessary to note that several remained on part-time shifts for the rest of their working lives and were happy with that work–life balance.

For example, as Jacky, who worked part-time in Scotland, observed:

> it was just perfect. It just worked and I felt I could give my job 100% and I could do it to the best of my ability and I loved it. Then I could also have some balance in my home life. Again, I feel very fortunate and that's just great. (Jacky)

Interestingly, some nurses successfully adapted to night work and continued to do so for the rest of their careers. Deborah, as noted in Chapter 4, was an auxiliary nurse. She had a long career on nights: 'Always nights ... I got used to it ... it was an acute medical ward'. She reminisced about the cordial relationships she developed with some members of staff over the years, especially one Indian consultant:

> he'd come down and I'd ask him, 'Do you want a cup of tea?', 'Are you making it?', 'Yeah', because he knew I washed the cups and boiled the kettle. He'd only take tea if I was making it, and he never forgot it, as a consultant, because some of the consultants are a bit, [loud sniff], they don't want to know the bottom of the pile. But no, he's a lovely man. (Deborah)

By contrast, others hated night work and could not deal with the disrupted sleep patterns. For instance, Aine did not like nights, so she worked part-time day shifts: 'I used to only work weekends for a start and my husband used to have them at the weekend. I used to do two days then, just a weekend job.' Gradually she increased to three days per week and then remained on that shift pattern for the rest of her long, working life: 'I stayed with the three days and then I retired.'

By going back to work, particularly in the 1950s–70s, these mothers were very much going against the norm of the era.[3] 'In those days', as Sheila explained, the general view was that being 'a wife and mother was more important than career'.

---

3 For discussion of social attitudes towards working mothers during this era see Helen McCarthy (2018) on women, marriage and paid work in post-war Britain.

Sorcha was among the few interviewees who completed general nurse training in Ireland. She moved to Britain to study midwifery and married soon after qualifying. Her experiences of combining career and motherhood in the 1980s occurred several decades after our older participants. Nonetheless, even by the 1980s, her decision to carry on working as a midwife, while having young children, was considered unusual.

> I was the first married sister at (hospital) to come back to work after having my kids, so I was the first one to get married, I was the first midwife on the labour ward to get married. All the other 'coordinators', as we were called in those days, in that position were single women, because in those days, well previous to that you had to give up nursing if you were married … you couldn't be married and do the job. (Sorcha)

She was especially appreciative of the opportunity to work part-time within the NHS:

> they were very flexible so I could work whatever I wanted, so they gave me whatever hours I wanted, and it was a great time being a young mother bringing up her kids and working and the NHS was a great place to be. I've never had any regrets at that level because yeah, I could do nights, I used to do a week's nights. (Sorcha)

The opportunity for flexible working in the NHS was a recurring theme in our data. As Eilish stated, the option to work part-time and especially to work night shifts: 'I always felt was fantastic with nursing'.

Yvonne, who trained as a radiographer, made a similar point: 'Well, I chose to work part-time, so I could do various hours … radiography's a 24-hour job and there was always shifts in casualty, so there was always an opportunity to work around the family'. This enabled her to strike a convenient balance: 'It was quite accommodating.'

However, over time, others wanted something more and were keen to advance their careers. Sheila felt that working part-time and especially on night shifts 'wasn't very good as a career move'. Similarly, Angela also noted that it was difficult for a part-time member of staff to progress: 'you're part-time and if you want to progress to, I was a staff nurse then, and become a sister, then you'd have to be full-time'.

Having returned from the USA, Pauline married and worked as a midwife in Liverpool. She explained that working on a fractional basis limited her interaction with colleagues, 'it didn't feel then as if you were part of the team'.

Echoing the points made by Sheila and Angela, above, Pauline also noted that, while working part-time, it was more difficult to develop your career and pursue training opportunities.

Among our interviews, there are many interesting stories of how nurses managed to advance their careers by undertaking new training opportunities.

'A REAL PUSH TOWARDS LIFELONG LEARNING': OPPORTUNITIES TO DEVELOP

As noted in the opening quote of this chapter, by Fiona, a career in nursing offered opportunities to 'turn your hand' to many different sides of the profession.

In the Midlands, Aisling recounted her insightful story of career development over time and, in so doing, illustrates the available options for further training and different specialist pathways within the NHS. As noted above, Aisling took many years away from nursing while rearing her family. She then got 'itchy feet' and went back to do some night shifts. But, as time went by, she decided to pursue her career and undertake additional training.

> I decided that I would just take a new path altogether and I went into district nursing. I applied and I did that training for about 6 months and I worked as a district nurse for three years … I loved it actually, it was absolutely fantastic and it suited my home life as well.
>
> When you worked as a district nurse you came in contact with the district midwives and health visitors and school nursing services. I looked around and I thought I was ready to do something else … I was talking to a health visitor one day and she said to me: 'would you not think of doing health visiting, are you going to stay in district nursing forever'?
>
> I decided that I would give that a whirl and I applied to do health visitor training which I did. I was sponsored by (local) Council to do my health visitor training which I did at college in Durham and that took a year to complete. I passed that and got my certificate and because I was sponsored by (the council) then I felt that I had to come back and work for them which I was happy to do anyway because it was where I lived. So, I came back in health visiting in 1968 and I worked as a health visitor for the rest of my career. (Aisling)

After a long career, spanning four decades, Aisling decided at the age of 60: 'it's time to hang up my boots'.

An interesting feature of Aisling's story is the conversation with the other health visitor who asked her 'are you going to stay in district nursing forever?' This question suggests an expectation that nurses could and should explore new opportunities and not simply do the same role for their entire careers.

Ruth also emphasized the support and encouragement to undertake new training throughout her long career: 'There was a real push towards lifelong learning, you just couldn't sit back.' After many years working in a surgical ward, Ruth decided: 'Oh my god, I need to get out of this surgery, I need to do something totally different'. Thus, in 1992–3, she retrained as a district nurse: 'So, I went out in the community, working in and out of patients' homes. I loved it, it was just a lovely, lovely, lovely thing to do'. Ruth loved district nursing not only because she enjoyed working with patients but also because of the flexibility and convenience: 'It was great. I could pass my own house, I could run in and put my washing on the line. Put it in the washing machine before I went to work'.

Although she continued to do more courses and enjoyed studying, throughout her career, Ruth explained that: 'I was never actually ambitious enough to go into the management side of it. Because I think you move away from the patient side, and I actually enjoyed looking after the patients and the patient contact. I enjoyed that side of it.'

Nessa also moved from nights to day shifts in a new setting when her children got older: 'a post was advertised for a practice nurse near where I lived, so I applied for that and yes, I worked three days a week to start with and then as the boys got older, I went full-time'. After years of combining night work in a busy acute reception unit, with childcare, Nessa relished the move to daytime working: 'it was nice to be able to come home and have a night's sleep'. She continued to work at the GP surgery for the next twenty years and eventually retired in 2009: 'I worked till I was 68.'

The opportunities for lifelong training are particularly apparent in the stories of two nurses, Eilish in Yorkshire and Claire in London, who both moved from SEN to SRN later in their careers. Claire began her career as an SEN after failing her final exams.

> to be fully honest I messed up a bit because I failed two of my exams and obviously met my husband, planning to get married ... In the end, I thought, 'This is not going to work out' so I went for the SEN role. (Claire)

After her children were born, like so many other nurses, Claire returned to work on 'twilight shifts': 'so that was just working in the evenings, three or four evenings a week which fitted in with family life'. However, once the children were at school, Claire wanted to quit her part-time evening shifts and switch to daytime working and get a job as a community nurse. In order to achieve this career move, she needed her SRN qualification: 'I decided to do my conversion to SRN, so I did a conversion and that went very well'. Claire then worked for a further nineteen years as a community nurse: 'I'm very proud of what I achieved from nothing to the career I forged out for myself, yes. I was always very proud of my nursing'.

As noted in Chapter 3, Eilish was disappointed when, as an 18-year-old in Ireland, she received her Leaving Cert results and realized that she would not get on to the SRN training and so opted to do SEN instead. Having completed her SEN training in Yorkshire, she got married and, while her four children were young, she worked nights for many years: 'I worked in a really busy unit, which I loved, called the acute reception unit'. However, as time went by and especially as her children entered secondary school, Eilish began to consider a new chapter in her career. Her colleagues at the hospital were very encouraging: 'and it was them that encouraged me to go on and do my SRN'.

> I decided then to go back to university and do my training ... and I qualified in the millennium year, which I thought was a great thing to do, to say, 'Well now I've made it after all that.' (Eilish)

After completing her qualification in 2000, Eilish briefly returned to nights and vividly narrated how, one Christmas, she had an epiphany when she spotted a poster on the wall of the hospital.

> I got in the lift one night and it was a Christmas and I was working Christmas, I remember working Christmas Eve and Boxing[4] night, so you might as well have worked all through, because you slept all day Christmas Day ... and it was millennium year, and there was a poster on the wall that said, 'How would you like to never have to work another Christmas, Easter or Bank Holiday?', and I just thought 'this is for me'.
>
> So, I went into day surgery then, which was Monday to Friday, and I applied and got the job, and that was like me saying, 'Well now it's millennium year,' I'd done my conversion course, and I want to do something for me now that my children are that bit older, so I then went back on working two days a week, which was lovely, working in day surgery. (Eilish)

---

4 Boxing Day is the name in Britain for 26th Dec., a bank holiday (St Stephen's Day in Ireland).

It is noteworthy that nursing provided people, like Eilish and Claire, with a chance to convert their qualifications, undertake new training and shift directions, especially after time out to rear their children. This meant that even in middle age, there were new opportunities for those who wished to explore them.

Through these career moves, many participants left hospital-based nursing to pursue community and primary care health provision. In the next section, we explore some stories of those who became school nurses and specialized in sexual health in community settings.

'I FELT SO PROUD': SCHOOL NURSES AND SEXUAL HEALTH

Sinead began district nursing while still in her early 20s and found the role quite stressful, especially driving around unfamiliar parts of north London:

> So, I worked as a district nurse for two years and didn't really, didn't get on with district nursing to be honest with you, I just found going into people's houses and driving and I suppose I was actually very young to be a district nurse. Most of the district nurses were older, I was still quite young, I was 23 and I was doing district nursing and I used to just find driving around quite stressful, I hadn't long passed my test. (Sinead)

Then an unplanned career move was sparked by the sudden illness of her mother-in-law who had been Sinead's main source of childcare. Without childcare, Sinead decided to do part-time shifts 'on the bank'.[5] She continued to work part-time for ten years while her children were young. However, she vividly recalled how a new career opportunity opened up: 'And then I just saw an advert in the local paper when my youngest started school, I just saw an advert in the local paper for a school nurse, so I said, "Okay that sounds interesting".'

There is a lovely symmetry in the fact of this opportunity coming about through a newspaper advertisement, given that so many Irish nurses began their careers in the NHS through ads in newspapers. Sinead continued to work as a school nurse for years but there was growing pressure to get formal qualifications in that specialism.

---

5 'The bank' is like an internal agency within the NHS to provide staff cover when there is a shortfall in the workforce due to holidays or illness leave etc.

even though I had years and years of experience, I didn't have the degree, the piece of paper to say I was fit to do the job. So, I did a public health degree and I got a first-class honours. (Sinead)

Sinead, who was still working at the time of our interview, said she had no ambition to climb the career ladder and was happy with her work/life balance:

So, I've never wanted to really go up the ladder … and I mean I couldn't because I had four children and they were my priority and I don't want a lot of stress in my life and I've got my term time only, and I still work term time only and I wouldn't change it for anything. It keeps me, it would keep me at work maybe longer because I know, I have a week off now next week and then I have six weeks off in a few weeks' time and then half term. I love it … my job is very stressful. It's in the amount of work and the nature of the job, you know it can be quite distressing … I can't imagine not working and I am passionate. I think I do a good job. (Sinead)

It is interesting to note that the opportunity for part-time and flexible working enabled many of our participants to carry on with their careers well past usual retirement age. Indeed, as will be discussed later, several of the nurses we interviewed were still working into their 70s.

In south London, Fiona became a school nurse, following her divorce, as a pragmatic decision to fit around childcare: 'because I thought at least I'll get the school holidays so I don't have to rely on anybody to mind the kids.' She recalled quite clearly the day the letter arrived offering her the job:

It was the following Tuesday, because the interview was on a Thursday, that the letter came through the door and I said to my daughter, 'Go down and get it.' The three of us were on our own – her running up the stairs and we opened it and it said: 'we are pleased to tell you …' We were dancing on the beds … That's when I felt so proud. So proud. It helped me because then I was getting my wages, I was able to drop the kids at school, pick them up in the evening. (Fiona)

Being a school nurse, working across a wide range of schools in her local borough, meant that Fiona did sometimes encounter her own children. She related one embarrassing situation, when she was running a class on sexual health and contraception:

> one afternoon we got a phone call saying that the sixth form, so they'd be about 16 ... Could somebody go in and do some talks with the boys because three teachers are down sick. I said, 'Okay.' Honestly, I did not know which class I was going into but walking into the room and the boys said, 'It's your mum.' Standing up in front of the class with you know what, all the demonstrators and everything else, and (my) poor son. Like me, he was like, 'Jesus.' (Fiona)

Linda also worked in sexual health. After many years in occupational health, she wanted a new challenge and decided to retrain in sexual health. By this time, she was in her 50s and felt like a complete change of direction.

> So, I did occupational health, and I got my degree in that ... I also did a diploma in family planning and cytology in 1997 in-between doing full-time occupational health work. ... So, I did my family planning and I liked it and I did my cytology, which is obviously basically smearing, and I did them. So then when I gave occupational health up, I went to a local clinic and did family planning and cytology, and I loved that, I loved it.

Linda was aware that patients may have had particular perceptions of her as a middle-aged Irish woman based on stereotypes about Irish Catholicism and attitudes towards contraception.

> I used to think, when they'd come in and see me, and as soon as I opened my mouth I'm sure they'd go, 'Oh my God, this Irish woman, Catholic obviously, what would she know about what's going on?' I certainly learned a lot, I can tell you, but I did enjoy it so much and trying to put the girls at ease or the lads at ease when they came in ... we used to have a great laugh. (Linda)

As noted, throughout this chapter, nursing enabled all sorts of career moves, as in the case of Linda after years in occupational health to undertake new training, in her 50s, and move into sexual health. As well as occupational mobility, nursing could also enable geographical mobility perhaps in ways that might not be so easy in other professions.

'THE WORLD IS MY OYSTER': GEOGRAPHICAL MOBILITY

Orla spoke for many when she said that nursing provided so many different opportunities that she felt 'the world is my oyster'. Although the primary focus of the book is the pivotal move from Ireland to Britain, in fact, many nurses were quite mobile and moved to new locations several times during their careers. In an earlier section, we mentioned young nurses who had seized the chance to travel to the US and Canada before settling down and having children.

Furthermore, several nurses relocated after they got married because of family considerations and work opportunities. For example, Bronagh moved to Birmingham because of her husband's job (we will hear more about her experiences in Birmingham in Chapter 8). Maeve moved to the south-west coast of England because of her husband's work commitments but later returned to her original hospital in London. Dervla relocated to, and settled in, Wales prompted by her husband's family connections and the promise of more affordable houses.

Having left Derry in the mid-1960s, Dervla completed her nurse training in a small town close to London. However, after her children were born, she and her husband decided to move to Wales in the early 1970s, partly to be near his relatives and partly because housing was more affordable. Dervla discovered that hospitals in Wales, possibly because of staff shortages, were amenable to accommodating working mothers:

> I found that in Wales they were more keen to try and encourage people, after they had children, to carry on nursing. So they were happy to accept that maybe you might only want to work say mornings and come in and do the morning shift, they were much more amenable. (Dervla)

Dervla got a job doing two nights per week in a critical care ward: 'that suited me fine and I still carried on working until 1989'. In a later section, we will hear more about how her career changed in new directions.

Una migrated to Liverpool with her sister in the 1960s (see Chapter 3). Like most of our participants, she married young, soon after qualifying, and had children. As her children got older, she returned to work part-time but then in the 1980s her career took a new direction and resulted in relocation to the south of England.

> in the 80s and there was a lot of funding around with the AIDS epidemic that came in at that time and I was a sister on an isolation infectious ward and there was a lot of funding around for AIDS, the management of it. (Una)

Una was keen to explore opportunities to train in this new specialized area of work. She went to Manchester to do a course on infection control. By this time her husband, a police officer, had taken early retirement and so the couple was willing to consider geographical mobility.

> then I applied for a job, I went down to Kent ... for 20 years, I worked down there in that role in communicable diseases and infection control and I went on and did a degree in nursing as a postgraduate student then down there. (Una)

Una's story is interesting for several reasons. First, unlike other nurses who had followed their husbands to new geographical locations, in this case, it was her husband who accompanied her to a new city. Second, her story shows how in middle age, a whole new chapter of her career opened up as she retrained and completely changed her specialty. Third, her experiences indicate how these Irish nurses were often at the forefront of key moments of health care history. While several of our older nurses had worked during the TB epidemic, Una was at the forefront of the HIV and AIDS epidemic and some of our participants were still working through the COVID-19 pandemic, as discussed in Chapter 9.

As well as geographical relocation across Britain, some participants also explored opportunities further afield. While some adventurous young women had set off alone to North America, as mentioned earlier in this chapter, a few participants also had the opportunity to relocate to the US with their husbands and children.

Miriam went to US in the late 1970s: 'my husband's family were all in America and he decided that he would like our children to get to know the American side of the family so we went to America for three years.'

Nursing is a career that travels well but some local qualifications may be required as Miriam soon discovered: 'While I was there, I did the Illinois State Boards because they recognized English training but they do not recognize the English exam'.

Miriam thoroughly enjoyed the experience and found some aspects of the US training rather surprising:

> That training was wonderful. For one thing it was the private sector. Then when we were doing our training one of the days was how to present yourself to your patients. I remember a makeup artist coming in saying to us, 'The last thing somebody ill in bed wants to do is look up and see a nurse that looks equally ill.' They showed us how to do makeup and hair. Not flamboyant, just very discreetly so that you looked nice when you presented yourself. So, we wore an all-white trouser suit uniform. (Miriam)

Nonetheless, despite the higher salary and the career opportunities in the US, she did not want to settle there:

> my salary was much more than the English girls were getting, but then it was time to come back because my parents were in Ireland and my heart was in England and I wanted to come back to England. I wanted the children to be educated in England. I did not want them to go into the American system. So, back we came. (Miriam)

Aileen and her husband also considered a move to the US and went to visit her brother who had already settled there. Her husband 'really, really, really wanted to move to America.' However, Aileen felt differently:

> I hated it – well, not hated it but I didn't like it and I never, I'd never, ever in a million years would I live there. And one of the main reasons that I didn't want to live there was it felt so far from Ireland, felt so far from home and the time difference. When I'd want to ring mam, my brother would say, 'We can't ring her now. It's 3 o'clock in the morning.' (Aileen)

In Chapter 6, we noted that most of our participants visited Ireland every year to see parents, siblings and friends. Moreover, as their parents aged, they also visited Ireland regularly to provide care and assistance (see Ryan and Doshi, 2024). Thus, geographical proximity and ease of travel between Ireland and Britain was something that our interviewees appreciated. By contrast, as noted by Aileen, America was just too far away.

As mentioned earlier, during her time in the US, Miriam observed that many nurses were already pursuing university degrees. Indeed, in contrast to how our nurse participants were trained, the whole system of NHS nurse training has transformed in recent decades. In the next section, we consider how our participants were involved in the transition to university-based nurse education.

'THE WRITING ON THE WALL AROUND NEEDING DEGREES': MOVING TO UNIVERSITY SETTINGS

Although all our participants had qualified under the old system, before nursing degrees[6] were introduced, it is noteworthy that several of them later became

---

[6] The move to university-based nurse training was part of Project 2000 in the UK and began to be rolled out in the 1990s. https://www.nursingtimes.net/news/history-of-nursing/a-history-of-nursing-in-britain-the-1990s-to-2005-26-08-2021/.

nurse tutors and eventually university lecturers. For example, in Liverpool, after ten years of general nursing on the wards, Kathleen was attracted towards teaching:

> I was still nursing full-time … I was allowed a day off, study day, to go to clinical teaching … I was on the wards teaching, clinical teaching on the wards, again, it was hands on patient care … and then I did a tutor's course. (Kathleen)

She especially enjoyed training nurses who were converting from SEN to the higher SRN or 'general' nursing qualification:

> some were enrolled nurses and they converted to general … So I was in charge of the enrolled nurse conversion and that was just heavenly. That was just the best job ever … I still have friends amongst those students that I converted from enrolled to general. (Kathleen)

A key part of her role was to support and encourage students who lacked confidence and self-belief:

> I'm not going to blow my own trumpet, but a lot of it still comes back to me, the appreciation of the support and the belief, because they hadn't the belief in themselves, particularly the enrolled nurses, so that was another forte that I really enjoyed. (Kathleen)

Earlier in this chapter, we discussed Eilish in Yorkshire and Claire in London who converted from SEN to SRN later in their careers. Their sense of achievement and accomplishment chimes nicely with the reflections of Kathleen in Liverpool who was delivering this type of conversion training.

As nurse training moved from hospital-based to university-based, Kathleen followed and ended her career as a university lecturer. She was not alone in this experience. Four of our interviewees ended their careers as university lecturers – Orla and Mairead in London, Ciara in Scotland, as well as Kathleen in Liverpool.

Mairead worked on the wards in a north London hospital but, after a few years, she wanted to explore new challenges: 'So, I thought, "Do you know, I'll apply to the RCN, and I'll do the clinical teachers' course".' She applied and was short-listed for interview. Funnily enough, she got the letter saying she was accepted on to the course the day before her wedding: 'and that's what I had to tell (husband), when we went to sign after we got married in the church.' So, soon after the wedding, Mairead embarked upon her training: 'it's a six-month course, I did that there and became a clinical teacher'. That was the start of a long career in education that would culminate in becoming head of department at a London university.

Ciara in Scotland recounted her career pathway through nurse education and, thus, reveals how the NHS encouraged and facilitated staff to develop their careers in new and exciting ways: 'I was interested in teaching, so I applied to do clinical teaching ... which was a year's course in Glasgow.' After doing clinical teaching for some years and supporting students on the wards, in a very similar way to Kathleen in Liverpool, Ciara decided that she too needed to shift to the university setting:

> I wanted to be a lecturer as well, because ... I could see the writing on the wall around needing degrees, and I applied to university to do a part-time degree in education, a bachelor's in education. (Ciara)

After teaching for some time, she decided to pursue further qualifications in order to enhance her skill-set: 'after that I did a part-time master's in education as well. Again, that was three years part-time, the last year was dissertation'. Throughout this process, Ciara was supported by the NHS and was able to combine her job with her studies. She eventually did a PhD in early 2000s. As will be discussed below, she ended her career by moving into policy advice.

Meanwhile, in London, Orla moved into university teaching and also completed her PhD. She worked as a university lecturer until her retirement in 2023.

As highlighted throughout this chapter, nursing provided an enormously varied range of options, including the opportunity to take on senior management roles, as will be explored in the next section.

'I GOT ON REALLY WELL': SENIOR MANAGEMENT ROLES

As noted earlier, Sheila worked as a night sister in a hospital on the outskirts of London for twelve years while rearing her four children: 'I did all the night duty because it fitted in with the family'.

In her 40s she made a significant career shift: 'I always felt people were pushing me to do more, you know what I mean?' So, she decided to pursue further opportunities to advance her career and eventually was promoted to: 'clinical nurse manager ... I was in the medical part of the hospital so you're looking after all the medical wards'. However, after a number of years in the role, the hospital went through a major restructuring and there was a threat of redundancies: 'I was now 50, so I was then thinking ... "Well, if I don't get a job, I'm fine, I get redundancy. I'll be alright".'

But far from being made redundant, after an intensive interview process, Sheila was actually offered a promotion: 'I was just totally flabbergasted'.

> so, I ended up as a general manager of medicine and I was reporting directly to the chief executive ... and being in charge of the budget, consultants, appointing consultants and doing all that. I loved it. I think also because I was good at maths and I was always good at maths at school, you know, so I had a good understanding of money anyway and managing a budget. And I never had any trouble, I got on really well. (Sheila)

The job was extremely demanding, responsible and time intensive. By then, her children were grown up and she and her husband had separated amicably, so, she could devote more time to her career: 'the job wouldn't have fitted in really with married life because I'd be in my office from 7 a.m. in the morning and probably didn't get back home until 7 p.m. at night'. Sheila explained how she coped with the role:

> I don't do stress. I just sit down and say, 'Well what are we going to do about it?' You just have to manage things ... I said, 'Okay, let's see, what can we do?' There's no point going mad, you have to work through these things. (Sheila)

Bronagh also changed her role and setting in middle age. She had worked as district nurse in Birmingham when her children were young as that enabled her to combine childcare with paid employment.

> after my district nurse training I'd done my health visitor training. When I had (son), I was working as a health visitor, at least it was regular hours during the day. But I then got promoted into management and manager of health visiting, and I was safeguarding lead, so I got into that part of it. And again, the money was a bit better, but long hours, and, you know, school and picking up him always came first. But after that it was a matter of well, whatever had to be done, I did it. (Bronagh)

Having worked on the district for many years, a new opportunity presented itself in 2000 when Bronagh was in her early 50s: 'a group of GPs that got together and they asked me, would I come and join them as a manager. So, I joined them. I went into primary care general practice.'

At this time, enormous changes were taking place in the management, organization and funding of primary care as GP surgeries were now responsible for their own budgets.

> GPs, for the first time, had been given this budget, and few of them had any experience in dealing with it. I mean fortunately by then I was a fairly experienced manager, nurse manager, but I mean it was just purely all contract commissioning, and that's what I did for about, oh crikey, I don't know, ten years. (Bronagh)

In a similar way to Sheila, discussed earlier, Bronagh also now found herself in a senior role, managing a large budget and making key strategic decisions, as the NHS began to move to a more business model, and significantly different from the more traditional nursing roles at the start of their careers. Bronagh reflected on the changes to health provision:

> We had a contract for psychological therapies. We had a contract for drug and alcohol service. Several contracts we won ... But I mean they deregulated the market to quite a degree. I don't know whether the historians will say it was good or bad, but it was a very exciting time for us and we were successful. Both centres are still operational today. (Bronagh)

In south London, Finnuala also took time off to have children. Upon her return to work, a completely unexpected opportunity came her way that led to a whole new chapter of her career and eventual promotion to the role of 'modern matron':

> (son) went to school, and then I joined 'the bank', they call it, it's like an agency within the hospital. I joined the bank on a Friday, and then Monday morning I got a call, 'Oh, can you work tomorrow?' And I go, 'Oh yeah, whereabouts?' 'In the eye clinic,' I said, 'Oh God, I know nothing about eyes.' 'Don't worry, don't worry, come here.' So that's how I started off in eyes, cataract surgery and all that kind of stuff. (Finnuala)

From knowing 'nothing about eyes' and not planning to stay long in the area, Finnuala quickly discovered a love of the specialism: 'When I went into eyes, I didn't think I was going to stay there long, it wasn't my thing, but I learned so much, and I got my degree there – ophthalmology.' Over the years she was promoted several times: 'then I got a sister's post. Then a couple of years after that, I got a matron's post. They were bringing in I think they called them modern matrons – my title was clinical manager, ophthalmology'. When we interviewed her, Finnuala was still working, part-time, in the eye clinic as she approached her 70th year.

While most of our participants stayed in health care, even if they changed specialities, a few did change careers completely, as discussed in the next section.

CAREER CHANGE

Out of the forty-five participants in this study, only a few changed their careers in totally new directions. In several cases, this was motivated by childcare.

As noted earlier, when Fidelma married and became a mother in the 1960s, she had to give up her nursing career. Later on, as her children got older, she put her skills to good use and became a childminder. She continued in that job for twenty years until the COVID pandemic in 2020 when she decided to retire.

Meanwhile, in Liverpool, Jane also changed her career after having children. She began volunteering with the Red Cross and then started to do lots of training courses:

> I did the exam for Red Cross and for first aid training ... when I had finished all that training I did NVQ[7] as well and I went to the college for I had to do a couple of other courses so that I could do teaching, you see. (Jane)

Having qualified as a trainer, she then worked for many years delivering Red Cross first aid courses: 'I used to go out training all over the place, doing four-day courses, two-day courses, and the examination at the end and did a lot of resuscitation'. In addition to her Red Cross work, Jane also worked for a charity that took disabled children on holidays. Her many years of service were recognized when she was invited to Buckingham Palace on two separate occasions to attend celebration events.

Aileen and her husband at one point considered migrating to the US, as mentioned earlier, but after returning to London they embarked on a completely new career. Along with another married couple, they bought a care home in Kent.

7 National Vocational Qualification.

we opened a residential home for the elderly ... did that for about twenty years while the children were growing up ... so we job-shared really and it worked, it worked so well in terms of childcare and that sort of thing ... we were a huge part of the community in terms of it was all local families, it was all local staff that worked with us ... So that was lovely. (Aileen)

However, a downside of stepping away from nursing was losing her registration status.

> The saddest bit of it was I had to drop my registration, which did really break my heart. Because for years we could pay the RCN to stay on the register but then you had to do so many clinical hours for every year you were out. And at that stage I was out about ten years, so it would have meant paying for childcare, paying someone at Care Home to do what I should be doing. And just financially I just couldn't have done it, although I would have loved to have done it but it wasn't to be. (Aileen)

After selling the care home, Aileen then took up a new career in further education, running training courses for staff working in the care sector. Thus, over almost fifty years her career spanned three sectors – nursing, business and then education.

As noted earlier, several participants moved into education, especially nurse education. However, in some cases this meant moving into university education more broadly and leaving nurse teaching. Having started out as a nurse tutor, Mairead moved into management and became head of department in a London university. Similarly, after completing her PhD in the early 2000s, Orla became a senior lecturer in health education. Meanwhile in Scotland, Ciara, who also moved into university lecturing, gradually moved towards research and policy advice. Indeed, Ciara went on to a role as a health policy advisor for the Scottish government.

Dervla also made a career move into education. As noted earlier, Dervla and her young family relocated to Wales in the early 1970s and she worked part-time on a critical care ward for many years while her children were growing up. She then decided on a change of direction:

> I had a job lecturing in a further education college and I did that for about 15–20 years and then I just thought I've had enough of this, there's a hospital down the road, literally two minutes from the house when I thought 'why am I driving miles to do this and doing all this prep work

lesson/lecture planning and marking exams when I could go back to there?' So, I did a return to nursing course which the Welsh government was sponsoring at the time, we didn't have to pay anything ... So, I did that and I got a job on the wards as a staff nurse and there was a vacancy come up in endoscopy unit so I did that until 2017 when I retired, eventually. (Dervla)

This career move, out of nursing for almost twenty years and then back into nursing, was somewhat unusual among our participants but, as Dervla explained, there was strong encouragement and sponsorship to attract nurses back into the sector. This observation echoes remarks made by many interviewees that because of staff shortages, it was very hard for them to retire and leave nursing even into their late 60s and early 70s (as will be discussed in Chapter 9).

CONCLUDING THOUGHTS

In this chapter, we have explored how our participants' careers developed over time. One of the great advantages of an oral history approach and interviewing older people is the ability to reflect on a whole biographical narrative that spans the entire life course. Having started with their initial recruitment into nursing, as teenagers, their interviews covered all aspects of their training and working lives up to retirement, although, interestingly, several were still working well past retirement age.

However, as noted, these stories were not simply linear progressions over time. In fact, some stories were complicated as nurses moved in and out of work, took long breaks for childcare, went part-time, pursued career moves and even changed specialities. Sometimes, the stories were so complex, involving numerous career pathways, that it was hard to keep track. Nonetheless, these biographical narratives offer fascinating insights into how nursing allowed all sorts of flexibility and opportunities to 'turn your hand' to so many varied aspects of the profession.

Of course, that is not to be naïve or overly celebratory about the long hours, hard work, and challenges of juggling career and childcare. As noted in this chapter, these demands could leave the participants feeling like 'robots'. Nevertheless, the option to combine paid employment and parenthood, especially during the 1950s–60s, afforded these nurses opportunities which were not available to many women at that time. Indeed, several of our study participants seized these opportunities and developed their careers into senior leadership and managerial positions.

While so far, the focus has been on very positive stories of long and valued careers as care providers and educators, it is important to note that our participants also had some difficult experiences as Irish migrants, especially during decades of anti-Irish hostility in Britain. In the next chapter, we will hear the nurses' stories of how they encountered and navigated anti-Irish abuse and hostility both within hospitals and outside in wider British society.

CHAPTER 8

'You're OK, even though you're Irish': experiences of being Irish in Britain

> She had made comments you know, about the Irish nurses … I can't remember really, she just said, 'The Irish coming over, taking over. Isn't there any decent English nurses?' I remember she said to me one day, but I used to let it go over my head (Claire, began nurse training in London in 1971)

As noted in earlier chapters, most of our participants had been actively recruited to migrate to Britain and work in the NHS. They fulfilled a vital role in the British health service and most said they felt very valued and appreciated as nurses. However, they were also Irish migrants in Britain during periods of heightened tensions between the two states, especially around the so-called Northern Ireland 'Troubles' (1960s–90s). Moreover, the legacy of anti-Irish stereotyping and prejudice, with deep roots in colonial history, as discussed in Chapter 2, was very much present in British society particularly during the 1950s–70s and amplified during IRA bombing campaigns across England (Hickman and Walter, 1997; Hickman and Ryan, 2020).

We were curious to understand how this wider context impacted on the nurses. Their stories reveal complex and, at times, ambivalent positioning as both respected key workers and demeaned Irish migrants. Geographical location also mattered as attitudes towards Irish people were shaped by local contexts and events, especially around specific bombing incidents.

This chapter relates those stories and, in so doing, contributes to understanding the specific impact of prejudice and hostility on Irish migrants, especially those performing a vital role as nurses. While many asserted that they sought to 'brush off' anti-Irish remarks, and let them go over their heads, as Claire states above, others adopted specific strategies to avoid confrontation, while some actively challenged what they perceived as racism.

'I LOVE YOUR ACCENT': BEING IRISH IN HOSPITAL SETTINGS

Many nurses stated that they had not experienced any form of discrimination or anti-Irish hostility in their professional careers and particularly not in hospital settings. For example, Orla said that overall patients were 'really appreciative', while Anita commented: 'we were always treated nicely by the patients'.

Finnuala, who trained and worked in London, also emphasized positive reactions from patients:

> I talk for myself, I was never made to believe like that, that I was different, apart from the early days. But from now on, a lot of people are very pro-Irish now, because when I'm at work with the patients, they'll say, 'Oh I love your accent.' The Irish accent. Oh God, if I got a pound for every time, 'My mother was Irish, my grandfather came from Mayo.' They feel a bit of a bond with you already! (Finnuala)

It is noteworthy that she says 'apart from the early days' and later in the chapter we will hear more about one of her earlier experiences.

Eilish in Yorkshire also noted that patients liked her accent:

> They'll say, 'Oh I love your accent. Have you only just come over from Ireland?' and I'll say, 'No, next year I'll be here fifty years in 2024.' I think it's very important to keep your accent, because I think it's who you are, isn't it? (Eilish)

The significance of accent as a marker of identity was a recurring theme in the interviews and will be discussed throughout this chapter.

Meanwhile in Liverpool, Kathleen, who arrived in the 1960s, emphasized: 'there was no prejudice, absolutely nothing, nobody ever said you're Irish or nothing, nobody ever said that.' Nonetheless, as we will hear later in the chapter, experiences in Liverpool were not always so positive, especially for Irish migrants who arrived in the 1950s.

In Glasgow, Jacky, who worked as a midwife, noted how friendly and welcoming the city is: 'The friendliness was amazing and we never felt in any way treated differently from, if you like, the other Scottish girls ... because they're exceptionally friendly anyway in Glasgow.' However, as will be discussed later in this chapter, Glasgow, like Liverpool, had a history of religious sectarianism which sometimes confronted the nurses in unexpected ways.

In the English Midlands, Aisling highlighted the prevalence of Irish and Catholic senior staff in hospitals as evidence of the fact there was no discrimination: 'never any religious bias ... The matron at that time was Catholic, maybe that helped quite a bit, but I never felt that they looked down or anything like that, I felt that [we] commanded just as much respect as anybody else really.' Indeed, the prevalence of Irish staff in hospitals was noted by many participants and contributed to making those settings more receptive and welcoming for Irish nurses.

Interestingly, a nurse who worked in Manchester and became a single mother in the 1960s said she would have been treated less well in Ireland and may have faced more discrimination there.

> I never found being put down or anything as an Irish nurse, and I worked in quite a lot of places, you know, I worked in different hospitals in Manchester ... I think if I was in Ireland, I might have been downgraded but not in England. They always treated you very well. (Caitriona)

While many of our nurses who arrived in the 1960s generally reported positive experiences, especially in hospital settings, those who arrived earlier, particularly in the late 1940s and early 1950s, had more varied experiences.

Gretta, in her 90s and our oldest participant, was recruited from Cork to work in London in 1948. Upon arrival she was surprised to be confronted by a colleague who stated bluntly: 'I hate the Irish'.

Helen, also in her early 90s, arrived in the early 1950s in Liverpool and explained that 'There was great discrimination, that's what there was. Then of course they used to blame the Irish girls for such and such'.

Several participants described so-called jokes or banter from patients which reinforced anti-Irish stereotypes and undermined the professionalism and authority of these young migrants. For example, Bronagh described an incident that occurred when she was a student in Kent:

> ... I felt that my Irishness was used as a figure of criticism shall we say ... and I can remember, there was a couple of rather large East Enders in the beds, and going round with a tea trolley, and they were very loud anyway [laughs], and I'm not caricaturing or anything like that, and sort of whistling at each other, and says, 'Here comes the pikey brigade.' ... I'd never even heard the word 'pikey'.[1] I didn't even know what pikey was ... They would have thought it was a joke, but I didn't quite understand. (Bronagh)

Aileen also noted that there was a lot of so-called banter and teasing from patients. At the time, she let it go but now she might challenge such behaviour: 'Looking back, there was a lot of, you know, "top of the morning to you" and

---

[1] Pikey is a derogatory term used in Britain to refer to travellers and gypsies.

all that sort of thing, which if it was said to me now … they probably wouldn't say it a second time'.

In the 1960s, in a London hospital, some of Sheila's colleagues called her by nationality instead of by name:

> They used to call me 'Irish' but it didn't make any difference, but I felt it was in an endearing kind of way. You'd go in, when you were in the operating theatres, you'd go in on a Monday morning, you'd be in there and the consultant would come in and say, 'Morning Irish, did you have a nice weekend?' or something … I can't ever remember it offending me. (Sheila)

It is important to note that some nurses did not take offence and did not perceive any negative intention or racism in hospital-based banter and 'jokes' with colleagues and patients. For example, Aisling explained that while she did get 'a few comments about my Irish accent … you didn't think of it as racism or anything like that'. Overall, she never felt that her professionalism as a nurse was undermined: 'I never felt that I was treated any different to any of the other nurses'.

In the same manner, Sinead did not perceive teasing about her accent as racist:

> honestly since I have come to London I have never, ever experienced any form of racism or, never, I mean I just remember there was a patient once and she kept going 'Tirty Tree and a Tird'[2] and I said, 'What's she going on about? What is she saying? Why does she keep saying that?' and somebody explained it to me and I said, 'Okay'. (Sinead)

However, other participants found repeated remarks and mocking about their accents irritating and somewhat undermining. Sorcha explained: 'your accent, I've always found that very difficult. Not so much to this day but people would take the Mick out of your accent and, you know, that was never nice, and I never liked it'.

Similarly, Orla was shocked and enraged when a senior member of staff made a remark about her pronunciation:

> this English cockney-type, elderly sister on a medical ward, I was helping out getting somebody a commode or something and she heard the way I

---

[2] This is a reference to dropping the 'th' sound in words like 'three' which is common in some parts of Ireland.

said 'commode' which I said in a very broad tone and she kind of imitated me and I was really enraged and I thought, 'I hope I never bloody come on her ward' and I didn't luckily! I was a bit shocked that she would do that and I thought, 'How dare she really?' That's just rude really and I felt, 'Gosh' and I didn't get that from the others. (Orla)

Overall, it is fair to say that our participants' reaction to being teased or mocked about their accents depended largely on the context and who was involved – for example whether it was an individual patient, a group of patients or a work colleague, especially a senior member of staff. Moreover, the intention behind the remark also mattered. Some nurses were willing to overlook what they perceived as harmless banter, while others took offence at what they perceived as a deliberate attempt to undermine them in a professional environment.

In the nurses' stories, anti-Irish attitudes were often attributed to one particular individual rather than being generally pervasive or systematic in hospital settings. This strategy may have made such encounters easier to deal with, as Orla explained: 'I shook it off I think pretty efficiently, I didn't let them bother me.'

Yvonne also felt able to deal with 'banter' and 'jokes': 'We were treated very fairly. Things like accents, there's a certain amount of mickey-taking but personally, I would honestly say few, if any, bad experiences. Some jokes about Saint Patrick's Day and Saint Patrick's night in casualty[3] but overall, I think we were treated very fairly.'

Several nurses talked about remaining polite and avoiding confrontation. Ruth noted that sometimes there were 'undercurrents':

> we didn't get offended by it or anything like that. In general, I think we were treated very well. On a personal level, I mean if you were nice to people, they would be nice back to you. Politeness goes a long way really, and I think what you give you get back. (Ruth)

Linda echoed this point: 'if you treat somebody nicely ... if you treat them well, people will treat you well in return'.

Pauline, while stating that she 'didn't have any problems', noted one isolated incident: 'The patients were lovely, just one slight hiccup, one woman sort of said, "You're okay even though you're Irish"'. This comment is revealing in suggesting that nurses may have been perceived as 'different', somehow 'set apart'

---

3 A reference to too much drinking by Irish people.

from the negative stereotypes associated with the wider Irish migrant population (see Walter, 1989). As Jacky observed, nurses were respected and somehow 'above it all'.

Furthermore, as discussed in more detail later in this chapter, the political context also mattered as Irish accents could become targets for abuse especially around the time of IRA bombing.

Indeed, nurses were not always protected from anti-Irish stereotyping. Angela related an anecdote about what a patient said to her during her student days:

> I did come up against a little bit of racism, one was a patient ... I was only about a second-year student, which is really young, I was early 20s, and he said something one day, something about, 'Men are first-class citizens and women are second-class citizens' he said, 'but you're different you're a third-class citizen: you're Irish.' Well, I went scarlet and a man across on the other side, we had open wards then, he said, 'That's uncalled for.' I had to walk out because I knew I blushed, I went scarlet.
>
> When I came in, I said, 'As he said, that wasn't called for;' he said, 'I was only joking.' I said, 'Actually it's not a joke.' The next day he was going to theatre, he had major surgery ... and I was caring for him, so I said, 'Are you okay for me to care for you now, even though I am a third-class citizen?' I didn't let him get away with it, and I thought it's not a joke. (Angela)

This incident is revealing because another patient challenged the racist man, this support gave the young student nurse the courage to repeat that challenge and echo the words '*As he said* – that wasn't called for'. Moreover, the next day, having regained her composure, Angela was able to remind the patient of his nasty words.

It is apparent that some patients perceived these nurses as first and foremost 'Irish migrants'. Delia recalled one particularly hurtful remark: 'the patient said to these two young Irish girls "you know my husband's taxes pay for you girls to come over here from Ireland and you are having all this on my husband's taxes".'

In a similar way, Sorcha encountered the attitude that Irish nurses should be grateful for everything the NHS had done for them:

> Like when I came over I remember somebody saying to me, 'NHS England has given you everything,' and I remember saying 'I've given it to the NHS, and it is so lucky to have me', and she was completely taken aback, and I think she wasn't able to talk to me for a while after that. But that was the

attitude, you know, England gave Ireland everything, but instead it was the other way around. (Sorcha)

Sean stated that he encountered some racism but it was 'under the surface', rather than explicit, and hence not easy to call out and challenge. He related one incident with a manager during his psychiatric nurse training:

> there was comments made about, you know, 'You lot, you people are always looking for something, always want something for nothing' and stuff like that, snide comments.
>
> I mean, one of the managers said to me 'You lot are always looking for something for nothing' and at the time I thought he was talking about us as students because I was one of the gobby ones, you see, so when there was a problem, students, we'd all get together and discuss it and I'd be the one nominated to go and try and get something done about it.
>
> So, I went to deal with it and that guy just said that to me and at the time, I thought he was just talking about the students but later on, I realized he was talking about 'you Irish'. There was racism just under the surface. (Sean)

As noted earlier, it mattered who was making an anti-Irish remark and the intention behind that remark. Furthermore, it also mattered if the incident occurred while they were young students or later on when they had more experience and confidence. For example, Maeve related an anecdote in which her Irishness was used in a direct criticism by an angry senior colleague:

> I had the patient and I was to take him up. It was only 8 o'clock and we had just handed over and in he comes. The doors open and he goes, 'Why isn't this patient upstairs?' I said, 'Oh, Doctor, I'll be up in a minute.' 'What do you mean up in a minute?' I said, 'I'll be up in a minute. I need to disconnect, reconnect him on portable batteries and I'll be up in a minute.' 'Oh, you stupid Irish woman, what would you know?' I said, 'Doctor, an old boy like you, heart attacks, palpitations and all that sort of stuff, it's bad for you. Now will you go away, leave me alone? I'll be up after you.' I could not believe it. He turned on his foot and went. I think it was about challenge at that time, about how you challenged them. I wasn't rude to him or anything. (Maeve)

As an experienced nurse, Maeve felt well able to challenge this doctor and, by drawing attention to his angry outburst as bad for his health, underlined his over-reaction and lack of professionalism. Rather than directly tackling his anti-Irish remark, instead she diffused the situation by asserting her medical knowledge in the face of his temperament.

Of course, as discussed in Chapter 2, Irish nurses were not the only migrants working in the NHS. With the passing decades, more nurses were recruited from overseas. Several participants mentioned moments of solidarity with other migrant nurses. For example, Helen talked about how Polish and Irish nurses used to support each other in the 1950s. Moreover, as mentioned in Chapter 6, there were friendships among diverse migrants in the Nurses' Home. But a few nurses mentioned uncomfortable incidents when some nurses were treated differently because of their ethnicity.

Despite the fact that she clearly felt very awkward discussing the subject, Delia recalled that some older, English patients on geriatric wards, especially in the 1960s, were wary of black nurses.[4]

> The relatives would say: 'it's great to have you here, you white people' because their old grannies and parents were there and they weren't used to the black people and the black people were always sent to the geriatrics … a quiet patient asked me to give him the injection … he called me over and he said: 'nurse, will you give the injection? Because you might be a little more gentle' … So yeah, now I think I've said enough about that, it's a very uncomfortable place to be, but that was the way it was. (Delia)

Similarly, Aileen observed that some patients made negative remarks to nurses from different nationalities: '[I] did see other nationalities being, not being treated as well as we were. You know, that was kind of quite clear. And, you know, as a youngster you just don't know anything about that sort of thing, do you? You just think, "Oh, why did they say that to her?"'

As noted in Chapter 2, there is evidence that nursing recruits from the Caribbean and Asia faced discrimination within the NHS (Markey and Tilki, 2007). Many were encouraged down the less prestigious SEN route, despite meeting the criteria for the academically recognized SRN (Bheenuck, 2010). In Bheenuck's study of overseas nurses in Britain, participants repeatedly referred to the glass ceiling for people of colour in the NHS, a finding that seems in line with studies conducted by Carol and David Baxter (1988), Beishon et al. (1995) and, more recently, the inquiry into why disproportionately more ethnic minority staff died from COVID-19 (Chaudhry et al., 2020).

---

[4] For discussions of racism in nursing see Okougha & Tilki, 2010 and Markey & Tilki, 2007.

Although it is clear that Irish nurses were not immune from 'jokes', 'banter' and even open hostility from some patients and colleagues, it is also the case that the sheer numbers of Irish staff in hospitals, especially in the 1950s–70s, acted as a source of protection and solidarity. Echoing a point made by several participants, Maeve noted that Irish staff in hospitals supported each other and challenged any negative behaviour against them: 'On the day-to-day working front, I never found that I had any issues with people generally and I think that was probably because there was a huge collection of Irish nurses and students that we could support ourselves.'

Ciara, like many participants, noted that many of her fellow students were also Irish. Thus, because there were so many Irish nurses, they became the norm: 'I think there was so many of us that it really, it was just taken as normal'. Similarly, Joseph who trained as a psychiatric nurse also noted that 'because of the numbers I suppose' there was a sort of protection for Irish nurses.

The number of Irish recruits expanded massively into the tens of thousands, through the 1950s–70s (Daniels, 1993; Yeates, 2004), and it is noteworthy that it was the earlier arrivals, Gretta and Helen, our oldest participants, who described the most explicit forms of anti-Irish hostility in hospital settings. Over time, with increasing numbers, as Ciara observed, Irish nurses became the norm in many hospitals.

Of course, the idea of 'safety in numbers' also applied to other ethnic groups: 'I think what happens when you emigrate, we were inclined to stay in little groups ... when I reflect on other cultures, I can understand why you stay in that little group for a while till you gain confidence' (Yvonne).

The presence of senior Irish staff in the hospital was sometimes a source of support to young Irish students.

> We had no bother, and that is the truth. I think because number one, there were two Irish nurses working in the hospital and one of them there's no way you would have said 'boo' to her. She was from Donegal, and she ruled the ... she was the theatre sister, she was in charge of all of that. She was small and she was mighty. (Julia)

But that is not to imply that senior Irish colleagues were necessarily supportive of young Irish students. As mentioned in Chapter 5, some Irish sisters were perceived as unsupportive, especially during student training. One participant told us that she had encountered senior Irish nurses who were 'absolutely, horrible' (Linda).

So far, we have focused on the hospital setting and, as Dervla emphasized, this was quite a specific context or protected 'enclosure': 'there was a lot of Irish people nurses, students as well, so it was different in that sort of enclosure'. For nurses who worked in hospitals and lived in the Nurses' Home, they could feel quite insulated from wider society. However, moving out in wider British society could be 'a shock to the system' (Dervla). Fiona also noted, 'within the hospital walls' was quite protected but 'outside was a different story'. We now begin to explore this 'different story' in the sections below.

'AN EFFING IRISH COW': ENCOUNTERS ON THE DISTRICT

Bridget, who migrated in 1952, stated that she never had any negative experiences because of her Irishness within the hospital setting but that changed when she started the next phase of her career: 'I did when I became a district nurse, and I was out in the district in Edmonton which is rather a rough area. I was a health visitor'.

She related a particularly upsetting case of an older woman who was being neglected by her family and was in a pitiful state when Bridget visited the house. After several visits and raising concerns with the social worker, Bridget arranged for the woman to go into a care home. This resulted in a massive backlash not only by the family but also their friends and neighbours. Interestingly, Bridget's Irishness then became a target for abuse.

> of course, I got tormented by her daughter. They came round to where I worked in the office and called me various Irish names. On a Friday lunchtime there was a big market in Edmonton, a fruit market. I used to go and get my shopping and a man came out of the pub and accosted me, called me an 'Effing Irish cow' because I'd got his neighbour's mother put in the home and they were made homeless and it's all my fault. And he threw a glass of beer on me. (Bridget)

Claire, who also worked on the district, related an incident where her Irishness became a marker of identity.

> one lady who rang up and said, 'I don't want the Irish nurse anymore,' but only because she always got pressure sores on her heels, but she used to wear the most tiny little slippers with tiny little heels. And of course, I'm not that tolerant and after a while you think, 'The reason you're in this situation is you just need to get a proper pair of slippers.' So, when I went back one day (to office) they said, 'We've just had a phone call, they don't want the Irish nurse anymore.' (Claire)

In this story, it is not obvious if the lady did not want Claire anymore because she was Irish or simply because she did not like being told off about her choices of footwear. In any case, Claire's Irishness was used as a marker of identity. However, the patient in question had made an anti-Irish remark in the past, as noted in the opening quotation in this chapter, about the Irish taking over and why were there no 'decent English nurses'. So that statement may add further insights into her attitude.

Being on the district meant that nurses were going into patients' homes as individuals and thus the context and the dynamics were markedly different from a hospital setting. Without the direct support of colleagues, a district nurse, in that moment, had to find strategies for dealing with and diffusing potential conflictual situations. Julia recounted her relationship with one patient who was a member of the Orange Order[5] in Scotland and puzzled by her non-Irish sounding surname.

> when I'd go in, I'd say, 'Good morning, I'm Sister (surname)'. 'So where are you from, sister?' 'I'm from Ireland.' 'Yeah, but where?' Well, I said 'I'm Dublin, but I lived in Co. Antrim.' 'Right. And your name is "..."?', 'Yes.' 'What was your maiden name?', 'E.' You see, that didn't click with anybody. He was trying to find out what denomination I was and this was his way of going round it ... and eventually he said to me, 'Okay, what religion are you?' I said, 'I happen to be a Catholic.' And I said, 'Have you a problem?' and he said, 'No.' But he said, 'I thought Catholics weren't supposed to do this and do that and do the other.'
>
> He was somebody big in the Orange Lodge here in Scotland, and he had two ulcers on his leg so I was bandaging them, and he asked me if I could come and bandage them on the 12th (July) morning before he would go to the parade, and I said, 'Of course I would. What time would suit you?' I did, and he never forgot that. But he couldn't understand at the beginning why it didn't bother me, because he was under the impression that if you were Irish and you were Catholic, that you didn't really do anything to anybody else, only your own. That was about the only time that I encountered anything. (Julia)

Through her long career in Scotland, Julia said she encountered very little animosity, although patients were often curious about her religious background and tried to position her through the marker of football loyalties: 'Oh you're

---

5 Orange Lodges are groups of Protestant Unionists usually found in Northern Ireland, though some Lodges also exist in Britain. They are known for organizing marches on the 12th July as a way of promoting Unionist identity.

Irish, are you a Celtic supporter?' and I used to say, 'No, I'm a Manchester United supporter,' which I always have been and I still am ... that was the only time it came up was Celtic or Rangers'.[6]

Yvonne also commented on how patients tried to place her geographically in Northern or Southern Ireland: 'particularly with the elderly English patients ... they all say, 'That's a lovely Irish accent,' or, 'Where are you from?' ... 'Are you from Northern Ireland or Southern Ireland?' However, Yvonne did not perceive any animosity in that question: 'I wouldn't have said that I was uncomfortable about it.' However, as we will discuss below, being placed as coming from Northern or Southern Ireland sometimes did take on more hostile meaning.

Despite some unpleasant encounters in their role as district nurses, these professionals were still part of a medical institution and could call on managers or colleagues to assist them if needed. However, across wider society in everyday encounters, it was often much more difficult to deal with experiences of anti-Irish hostility.

'NO IRISH': EXPLICIT ANTI-IRISH RACISM IN BRITISH SOCIETY

It is interesting to observe how many nurses, across different generations from the 1940s to the 1970s, described seeing 'no Irish' signs. We did not specifically ask about seeing such signs but, nevertheless, we were fascinated to observe that participants, unprompted by us, raised this issue.

Gretta who arrived in London in 1948 said there were 'plenty' of 'no Irish' signs: 'mostly in the houses that let rooms.'

A nurse, who arrived in 1961, first saw the 'no Irish' signs on a day trip to the seaside:

> there was a trip out and we went to the seaside and there's landladies with vacancies and things and you know on the doors there's 'No blacks, no Irish, no dogs' ... and I remember saying to people, 'Why are they saying that?'... you know and I'm thinking, so in my brain I'm thinking, 'God, they've been over in Ireland recruiting us to staff their hospitals and here I couldn't even stay in somebody's house if I wanted to!' I mean I literally wouldn't have been able to stay. It said, 'No dogs, no blacks, no Irish', well I think that's well known, isn't it? (Sheila)

---

6 Celtic and Rangers are the two main Scottish football teams and are strongly linked to Catholic and Protestant identities especially in Glasgow.

This experience was echoed by Dervla who arrived in the mid-1960s. She contrasted the rather protected environment of the hospital, as mentioned earlier in this chapter, with the explicit anti-Irish racism she observed in wider society:

> when we used to go up to London to the markets and things and the shows, I started realizing that in Paddington there were a lot of signs on the windows of lodging houses saying: 'no gypsies, no blacks, no Irish and no dogs'; it was an eye opener really, a shock to the system because in the hospital there wasn't any of that at all in the hospital you know ... I do remember being probably demeaned as well, when I think about it now, angry. It's not on, you know. Maybe I was naïve, I should have shouted a bit louder but I don't think it would have made much difference honestly. (Dervla)

A decade later, in the mid-1970s, Maeve described seeing a 'no Irish' sign on a shop door, while out for a walk near the hospital in south London: 'I thought, "I'll get a bar of chocolate or something." On the door was written "No blacks, no dogs, no Irish." I thought, "Ah!" That was the first time I thought "ooh" and you're sort of taken aback'. Maeve reflected on her reaction to seeing this sign.

> I thought if you're that rude you don't deserve business ... it was a little shop on the side. It was only a sort of single door frontage and I just thought, 'You're just ignorant,' was the way I felt about it ... I said it to my sister and to (friend) – 'There's a rude note that they put up.' I think probably, I thought, 'That wasn't very nice.' I said I would never go in there again and I wouldn't and I didn't but that was the only time where you could blatantly see. That was the only time where I thought, 'Woah, so people are noticing the blacks, the dogs, the Irish, three *persona non grata* ...'; you feel you are down on dog level. When you think about it, I mean that is not that long ago ... 1975.
>
> I suppose the thing about it is, looking back, there was probably a fear if I did go in and they turned on me would I be able to defend myself? I think from my own self, I think I avoided direct confrontation because I could have gone in and said, 'You ignorant man. What sort of a note is this?' or pull it off the door which is probably what I might be more tempted to do now that I feel much more established. I'd just pull it off the door, but then you were sort of the newbie. You hadn't even learned probably another street if you had to run to the hospital. I thought if I had to run, I probably wouldn't know if there was another road that could

take me round, so I didn't. I just probably was a bit of a coward when it came to dealing with that. (Maeve)

Maeve linked this anti-Irish hostility to the spate of IRA bomb attacks during the 1970s: 'Birmingham bombings have gone and a couple of years later Mountbatten[7] is killed and you think, "Oh my lord, where has all this gone so awry?" We will hear more about the impact of the Northern Ireland Troubles and the IRA bombing campaign in a later section.

'HOW DID YOU KNOW THAT? YOU'RE IRISH!': ANTI-IRISH STEREOTYPES IN EVERYDAY ENCOUNTERS

Several nurses described incidents of anti-Irish racism in everyday encounters across a range of social settings. While a student in the 1960s, a nurse related one such incident after she was invited to tea at the house of an English student nurse:

> while I was there the insurance man came to visit to collect the insurance money and he said to 'J': 'what are you doing?' And she said nursing and he said, 'oh how's it going?' 'Well, I'm sharing a room with an Irish girl', and he said: 'is she a clean one?' That just stopped me in my tracks because I never really thought, and she was so embarrassed and her family. Nobody said, you know, that I was the one so we all just sat there in horrified silence. (Dervla)

For Dervla, an 18-year-old student, to be confronted with such blatant anti-Irish racism was deeply shocking. As noted by Bronagh earlier, who was stunned and confused by the reference to being a 'pikey', such hostility was unexpected by these young Irish women. As Sheila stated when she saw the 'no Irish' signs during her trip to the seaside, these Irish student nurses had been directly recruited to Britain to deliver vital health service and so they were unprepared for the hostility they encountered.

Fiona told the story of going to a restaurant one evening for a meal with friends. One guest brought his English wife who asked about getting into nursing:

---

7 Lord Mountbatten, a cousin of Queen Elizabeth, was killed by the IRA while on a fishing trip to the Irish Republic.

> 'What qualifications do you need for nursing?' I said, 'Well, you need the equivalent to A Levels really.' I had the English, Maths, whatever else. She said, 'Surely they must have been Irish exams.' Something like that, in the restaurant. Me thinking, 'Excuse me!' She said, 'They're not like our A Levels. Anybody can get into nursing.' So that was really, really horrible at the time. I was very young. They didn't seem to pick up on it. Everybody laughed at the time but my heart was breaking and I thought, 'How dare she?' I didn't know how to respond. I wish I had. I was kind of quiet. (Fiona)

Another participant related an experience she once had in a pub. While she waited to be served, two men nearby were having a conversation:

> He swore at his friend, I didn't hear him swear and he turned to me, and he said, 'I'm sorry, there's a lady.' I said, 'That's okay,' so he recognized my Irish accent, he said, 'Oh, she's Irish, let's move away.' So, they moved to the other side of the pub. (Angela)

It is often difficult to interpret such brief encounters and passing remarks. What did the man mean by 'oh, she's Irish', why did they move to the other side of the bar? In a way their motivation is not really the issue here. Instead, it is important to pay attention to the impact of such encounters on Irish migrants. Exposure to such incidents, particularly if they are repeated across different settings, can result in a heightened sensitivity to one's accent and identity to the extent where one is continually preparing for some negative remark (Hickman and Walter, 1997; Walter, 2002). Over time this can impact on self-confidence.

Experiences of hostility meant that some Irish migrants sought out the safety and security of Irish networks (Gray, 2004; Ryan, 2008). A participant from the 1950s generation, Colette, told us that she never had any negative experiences because of her ethnicity. However, her daughter, who was present during some of the interview, added that 'you were in this Irish cocoon, you had the church and the social clubs, that's what you did'. The daughter's intervention was quite revealing and may explain, at least in part, why Colette had not been exposed to anti-Irish hostility.

As the years went by, some participants felt more able to challenge anti-Irish stereotyping. For example, Aileen described how a tutor on an IT course made a snide remark that she perceived as anti-Irish.

> I did a computer class and a South African woman was teaching and one day I said to her, I said, 'Oh, I don't know what's wrong with this

computer today. It's really slow.' And she said, 'Like the person that's using it.' And I said, 'Actually we don't take that anymore.' She went bright red. I said, 'We really do not take that anymore.'

And she did apologize and I thought, 'Well, you know, sometimes you just have to stand up a bit for yourself and not let them.' You know, not let people make remarks like that and whereas probably twenty years ago I'd have thought [tutting sound] … you do mature as the years go by and, you know, you just don't take it really anymore. (Aileen)

Sean, who was a psychiatric nurse in Yorkshire, recounted an incident during a pub quiz which he was able to challenge with some quick-witted repartee:

I was in the pub at a quiz and I answered a question and what happened, you had a normal quiz and then you got a lottery ticket at half time and if you won that, you could go up to the bar and answer one, open a sealed envelope and there was a question in there, the question was, I remember it very well, it was 'What is a sinologist?', and I worked it out, so I said 'it's someone who understands all things Chinese', and I won £25 and as I'm going back to my seat, a woman at the bar said, 'How did you know that? You're Irish!' … Well, I used to say to people, I've been called a stupid Irish bastard, but I always used to say, 'whoa hang on a minute, I'd have been just as stupid whatever nationality I was'. (Sean)

As noted earlier, most nurses stated that people, in general, were friendly and open. Particular geographical areas, such as Liverpool, were considered to be especially friendly. Because of its history of Irish migration over centuries, Liverpool had an affinity with Irish people: 'everybody you meet is Irish descent, everybody' (Katheen). Nonetheless, even Liverpool could hold some unexpected surprises for Irish migrants. Kathleen, who came originally from Northern Ireland, was shocked to discover sectarianism in Liverpool.

I didn't realize that Liverpool was quite sectarian, I didn't know, I didn't realize because it was a very sheltered life in Ireland. I didn't realize. The first time I think was when I saw an Orange Order parade … I remember being somewhere, in Southport or somewhere, and I saw, and I couldn't believe it, I didn't realize there was that sectarianism and it's probably still around, I don't know. But at the time it was there but it didn't affect me, I didn't feel any prejudice against an Irish Catholic or nationalist or whatever, you know. (Kathleen)

Indeed, Joseph found that being Irish in Liverpool was not entirely plain sailing: 'It was strange at first and my accent, people were, "What did you say Paddy?" Everybody calls you Paddy! It was no good protesting, that was the way it was. And I had to repeat myself all the time'. After living in the city for over sixty years, his accent has modified a little: 'I had a bit of a Liverpool accent, it rubbed off on me!'

Earlier Sheila remarked that some colleagues in the hospital used to address her as 'Irish'. She also mentioned that her brother, who worked in construction, was rarely addressed by his name and more usually called 'Paddy'. It is noteworthy that our male participant, Joseph, was repeatedly called 'Paddy'.

As noted earlier, people were often curious about names and accents, as a way of trying to place nurses within the geo-political context of Northern or Southern Ireland. Like Julia above, all our Scotland-based participants mentioned how names, accents and even schools were used to try to place them within specific religious, ethnic and political affiliations.

> in Glasgow would be – 'what school did you go to'. That would determine a lot. If you said 'Saint whatever', then they knew you were more than likely Catholic. (Jacky)

A similar point was made by another Scotland-based participant:

> the religion thing, you did need to be careful ... Glasgow in particular, even now to this day in Scotland, if you're asked what school you went to, you're asked because they want to figure out if you're Catholic and you went to a Catholic school. (Ciara)

As the political situation grew more tense, these perceived affiliations took on a deeper meaning, as discussed below.

'DO YOU HAVE A BOMB IN YOUR BAG?': BEING IRISH DURING THE TROUBLES

Geographical location mattered and being in a particular city around the time of an IRA bombing[8] could have very real consequences for Irish people. Bronagh, having originally trained in Kent, later moved to live in Birmingham after she got married in the 1970s:

---

8 As the armed conflict in Northern Ireland intensified, the IRA began a bombing campaign in England in the early 1970s that carried on until the ceasefire in 1994. The most notorious of these included the Birmingham, Hyde Park, Brighton and Manchester incidents.

> ... and that coincided with a lot of IRA trouble, the Birmingham bombing which was absolutely, this was a bombshell blast out of the blue, and we were all damned by association. You spoke with an Irish accent so you were a terrorist ... I was out in the community as a district nurse, and you would have kept your head down. You would only go shopping ... You'd have had to go into the butcher's and the baker's and ask for bread and meat with my very broad Irish accent, which I never chose to change in one shape or form.
>
> So it was certainly a period when we were singled out, it didn't matter whether you were a nurse, I mean the patients were always very grateful to you, but the caring part of you, what you were doing, they would be very grateful to you, but there was also the fact, the association with the fact that you were Irish, and 'all the Irish over there were bombers and you never knew what they were going to do next' ... it was certainly not comfortable having an Irish accent there. (Bronagh)

She recalled how the general atmosphere of suspicion about Irish people could lead to sensitivities about accent and identity in everyday social encounters, such as in shops:

> I do actually remember, and the reason why I mentioned the butcher's is because ... there was this row of shops along there, and I'd always gone in and picked up my meat. And I can remember them saying to me, 'Oh here comes trouble.' And maybe I was being terribly sensitive, but I sensed that I was being watched, in other words ... everybody was talking about what the Irish were doing, what the Irish had done in Birmingham, and how we were made to feel. (Bronagh)

Bronagh's point about being 'damned by association' is important. All Irish people came under suspicion of being associated with or supporting the IRA (Hillyard, 1993; see also Walter, 1989).[9] In London, Aileen remembered an incident related to the bombing in Woolwich, which was located near the hospital where she worked: 'I do remember a male patient saying that his son was in Belfast fighting us lot and he'd rather he wasn't attended to by an Irish, I do remember. And I remember that vividly because it was probably a one-off, I think'. Aileen went on to reflect that Irish nurses never received any kind of training from the NHS about how to deal with such situations: 'we were never

---

9 Paddy Hillyard's pathbreaking book *Suspect community* vividly explains the impact of 'the Troubles', and how the British state reacted to bombing campaigns, on the everyday lives of Irish people in Britain.

taught how to react ... we didn't ever, ever have any talk about that sort of thing. We were just, you just got on with it.'

In Yorkshire, Nessa also remembered an incident when a patient refused to be treated by an Irish nurse:

> I was working in one hospital that took the soldiers from Northern Ireland. We used to get the soldiers from Northern Ireland over for neurosurgery and we never had a problem with them. It's I think because of ... I know with the soldiers that we had over, it didn't bother them that we were Southern Ireland. There was a nurse – she only came from Donegal but she had more of a Northern accent and one of the soldiers complained he didn't want her looking after him because of where she came ... (Nessa)

In this incident, accent was clearly used to identify and single out one particular nurse as 'Northern Irish' and therefore unacceptable to the soldier. The fact that she was actually from Donegal, and thus from the Irish Republic, was immaterial to how he perceived her. He seemed to have no problem with nurses who were clearly from the South (as defined by their accents) caring for him in the hospital.

Indeed, one nurse recalled a situation where she felt the need to challenge a patient who expressed anti-Irish views:

> he suddenly, out of the blue one day, started going on about the Irish because obviously he had a different view of what was happening, and I was not denying what was going on at the time as well. It sounds awful but I think I started arguing with him and as luck would have it, I think whoever was in charge that day decided to send me off someplace else because obviously I shouldn't be arguing with a patient, but he had very strong views about the Irish, what they were doing ... and I think I was probably upset about the whole thing because there we are, we're looking after him, mostly Irish nurses. (Claire)

Although there is a power relationship between sick patients, lying in bed, and medical staff providing care, it seems that in several cases, Irish nurses did not feel they had any power to deal with unpleasant and confrontational situations. Some patients obviously felt they could make anti-Irish remarks with impunity particularly in relation to the IRA.

In Yorkshire, Eilish talked about the pervasive 'joke' about the Irish carrying bombs: 'the time of the Birmingham bombings and things like that. People were a bit more like, "oh she's Irish", or they might make a joke saying, "Oh just check what's in her bag," but you just sort of let it go over the top of your head'.

Similarly, in London, Finnuala observed that remarks about bombs in bags were often presented as 'jokes' or banter: 'Some of the patients would make comments. They wouldn't get away with it now, "You haven't got a bomb in there have you?" ... but we were nurses, we're not into maiming people. But they thought because you were Irish, that you were the same as the IRA and all that kind of thing'. Finnuala also related a much more explicit experience of anti-Irish hostility, while working on the district.

> In the 80s, when I worked in the district, it was the Harrod's bombing ... So I went in to put this man to bed – I'd been going in there like for about four years, and I went in, and he said, 'That was a nice job you did today.' He said, 'I don't want you, I don't want to have you near me, you're dangerous.' The next day – we didn't have pagers in those days – I rang the manager, and I told her, and she said, 'Right, we're withdrawing the service from him.' And his wife was embarrassed, but that was what it was like then. It was ignorance really. (Finnuala)

In this particular story, it is noteworthy that Finnuala had been caring for this patient for four years without incident. However, the Harrod's bombing resulted in the man refusing any further care from his Irish nurse. It may seem a massive over-reaction, and clearly the man lost out as the care was withdrawn, but this story suggests how anti-Irish hostility in wider society can impact even on long-term, established relationships. The story is also noteworthy because earlier in her interview Finnuala said she never had any negative experiences as an Irish nurse. This was not unusual among our participants. The interviewees tended to minimize or downplay experiences of anti-Irish racism and, when such experiences did occur, they tended to blame one 'rude' or 'ignorant' individual. This may be an important coping mechanism to deal with negative encounters as isolated individual incidents rather than something which is deep-rooted and pervasive in society (Ryan, 2007).

It is apparent that, back in the 1970s and 1980s, many Irish nurses found it hard to defend themselves and tended to just try to brush it off or, as one nurse said, 'rise above it':

> like the Guildford bombing, the Birmingham and all this type of thing, people would say, 'Your relations are at it again' ... It was actually quite embarrassing ... You had to actually rise above it. (Ruth)

The IRA bombing campaign went on for decades and involved various parts of England. Our participants often had very clear memories of bombs in their cities and the impact on the local Irish population. One nurse vividly remembered the Manchester bombing in the early 1990s:

> I was on duty, we were all called in on duty for that day and the abuse the Irish doctors and nurses got that day was – and we weren't even involved in it – but that was terrible. But we just got on with it. (Caitriona)

In Scotland, Julia told us a story related to the Enniskillen bombing. Although that took place in Ireland rather than in Britain, the impact was felt powerfully.

> I was out on district and it was an elderly lady and I was going in to do a general nursing care. You'll remember the Enniskillen bombings, and they happened on the Sunday, as you know, and then the Monday morning I was going in to do the general care on this lady, and I came in and her son-in-law was there and he wasn't working, and I knew that he wasn't a nice man from some of the things the mother-in-law had been saying to me.
>
> Anyhow, I came in the door and I said, 'Good morning, how are you all?' and immediately he started on to me, 'So what have you to say for yourself your lot did yesterday, that was blah-blah-blah-blah,' and he stood and he shouted at me. To be honest, I didn't know what to do, so I let him rant on and I said, 'Look, it's got nothing to do with me.' 'Yeah, well you're Irish, you're a Catholic.' I said, 'You don't know what I am. Yes, I'm Irish, but you don't know anything more about me.' 'Well, you're still Irish and you're here. You've got cheek to put your face in here.' He went on like that to me.
>
> His daughter by this time was in tears, so I just said to him, 'Will you excuse me a moment,' and I said to her, 'Come on and we'll go up and do your mum.' I went upstairs, I got her mother fixed, got her mum, gave her a hug, gave the daughter a hug, came downstairs and I just said, 'Excuse me,' and I walked out. I went straight to my boss and explained to her. And I didn't retaliate in any way because it would have made matters worse.
>
> I forgot about that. That's probably the only incident that I ever had that turned against me. But I went back to the house the next day because she was still on my list, and he always walked out of the room whenever I walked in, which was fine. My boss went down to the house. I forgot about that. (Julia)

It is noteworthy that Julia twice says 'I forgot about that'. As with Finnuala earlier, who also appeared to have forgotten about a very similar incident, it seems that our participants put these difficult and painful memories to the back of their minds and tried not to dwell on them.

While in many of these examples, nurses seem to just 'get on with it' or 'rise above' such incidents, this was not always possible, particularly when a formal complaint was made. One nurse,[10] during her student days, was stunned to discover that a patient had written a letter of complaint about her:

> I was called to matron's office. She said, 'There's been a complaint made against you.' She said, 'A gentleman said you refused to give him medication when he asked for it and that he nearly had an acute asthmatic attack because you refused the medication.' At the time I couldn't even think of what it was about

Luckily other nurses, who had observed the incident, were able to confirm that the student nurse had acted appropriately and the man, in fact, did not have an asthmatic attack. At first the student nurse could not understand why the man made a complaint against her but later on she discovered that:

> his son was fighting in Northern Ireland and it had nothing to do with his asthmatic attack, it was just, I happened to be an Irish girl, he was an English man with a son in Northern Ireland. So, the matron got a written apology, which she gave to me, from him saying I was actually doing what I should have done but he apologized.

This nurse considered herself to have been 'lucky' that others could verify her side of the story. The situation could have become quite serious if he had pressed his allegation. The incident was 'the first time I suppose that the so-called "Troubles" came knocking at my door', prior to that 'they hadn't even entered my head.'

Sometimes the remarks were not coming from patients but from nursing colleagues. Sorcha recounted an incident that occurred after the Hyde Park bombing.

> in the 80s ... that was a really difficult time being in London, in the UK, because the IRA were bombing ... I remember one day I was ... walking down the corridor with the people I'd been socializing with the night

---

10 We will not use her pseudonym here for added confidentiality.

before and one of the junior obstetricians; a bomb had gone off in Hyde Park, I remember saying in all innocence, 'Who let the bomb off?' She said, 'Who do you think? The bloody IRA.' I was mortified and she just walked away from me, and it was just terrible. (Sorcha)

Thinking back to those years, Sorcha concluded: 'Yeah, it was a horrible, horrible, horrible time.' She felt that this political context and the backlash against the Irish impacted on her initial attitudes about settling down in Britain: 'It was difficult to settle because, it was difficult being Irish for a long time here'. She added that attitudes have changed enormously over the decades and being Irish became much more acceptable in recent years: 'it really was only, when did it become fashionable to be Irish in London, in the early millennium'.

Experiences of anti-Irish prejudice, stereotypes, snide remarks, insinuations as well as open hostility, clearly have an impact on Irish migrants' self-confidence in particular situations (see Hickman and Walter, 1997; Gray, 2004; Ryan, 2007). Earlier Bronagh spoke about her experiences in Birmingham in the 1970s and how self-conscious she became of her Irish accent, especially in shops. As Miriam stated: 'We wouldn't make ourselves very known, very vocally, like if we were on the Tube or something like that. We would speak quietly to each other. It wouldn't be loud. Just in case.' Similarly, Claire recalled being wary of meeting new people or going to unfamiliar places because she feared a negative reaction to her Irishness: 'I was always a bit dubious about going places and people.'

Fiona put it rather succinctly when she simply stated that: 'in the 70s it was very, very scary to be Irish really because of the IRA bombs and everything else'. Yvonne echoed a point made by many participants when she spoke about avoiding any discussions of the 'Troubles': 'we never got in conversations about it really but there was an awareness of it. We were hearing it all the time.' Similarly, Fidelma also spoke about being careful about what she said in particular places especially with people she did not know well: 'you were a bit more reserved if you were outside of your comfort zone'.

Angela powerfully narrated how the anti-Irish prejudice and hostility circulating in Britain during those years impacted on her self-confidence, especially during interactions beyond the hospital and her professional identity as a nurse. For example, when interacting with other parents at school, she felt very aware of her Irishness and was nervous of encountering hostile reactions:

I remember at the school gate, I wouldn't try to speak to anybody. I was so conscious of my Irish accent, and if you spoke to me I'd speak to you, but I really was, yeah, I was very conscious of my Irish accent ... it was the 70s and 80s, with the real Troubles in Ireland. I mean there was that bombing in Westminster at the time, we were all here, so those things were close to home in London, you know. (Angela)

Another nurse recounted her experience of wanting to use a toilet in Marks & Spencer's department store in London.

I was bursting to go to the toilet. I was absolutely bursting so I said to this girl could I go into the toilet, and she wouldn't let me in. I think she wouldn't let me in, and I was thinking, 'Does she think I'm going to plant a bomb or something?' (Linda)

Eventually, after much persuasion, the shop worker did allow Linda to use the toilet but insisted on accompanying her: 'she did actually walk in with me and sat there, kind of sat outside the toilet and walked me out'. Linda acknowledged that access to the toilet may have been restricted for other reasons and may not have had anything to do with her Irishness but, nonetheless, she had a suspicion that her ethnicity was a factor: 'But I felt my Irish accent, maybe, because I had an Irish accent, that they were very heightened to it.'

For most of the young Irish nurses, who came originally from Southern Ireland, the impact of 'the Troubles' on their everyday encounters in Britain often came as a surprise. As one participant noted above, it 'never entered her head' and she was stunned when it 'came knocking on her door'. Some nurses from the South said they knew very little about the political context in the North. However, for our participants who came from Northern Ireland, these issues were all too familiar. Kathleen was originally from Derry:

Yes, we did have quite traumatic times ... because I went to school in Ireland with a mixed, it was a mixed school, Catholic and Protestant, but in the trouble times obviously there was that division ... my brother had a bad, he had a tough time really ... we would have problems being stopped and searched and all that all the time. (Kathleen)

A few nurses talked about being very mindful of 'the Troubles' when they visited Ireland on holiday especially if they drove across on the ferry in cars with British registrations. For example, Sheila recalled her daughter's reaction to these visits: 'I can only remember we used to go over in the car and you had GB plates on it', this was when all the trouble was going on in Northern Ireland and she said, "Everywhere we'd park, dad would get out and look under the car to make sure there wasn't a bomb under it!"'

Similarly, Mairead recalled: 'when we were going home to Ireland, and Bloody Sunday[11] happened, I remember that. We had children, we had an English car, that kind of thing, and you'd see the black flags flying in Galway and places. So, I was more aware of it from a personal point of view rather than a political because I'm not politically-minded.'

Compared to the reality of living in the midst of the Northern Ireland Troubles, the occasional rude or derogatory remark made against those living in Britain may seem like a minor inconvenience. However, as noted, the cumulative impact of this anti-Irish prejudice and hostility definitely took a toll on many of our participants. Sean spoke about the pervasiveness of anti-Irish stereotypes in the media and in society more generally.

> Oh yeah, there was lots of stuff going on, people would make comments like, 'Have you got a gun in your pocket?' and stuff like that and of course, during that period, the late 60s, early 70s, you had all these comedians on TV talking about the Irish in derogatory terms, so called Irish jokes and all that. (Sean)

While many participants said they kept their heads down and their mouths shut during those difficult years, Sean, who grew up in the North of Ireland, described how he tried to openly discuss the political situation and what was going on.

> during that period of the Troubles, so called Troubles, and people would ask me what was going on in Ireland and then when I tried to tell them, they'd get upset. I think people didn't understand what was going on and people who knew me, I mean I had good relationships ... they would ask me what was happening and I would try to explain it to them but like ... they didn't get, they really couldn't grasp what was going on. (Sean)

Delia, who also grew up in the North of Ireland, was rare among our participants in actually becoming involved in protest groups in Britain. She felt passionately about what was going on in the North and she went on protest marches in London in the 1970s. However, it was soon made known to her that the hospital authorities disapproved of her actions.

---

11 Bloody Sunday refers to an infamous event in Derry in 1972 when a civil rights march was shot at by British soldiers, killing 13 civilians.

> I was called up to the office. These two nursing officers, they were there at the table and they were ... They didn't know how to address me. They didn't know because they were apolitical. Those kind of people never had anything to do with the war, you know. I remember explaining about the war in Ireland. And I was just told by the two of them to be very careful. (Delia)

This appeared to be a veiled threat that her political activism could jeopardize her career. Clearly this was a very painful memory for Delia and she did not elaborate further.

In terms of terrorism and suspicions against particular groups, one nurse drew a direct parallel between the Irish in the 1970s–80s and Muslims today:

> I have an empathy for the Muslims now because I view them in the same situation as I was in the 70s. I didn't do anything wrong but yet you can imagine people hear your accent and they think, 'Ooh, she must be one of them.' That's what I think now when they say, 'The Muslims.' So, I do have this empathy for them because I can equate to what I felt, because I felt myself, 'God, I wonder what people really think of us being Irish and living over here' and either just not saying anything to our face but it's all happening behind our back. (Maeve)

CONCLUSION

As noted by Bronwen Walter (2002), Irish people have occupied an ambiguous position in British society, as much needed workers but also as undesirable migrants and potential terrorists. In this chapter, we have discussed some very difficult and painful experiences of the Irish nurses as they navigated those ambiguous positions. Despite their professionalism as health care providers, our nurses recounted incidents when they were undermined, criticized and suspected – damned by association with the IRA. Moreover, it is also clear that the NHS provided no training or support to Irish staff who were being attacked or humiliated by patients, especially during the 1950s–80s. There was an expectation to just 'get on with it'.

However, it is apparent that in many cases our participants had tried to forget these incidents. We are grateful that they chose to share their experiences with us. It is important that these stories are recorded and understood as part of the wider story of Irish people in British society.

In the next and final chapter, we discuss the overall contribution that Irish nurses have made to the NHS.

CHAPTER 9

Conclusion – 'Under the radar': reflecting on the contribution of Irish nurses to the NHS

> they put an awful lot into the NHS, right from the beginning. In the 1950s, 1960s, there was an awful lot of Irish nurses then ... hospitals would have been without an awful lot of staff if the Irish nurses weren't here then. (Nessa began nurse training in Yorkshire, 1957)

In this concluding chapter, our research participants reflect on the overall contribution of Irish nurses to the NHS. They discuss not only the sheer numbers of Irish nurses working in the British health service but also the particular qualities that they, as Irish people, brought to the job. Furthermore, the chapter explores the extent to which the nurses felt appreciated. The interviews suggest that most nurses felt appreciated, on an individual level, by patients and managers. However, most participants expressed the view that the wider contribution of Irish nurses to the NHS is not well known or appreciated by British society more broadly.

This chapter also considers change over time and how the NHS has evolved in recent years. Moreover, the ways in which our participants engage with the NHS is also changing. Now, as they grow older, many are also shifting perspectives – from care providers to care recipients. Our participants expressed varying views about whether health services have improved or worsened especially in terms of patient care. Overall, as demonstrated throughout this chapter, the interviewees feel a strong attachment to the NHS and a huge sense of pride in the role that Irish people have played over the decades.

Finally, the chapter ends by reflecting on how our oral history research adds new insights and understanding about Irish nurses in Britain and we highlight what more should be done to promote and celebrate their contribution to the NHS.

'THE BACKBONE OF THE NHS': THE CONTRIBUTION OF IRISH NURSES OVER TIME

As discussed in Chapter 2, there were over 30,000 Irish-born nurses in the NHS by the 1970s (Daniels, 1993) and by 1981, 17% of all Irish-born women employed in Britain worked in medical services (Walter, 1989). Our forty-five participants had worked in the NHS during those decades when Irish nurses constituted such a significant proportion of health care staff.

All the participants were unanimous in underlining the enormous contribution of Irish nurses. Sorcha put it succinctly: 'it's been phenomenal, it's been huge'. Sinead used very similar words: 'the contribution that Irish nurses have made to the NHS, I think it is phenomenal to be honest with you'. Sean emphasized that 'Irish nurses made an amazing contribution to the NHS'.

Many interviewees emphasized the sheer numbers of Irish nurses and their key role in staffing the NHS. As Bronagh stated: 'we were a significant part of the workforce'. Across our research, it was often stated that hospitals would not have had sufficient staff without Irish recruitment into the NHS. Fidelma emphasized that 'without the Irish nurses, and without their total contribution and their commitment, I think the health service would be in a really bad place'. As Nessa noted at the start of this chapter, Irish nurses were crucial during the 1950s–60s. This pattern continued into later decades: 'hospitals in the 1970s and 1980s would have struggled without the Irish nurses, in terms of numbers' (Aileen).

Ruth stated simply that 'the Irish propped up the NHS'. It was interesting how many participants used similar phrases to denote the key role that Irish nurses played in maintaining, supporting and 'propping up' the NHS. For example, Ciara said that Irish nurses 'kept it going', while Anita asserted 'they were the backbone of the NHS'.

Part of the reason why Irish nurses were needed in such large numbers was because, as noted in Chapter 2, English people seemed not to be attracted into the profession (Jinks et al., 2014). Indeed, several interviewees mentioned that the English were often a minority in their student cohorts and some even dropped out before completing the course. For example, Aileen stated: 'Four English girls started in our group ... One finished the course'. She went on to explain that hospital managers 'did recognize that if they were dependent on the English becoming nurses, they would have struggled for actual bodies on the ward.' Fidelma made a similar observation about her training set, underlining not only the scarcity of English students but the fact that those who started did not complete the course: 'maybe it's just because it wasn't what they actually expected it to be like ... I only knew two and one left'.

Reflecting on the hospital in Hertfordshire where she spent her entire career, Deborah remarked on how few English people worked there: 'you didn't get many English ... you got some but you didn't have that many English people coming into it ... Maybe an odd one or two but not very many.' Interestingly, she added that even those colleagues who were born in England many were second-generation Irish: 'But most of them would be Irish descent, they might be English-born but they would count themselves as Irish'.

Of course, it was not only Irish migrants who were recruited to staff the NHS. As noted throughout this book (see Chapters 4, 5 and 8), our participants worked alongside migrant nurses from around the world. Sorcha explained that in her north London hospital: 'you were black or Irish, that was the way it was'. Caitriona in Manchester made a similar point about the Irish 'and the Jamaicans and the Nigerians. The National Health wouldn't have existed without them.' In Yorkshire, Nessa, reflecting back on when she arrived in the 1950s and through her early career in the 1960s, echoed this view: 'the Irish and the Jamaicans, there would have been no National Health Service if it wasn't for them.' The changing migration pattern across the NHS, over time, was discussed in Chapter 2 and will be considered again later in this chapter.

'SOMETHING SPECIAL ABOUT AN IRISH NURSE': HARD-WORKING AND CARING

Beyond their sheer numbers, many participants mentioned that Irish nurses brought particular qualities to the nursing profession. A recurring theme throughout the interviews was 'hard work'. Most participants emphasized that Irish nurses were hard workers.

Nurses from across the decades and geographical regions reiterated the theme of hard work. In Liverpool, Jane, who trained in the 1950s, commented: 'They're good workers'. Similarly, Bronagh, who trained in Kent in the 1960s, said: 'Irish nurses were known to be hard workers ... Whatever they were told, that was it, you just got on with it.' Meanwhile in London, Aileen, who trained in the early 1970s, expressed the view that 'it was always recognized that we were very hard-working and that we, for the want of a better word, kind of got stuck in and did the job and saw the job through, didn't complain.' The point that Irish nurses got on with it and didn't complain was made repeatedly by participants from across the decades. Caitriona, who trained in Manchester in the 1960s, also stated simply: 'we got on with it'.

Trisha, speaking about the dedication and hard work of Irish nurses, also emphasized that they 'got on with it':

> They were very good, very conscientious. All of us we did our job. I know most of our group never took time off sick or anything like that. I can count on one hand how often I was sick, which was never really ... you just got on with it and that was it ... really worked hard. (Trisha)

Kitty suggested that growing up in Ireland prepared them well for the demands of nursing: 'they weren't frightened of work and they got on with people really, so, it wasn't hard work for them ... because they'd probably got used to (it) in Ireland'. As discussed in Chapter 3, many of our participants grew up on farms and drew a direct link between these farming backgrounds and an indefatigable work ethic. For example, Carmel reflected: 'We were hard-working, because I came from a farm – five brothers and me – a small farm. And even though I was the only girl in the family, I liked to be out on the farm as well'.

Growing up in Ireland, especially in the 1940s–60s, may also have engendered other traits in Irish people that equipped them for a career in nursing. This point was mentioned by sisters Aoife and Una in Liverpool as they reflected on why Irish nurses were recruited, in such large numbers, by the NHS:

> Una: the deputy matron, who was a rather robust lady, and she used to go to Ireland and recruit Irish nurses because they were hard-working.
> Aoife: And willing.
> Una: Yeah, willing to do things and ... I never heard anybody giving out about Irish nurses being lazy ...
> Aoife: Supportive, they'd be supportive ... They'd always look after you ... They were friendly and they could talk to people, they would talk to the patients, I found that ... and they were very caring about small things, making you cups of tea or that kind of thing. They weren't afraid to deal with things like death and sadness, they didn't hide away from death and sadness ... I think it had something to do with, you know from a young age everybody in Ireland goes to funerals and they get used to dealing with that kind of thing whereas in England you rarely get invited to go to a funeral. I think because of that, they were used to dealing with sadness and death and they grew up with it.
> Una: Aoife's pastime, she goes to funerals all the time!

As noted in Chapter 3, several participants attributed their desire to become a nurse to their childhood experiences in Ireland, especially coming from farming families and being familiar with cycles of birth and dying both among animals and humans. Hence, as noted by Aoife above, Irish nurses were not afraid to deal with death.

Therefore, beyond their capacity for hard work, several interviewees highlighted other qualities that made Irish people especially suited to nursing.

For instance, Kathleen emphasized that there was a special quality about Irish nurses: 'full of fun as well as seriousness, as well as conscientious ... There's always something special about an Irish nurse, even today I think, there's always something special'.

Similarly, Ciara, while acknowledging that it was a generalization, stated: 'I think the thing that Irish nurses bring, and I am really generalizing, is a bit of humility as well as humanity to it. I always say the hand that touches the patient makes the difference'.

These special qualities, particularly in patient care, were also described by Pauline:

> I was very quiet but always very attentive to people, so if somebody buzzed a buzzer, I would go immediately. If somebody was dying I'd like to sit with them ... to hold their hand while they were dying if they had nobody else. Yeah, I think they generally liked Irish nurses, appreciated ... I think they brought a different type of caring because they're very chatty ... I think possibly it's in most Irish people. There's a gentleness and a caring attitude about them. (Pauline)

Here, we see that Pauline spontaneously mentioned holding the hand of a dying patient, reiterating the point made by Aoife above. Indeed, this bond between nurse and patient, exemplified by holding someone's hand as they passed away, was mentioned by several interviewees.

Another nurse shared her saddest memory when a young patient, whom she got to know well during his long hospital stay, passed away: 'I held his hand'.

> and I said, 'I will never forget you. You're a lovely young man, I just wish we had you for a bit more', and a tear rolled down his face and I knew I was going to have to run to the canteen to get his people to come back. And they just got into the room, fell on their knees and he just went [sighs]. That was a horrible night. (Deborah)

Deborah also emphasized the tenderness she felt for her patients, stating that 'we were kind and caring.' The caring nature of Irish nurses was highlighted by many participants: 'great carers' (Sorcha), 'very caring' (Ruth) and 'very caring people' (Aisling).

In terms of 'going the extra mile' in order to put patients at their ease, the story of Julia is particularly revealing and amusing. As a district nurse in Scotland, going into patients' homes, Julia made an effort to forge a bond with all her patients through football. While she actually supported Manchester United, she feigned an allegiance to various clubs depending on her patients' interests.

> This is when I became a Celtic and a Rangers fan, a Partick Thistle fan, a St Mirren fan.[1] Because I love football and sport so I used to listen to all the matches, and then the next time you'd go to that house that would be all that they could talk about. One man sat and watched the Rangers' channel twenty-four hours a day. When he couldn't sleep, he got up and he turned it on and watched it. The only thing, his brother eventually ... he asked me what team I supported and I said Man United. 'Oh my god, if my brother knew you were a Man United ... he wouldn't have let you in the house.'
>
> But again I think going back from all the experience I'd had with different people, you learn so much from other cultures and other ways of living that it helps you the way you treat these people that you're looking after. That's how I felt. If I had stayed in either Ireland or in Northern Ireland, I don't honestly think I would have been as open as I am. We're all Jock Tamson's bairns[2] as they say here, and it is so true. (Julia)

Finnuala talked about Irish nurses being particularly empathetic: 'I think Irish people have a kind of an empathy built in. I don't know what it is, so it was easy to look after people ... we cared for patients and looked after them extremely well'. A sentiment that was reiterated by many others:

> the way I looked at it anyway as a nurse was 'that's my mother in the bed or my father in the bed or my brother or my sister in the bed and how I would like them to be treated'. I think that's what made the nurse, basically. (Fiona)

This empathy was also demonstrated in how nurses mediated between doctors and patients. As Joseph observed: 'nurses are much closer to patients than doctors'. This point was further elaborated by another participant:

> The observation, noticing things, our patients if they're upset or anything, we'd go and have a chat with them. We were able to make a cup of tea for them and I used to say, 'Oh, great. One for the patient and one for the

---

[1] These are all rival teams in Scotland and it would be impossible to support them all. [2] A Scottish expression meaning we are all the same, we are all equal.

nurse.' It was those kinds of things that they haven't got time for even the patients, to be honest … the doctor would tell the patient and then he'd walk off. You could see the patient like draining so, obviously, our job was to explain to the patient what they were going to do … We're there to do the job because we're trained to do and, as I said, because of our manners and respect we were halfway there. (Kitty)

The extent to which Irish nurses were 'special' and significantly different from other nurses is worthy of some reflection. Ciara, as noted above, was wary of generalizing. Moreover, a few participants added some nuance to the discussion. Miriam made the point that Irish nurses were often perceived by other colleagues as dedicated to their profession: 'They would say things like, "Oh, I want that Irish girl to do it for me"'. They had this thing that if you were Irish you were dedicated to nursing'. However, she noted that this was not always the case, and added half-jokingly, 'little did they know!' Angela, while noting that Irish nurses had a reputation as especially caring, was not sure this was always true: 'Now I don't know, I didn't see that myself really, but they seemed to think that we had a more caring nature'. She highlighted that 'Chinese nurses' were also very good and well-liked by patients. Some other nurses presented a similarly nuanced view:

> I think the Irish nurses were No. 1 more talkative as well … more friendly. I don't mean more friendly than other people, I think warm as well you know, they're caring. I'm not saying that others are not, but you know they were particularly kind of – especially verbally more caring. Just going that extra mile for people. Mind you, you could say the same for the Filipino nurses too, they are very good. (Veronica)

Sinead also added some nuance by stating that: 'there's shirkers everywhere you go (but), in my experience, most Irish nurses were the hard-working ones'.

The aim of our oral history research is not to assess whether Irish nurses were more caring and empathetic than other nurses. Instead, we aim to present the voices of our participants and highlight their perceptions and interpretations of their nursing experiences. As with all the topics discussed throughout this book, the participants expressed varied opinions. While many suggested that Irish nurses had specific qualities, including good inter-personal skills, others were wary of such generalizations. Moreover, these qualities were not necessarily regarded as innate Irish qualities but rather were attributed to their early socialization and the skills they learned growing up in Irish society during the twentieth century. For example, many participants explained how they had learned how to work hard as part of large families and looking after siblings from a young age. Several participants opined that other nurses, from similar backgrounds, such as Filipino nurses, had developed comparable caring qualities.

While most participants extolled the qualities of Irish nurses, the extent to which they were appreciated within the NHS was a matter of some discussion. We consider this issue in the next sections.

'PEOPLE WERE NICER': APPRECIATION BY PATIENTS AND COLLEAGUES

Interestingly, among some of our older participants, there was a perception that patients in previous decades had been more appreciative of nurses and more respectful towards staff. For instance, Aileen stated that 'people were so nice and respectful when I first came to England'. She expanded on this point:

> People were nicer to professionals, people were nicer to nurses, they were nicer to policemen, they were nicer – just nicer. You know, now you don't expect them … I think all of us now, we're waiting for someone to 'have a go' about something some place, on a train, on a bus, at work … People just didn't do it then … I think people generally were less confrontational. (Aileen)

Like Aileen, others also noted generational differences. For example, Kitty, describing herself as a shy and quiet person, reflected that she got on well with older patients:

> They were lovely. They were older people … I did like the older because they were more like us really as well. We understood them. A lot of the older people as well were quite shy whereas even the youngsters are not shy these days. (Kitty)

Reflecting back on her early years as a nurse in the 1950s–60s, Colette simply stated that 'the patients were very nice'.

Some nurses underlined a regional character to their relations with patients. As noted in Chapter 7, Dervla, after training in England, moved to Wales:

> nursing in Wales is different because they're very grateful. People in Wales are much more grateful than I found in the English people. You looked after them, they were much more appreciative of what you did. (Dervla)

A nurse who trained in the Midlands in the 1960s told us that grateful patients would sometimes invite nurses to their home for afternoon tea.

> going to people's houses was interesting, when I'd go for afternoon tea, because grateful patients would invite you. That doesn't happen nowadays, but in those days it did happen … I mean nursing can be very stressful, but then it can be great too when people appreciate. And you do get a lot of patients who are very appreciative, you really do. (Veronica)

Another nurse shared an anecdote about her experience in Yorkshire:

> I always remember, this lady came in once to have something done and we just got talking and she said, holiday times, she said, 'Where are you going?', so I said, 'Oh, I'm going to Ireland for a holiday,' so she said, 'Oh, when I go into hospital, as soon as I hear an Irish voice,' she said, 'I feel faith, I know I'll be well looked after.' (Nessa)

Several expressed a similar view that their patients had especially appreciated them as Irish nurses.

> … obviously the hospital was full of English patients … Oh, I think it was well known and patients loved the Irish nurses, you know even now you often hear them saying, 'Oh and a lovely Irish nurse'. They will say 'Irish', they don't say, 'Oh a lovely nurse', very often they'll put in, 'Oh and a lovely *Irish* nurse came', I even hear that being said now. (Sheila)

Several nurses shared stories of particular incidents that they would never forget and where their care had been especially appreciated by patients.

> There was a little baby, I think it was two days old. He was rushed in and he was extremely ill. I happened to look on his notes and it said he was a Catholic. I happened to say to the parents, 'Has he been baptized?' They said, 'No.' I said, 'Well I can give lay baptism.' So I gave this little boy, he was called J, I gave J lay baptism. Anyway, he had to go to theatre for emergency surgery and like that in A&E when somebody went off you concentrated on the next new patient so I didn't really think about him much. A few months later I got a lovely letter and a photograph of this lovely little baby and thanking me for giving him lay baptism and he had survived and progressed. And over the years they kept in touch with me. They didn't live in Leeds, they were just visiting Leeds, I think. They used

to send me photographs of his first communion and his confirmation. It was really, really nice. A nice experience. (Niamh)

Anita shared a story of a baby she saved from choking. Interestingly, this incident occurred not in a hospital but in her own house after her neighbours suddenly knocked on her door:

> they knew I was a nurse because they'd see me going in and out, the lady over the road, she had a little baby and a sweet got stuck in his throat ... she brought him over and I opened the door, she just threw him at me, and I just soon knew what to do and got it out, boiled sweet. I remember sitting in the kitchen and tapping his back to get it out, yes. The poor mum was so scared ... Well, I was scared because I thought, 'If I don't get it up, what's going to happen?' ... I think he was only about nine months old, something like that age ... I don't know how he did it, but he got the sweet, yes. You see him now, he's a big, tall guy. (Anita)

Beyond their particular encounters with patients, many participants talked about how they were perceived and valued by their colleagues on the wards. For example, Mairead stated: 'I always felt very valued ... 100%'. Finnuala, who was still working part-time up to the age of 70, shared a comment made by one of her colleagues: 'I love it when you're here, you never stop working'.

Fiona spoke about a letter she received when she retired: 'I got a lovely letter after retirement from one of the directors which really I thought "if I've got nothing else, I've got that". I put it in a frame actually'.

Several participants spoke about a general appreciation for Irish nurses within hospitals and among managers. Carmel said that: 'I always heard so much praise for the Irish nurses.' Similarly, Kitty had also felt that Irish nurses were valued: 'They said that the Irish nurses were the best'.

Maeve shared conversations she had been involved in at her hospital especially in relation to various recruitment drives:

> when we're short staffed and they were talking about where would they recruit and how would they recruit. They said the best nurses are Irish nurses ... This is one of the senior nurses, she said, 'They're absolutely brilliant. They're the sort of nurses you really want to work alongside.' (Maeve)

By contrast, some nurses felt that their hard work and dedication was not valued. Angela simply stated: 'you weren't appreciated one bit'. Indeed, some stated that nurses' hard work was sometimes taken for granted within an understaffed NHS.

> Talking about working late and overtime, oh my God that's a big bugbear with me and the NHS, oh my goodness, absolutely, the NHS owes me years of overtime, years of overtime. What was so annoying was that it was taken for granted, it was just accepted. If you looked up at the clock and you were meant to leave at 9.00 and you left at 9.05, you'd say, 'Oh I'm leaving early today.' You'd think, 'No hang on a minute, I'm leaving on time' but you never seemed to get any gratitude, it was so taken for granted, expected … If you didn't have a lunch break or you had it for ten minutes … that is a bugbear with me, no appreciation and taken for granted, it bugged me. (Linda)

A similar point was made by Deborah, who worked on a psychiatric ward. She described skipping breaks, putting in long shifts and working extra time without being recognized or properly paid. She gave an example of one particularly difficult night shift:

> Some nights were easy, some nights were – Jesus! And we didn't always get our breaks … we had a man go berserk about quarter to 12. One nurse had gone on her break and he started going at 12 o'clock until five in the morning. Oh my god, it was horrendous. He threw a cup of tea over me … he says, 'You can have your fucking tea', and he threw it over me. … 5 o'clock eventually he went to sleep. We'd had no break but we didn't get paid for that. (Deborah)

Interestingly, Bronagh observed that back in the 1960s and 1970s there was less emphasis on praise and feeling appreciated by managers than might be the case today: 'I don't know that anybody ever said many encouraging words about you in those days. We weren't as much into motivation and encouraging'.

As well as discussing their individual experiences and sense of being valued, we also wanted to understand if the overall contribution of Irish nurses to the NHS was known and appreciated by wider British society. In the next section, we consider how our participants responded to that question.

'UNDER THE RADAR': RECOGNIZING THE WIDER CONTRIBUTION OF IRISH NURSES TO THE NHS

Some participants expressed the view that the overall contribution of Irish nurses was recognized: 'I think it definitely was, I think it was appreciated' (Pauline). Some felt it was known in specific areas: 'I certainly find it here in Scotland, it was acknowledged' (Julia). However, others were less sure that the significance of Irish nurses' role in the NHS was valued in wider society: 'I don't think it was valued, was it?' (Claire). Sorcha was also not convinced: 'So I don't know if it's been acknowledged or recognized to answer your question directly, I'm not sure it has.'

Several interviewees actually asserted that the contribution of Irish nurses to the NHS was not recognized in British society. For example, Fidelma stated succinctly: 'they did make a big, big contribution, and they're not recognized for it, unfortunately.'

Caitriona emphasized that recognition was needed: 'there should be a lot of honour given to the Irish, both the Irish men who built the motorways and the Irish ... they contributed, they made the National Health'.

Sinead also noted that the 'massive' role of Irish nurses was not acknowledged or known about in wider society. Indeed, it was this lack of acknowledgment that motivated her to take part in our research project:

> To be honest ... I've never seen it in the media or it has never, to me it hasn't really been acknowledged, it's not very high profile and that's one of the reasons actually I did the interview because I thought, actually ... I'd never done anything like this before ever, right? And I just thought, do you know something, the contribution that Irish nurses have made to the NHS I think is phenomenal to be honest with you. I mean in every hospital you go to you will find Irish nurses, maybe not so much anymore but, and you'll still meet a lot of Irish nurses.
>
> ... some of my colleagues are Irish who came here the same as me, still working for the NHS. So, I think we've made a massive contribution but I feel sometimes it hasn't been acknowledged in ways maybe like the Windrush ... there was a lot of nurses came from the West Indies and brilliant, it should be acknowledged, but I feel maybe Irish nurses had been under the radar a little bit so that's the way I feel, anyway. (Sinead)

Like Sinead above, many of our participants spoke quite spontaneously about the role of other migrant nurses, not just the Irish. Dervla noted that some of the Caribbean nurses had felt unappreciated and even discriminated against within hospitals especially in the 1960s–70s:

> I think also some of the West Indian nurses felt that they weren't appreciated and yet they were one of the largest, outside from the Irish, group of nurses in the NHS at the time. And they felt that they weren't appreciated because a lot of them, the older ones, had actually trained as nurses in the West Indies and then came over and found they were in an auxiliary position which of course was very demeaning to them. (Dervla)

In recent years there have been efforts to recognize and celebrate the role that nurses from the Caribbean have played in the NHS – especially the so-called 'Windrush generation'. Several of our participants, like Sinead above, welcomed that recognition but added that similar recognition was also due to Irish nurses. Likewise, Aileen stated that the contribution of the Windrush generation of nurses was now better understood in society but work still needed to be done to celebrate Irish nurses' contribution.

Miriam opined that there was a tendency to take the Irish for granted. She explained that unlike other migrant nurses, the Irish had not travelled very far or had to learn a new language: 'you heard about the Malaysian girls and the West Indian girls, that they had come a long way (or) they had learned another language'.

Overall, among our interviewees and indeed, as noted by Sinead, motivating their desire to participate in this oral history project, there was a strong emphasis on celebrating and commemorating the significant contribution of Irish nurses to the NHS. Moreover, there was also a motivation to celebrate and protect the NHS itself and express concern about some of the changes taking place in recent decades.

'NURSING IS NOT WHAT IT WAS': HOW THE NHS HAS CHANGED OVER TIME

Many of our nurses expressed the view that the NHS had been better in earlier decades. Fidelma echoed many when she said: 'We were lucky. It was really, really good … We were looked after, so well looked after. Sad to say, today that's not the case, and it's such a shame'. She gave the simple example of the staff canteen to illustrate how things had deteriorated in recent years.

> And even if you were on night duty, kitchens were open at night, hot meals all the way through. Now, sandwich out of a vending machine if it works, if you get a break at all. It's tough for them these days. I feel for them. I do feel for them. (Fidelma)

Fidelma had quit nursing when she had her children, as discussed in Chapter 7, and did a refresher course years later to return to nursing. However, she found that nursing had changed so much that she no longer felt attracted to the profession: 'I thought I couldn't work like that anymore. No time for patients. No time for what I call "caring". And it's not the nurses' fault. It's just they haven't got the time. They haven't got the staff.'

We heard many similar observations about how patient care has changed over time:

> when I left nursing, I retired, I haven't missed it for one second, which is sad to say, because I just think it's not the nursing that it was. It's not the caring, I definitely don't think it's the caring profession that it was, that's my impression. (Angela)

As our participants age, many are now encountering the NHS as patients or as carers for elderly partners. Angela regularly took her husband to hospital appointments and reflected on how nursing had changed since her nursing days:

> I just feel sorry for the patients today, I think it's quite sad and frightening ... I do think the way we looked after patients I think was excellent care. Whether I'm looking at it through rose-tinted glasses, I don't think I am. But then the patients had the basic nursing care, mind you now ... there's basically no nursing care given to anyone. I think sometimes if you're a patient in hospital, sometimes a cup of tea means more, you know, someone being nice and caring and making you a cup of tea. I think that can mean more to some little old lady. (Angela)

Angela concluded that 'nursing is not what it was, I think it's very sad, but yeah, I am proud of what I've achieved'.

Most of our participants, as noted in Chapter 5, were very positive about the quality of training they received and the level of patient care that had been provided in the past. Aileen contrasted her nursing experience, when nurses were expected to know about each patient, with her recent experiences as a patient in the NHS:

when we, as youngsters, stood at the top of a Nightingale ward, instantly you knew, you knew what had to be done, who needed discharge papers, who was going ... You could just do that so easily. And I found that very lacking when I was a patient. You'd almost have to tell every single nurse, 'I'm in here because ...' and, 'I need this because ...' (Aileen)

Other participants discussed how the relationship between nurses and patients had changed in part because stays in hospital are now much shorter than before and so the turnover of patients is much faster than in previous decades: 'people were in hospital a lot longer and in bed a lot longer. Now they're in and out in a few hours' (Aoife).

This point was further elaborated upon by Kitty. She also noted that in the past patients spent longer in hospital and, for example, came in the day before an operation so the preparation work could be done in advance:

They'd come in the day before which was helpful to that patient and also very helpful to us, preparing patients for theatre and put them at their ease. So, it was a lovely way. They don't do that now. They come in on the morning, which is not fair. It's not fair for the nurse because you don't know the person and you're telling them all this and they can't take it in. (Kitty)

Like many other participants, Kitty stated that nurses no longer had time to chat with patients: 'we were always observant and we listened to people. An awful lot of people, these days, don't listen to patients'. She concluded that the NHS had now gone 'haywire'.

The changing uniform often came to symbolize how much nursing had changed. Carmel also drew upon her recent hospital experience: 'I was in hospital myself a few years ago for a few days, and I was horrified at the way they were dressed. Baggy trousers and tops, you wouldn't know who was who.' She contrasted that with the nurses' uniform when she began her career in the 1950s: 'The patients all knew who the first-year (students) were and who the second-year were, then the staff nurse and the sister'.

A similar observation was made by another nurse, who had also trained in the 1950s:

If you had one spot on your apron, you had to go to the Nurses' Home and change it straight away. This is what I find so difficult now, the nurses are very tatty looking in the hospitals. I've been in hospital quite a bit on and off over the years and they're untidy and they're wearing trainers that are all dirty and it's totally different and I don't like it. (Bridget)

Aine, although aged over 70, still works part-time in a care home and often takes patients to hospital for medical appointments. She also spoke about the changes to the nurses' uniform: 'The whole uniform is different as well ... I think it's terrible ... they go round wearing trainers at work.' Echoing the views of many other participants, Aine concluded: 'They should dress as nurses properly did in the olden days.'

Of course, not all our participants held the same opinions. A few were more positive about the new uniform. Aileen emphasized the advantages of the loose-fitting scrubs: 'they are more casual now, they're more comfortable, they're more practical, of course, everybody can see that.' Claire took a balanced view: 'Well yes, I mean there's pros and cons'.

But it was not only the uniform; several participants stated that the entire nursing profession had changed over time. For instance, Aine opined: 'I do reckon nursing is a vocation, I don't think it is anymore ... I don't think they have the same commitment really'. To indicate this changing level of commitment, she cited the NHS strikes:[3] 'because they're obviously going looking for more money. We never thought of money when we started off, it was a vocation, but now that's the way they think'.

Relations with patients were also impacted by increasing computerization according to several participants. As Aoife noted: 'it's more computerized and we used to say, "You need to look at the patient in the bed, look under the bedcovers to really see the patient".' Aoife, whose grandson is now training as a nurse, added humorously: 'I told that to my grandson, I said, "You're not nursing the computer, you're nursing the patient in the bed so that's the one you look after".'

Indeed, Bridget, who had carried on nursing in a GP surgery until she was over 70 years, also noted how computerization had been the final hurdle for her and led to her decision to retire: 'The reason I retired was the internet got me'.

Furthermore, several participants emphasized that nursing staff felt overwhelmed and powerless in the face of changing structures within the NHS. For example, changing work patterns have created a much more challenging environment for nurses:

> The twelve-hour shifts came into being, some number of years back ... It was a long day, I didn't particularly like those twelve-hour shifts, I didn't think they were good for anybody ... you know how things changed as the years went on and the services became very busy. Here in Glasgow there

---

[3] During the period of our research in 2022–3, staff across the NHS, including nurses and junior doctors, were involved in protracted strikes about pay and conditions.

was amalgamation of maternity units, then it just became a very, very busy unit ... It had changed dramatically in a short period of time due to amalgamation of another big maternity unit. (Jacky)

This point was echoed by nurses elsewhere in the country who also felt that shift patterns and working schedules were changing in ways that impacted negatively on them and on patients. In London, Sorcha, as discussed at length in Chapter 7, was one of first midwives to return to work after having children: 'it was a great time to be in the NHS and I was one of the first women that was allowed to have that flexibility'. However, like so many other interviewees, she stated that some of the advances made over time were now being rolled back: 'It's kind of gone back now again, it's changed again'.

Deborah had a long career as an auxiliary and, unlike most other participants, she had decided to work permanently on nights. She had fixed shifts which meant she always knew her schedule in advance and could plan her life around these set working nights. However, in recent years, 'the hospital was changing their attitude' towards 'set nights' meaning that she could no longer work the nights that suited her.

The changes in the NHS over recent decades, towards a more business model, were discussed by many participants. Several interviewees remarked that people were now coming into management positions in hospitals who had no clinical experience. Sheila put it succinctly: 'there was the theory ... that if you can manage Sainsbury's (supermarket) you can manage the Health Service.' As a result, according to Bridget: 'Now, they're walking round with their clipboards, and they know nothing about nursing'.

Julia echoed this point and went on to explain how the NHS has been 'belittled':

> ... changed from a culture of care to a business. You've got the secretary to the secretary's secretary because their chief executive's under chief executive's extra secretary's chief executive. You've got seven people in charge when it used to be matron. They don't know anything about the wee patient in bed number six ... It doesn't work, because the right hand doesn't know what the left hand is doing. I'm sorry, I feel so strongly about it. (Julia)

The passion expressed by Julia was not unusual and reflected the high regard that all our participants had for the NHS and the concerns they felt about recent changes.

The pressures on the NHS were made clearly apparent during the COVID-19 pandemic. One of our participants who was nursing throughout the pandemic described it as: 'the hardest time ever throughout the whole of my career. It was gruelling in very different ways' (Maeve).

The pandemic exposed pressures on staffing and resources within the health service. Some participants linked these challenges directly to government policies:

> the present establishment[4] do not care about the NHS because they're privatizing, they're handing it over lock, stock and barrel to private companies, private health care companies from America. So ... they're doing away with nurses' pensions and benefits and so on because they know that these private companies won't take them over if they've got a lot of expensive nurses to pay. So, all of this undermining nurses, refusing to recognize, they were out banging tins[5] for them during COVID but they won't give them a pay rise and the reason for that is because they want to privatize the NHS and they don't want nurses to be well paid because these private companies won't take them on. (Sean)

Deteriorating working conditions were linked, by several participants, with difficulties recruiting staff. Jacky observed how the number of Irish nurses during recent decades had dwindled: 'I'd say less and less were coming ... those numbers dwindled and now I don't think there are any Irish coming to do midwifery, not for a good number of years actually'. Sorcha spoke about some recruitment drives in recent decades to try to attract Irish nurses and students but without success: 'we started recruiting again, there was a huge shortage, I think it was about 15–20 years ago we started recruiting again in Ireland and some of the major hospitals went over to recruit'.

Given the lack of recruits from previous sources such as Ireland and the Caribbean, Sheila described how she had been part of active recruitment drives in the Philippines.

> I've gone full circle. Before I retired, I'd been to the Philippines three times recruiting nurses for the hospital ... 98/2000 and 2002 I went to the Philippines. In fact, we were the first hospital to go recruiting nurses for British hospitals. So, it's always been a problem ... We've never had

---

4 He was referring to the Conservative government in power at the time of our interview.
5 This is a reference to the practice during the Covid lockdown of people standing at their front doors, every week, and clapping or otherwise making a noise to support the NHS.

enough, there's never been enough people in this country to staff, you know we depend on people from other countries. (Sheila)

Of course, as noted earlier, there is a risk of looking at the past through 'rose-tinted glasses.' Oral history research relies, to a large extent, on how people recall and retell stories of the past, as discussed in Chapter 2. It is interesting to observe, therefore, that not all our participants believed that nursing had been done better in the past. There were a few dissenting voices. In a previous chapter Aoife and Una talked about how some practices had improved considerably over time (see Chapter 6). For example, patients had been kept in bed for months with bone fractures whereas now they were up and about much more quickly. Eilish expressed the view that patient care had been too rigid in the past and too much based upon routine without taking account of different patients' needs and preferences.

> I think the respect for people as patients grew much, much more as years went on. When I first started we were like, if you were on the elderly ward and somebody was confused, you were put in ... these sort of tip back chairs, and they were left sat there, because they were getting up and wandering round. Whereas as time went on, patients themselves have much more, their rights are much more important than they would have been back in 1974, 75. It was more a kind of a quick round and sort of clean them, put them back, and in and out of bed and things. There was no choice. Nobody was saying, 'Well I want to stay up and watch television.' Everybody was put to bed. Everybody was got up really early in the morning, whether they wanted to get up or not. So, I think from that point of view we have moved on. (Eilish)

This view contrasts with many others who felt that the order and routine of set time for getting patients up and putting them to bed was better in terms of overall care (see Chapter 6).

Another dissenting voice was around pay and conditions. While several nurses suggested that nursing was a vocation and pay should not be a primary consideration, this view was not universal. Interestingly, opinions were not clear-cut across generations. Indeed, it was one of our older participants who described going on strike over pay in the 1970s and how her husband had left the profession due to low pay in the 1960s. Colette, who was 88 years old when we interviewed her, showed us a fascinating photo of herself and colleagues on the picket line, in 1974, holding placards about low pay:

> we all said we'd all go out on strike, which we did. We went outside the hospital in uniform and our matron then, she was from Cork, her parents were from Cork ... she wasn't very keen on what we had done. But anyway, we stood outside the gate one day and we had all the cars tooting us ... We went to the Houses of Commons to see Barbara Castle[6] ... and anyway we got quite a good deal. (Colette)

A decade earlier, Colette's husband, also an Irish nurse, left the profession and went to get a job in the Ford Motor factory. During our interview, she showed us a newspaper article about his plight.

> we found it obviously a bit difficult to get the mortgage together, so (husband), he gave his notice and went to work in Ford. The papers came around looking for photographs ... and he'd got a big mention 'Why I resigned as a Nurse'. (*reading from article*) 'A man who loved nursing but gave the job up because of the low pay told *The Pictorial* this week "I was doing a worthwhile job at the hospital but have to think of my family".' (Colette)

The argument that the NHS is now very understaffed, in contrast to the past, was challenged by Bronagh: 'they talk about being short of staff now. I can remember being short of staff. We were always short of staff. But, you know, you had to rise to the occasion'.

While overall there was a perception that things in the NHS had deteriorated over time, this view was not shared by everyone. Indeed, some participants felt that, because of technology, some services had improved. Yvonne, who, despite being over 70, still worked part-time in a radiography department, stated: 'But things have improved and I think patient care is very good.' She added: 'we've got CT, MRI, endless different scans and tests'. Nonetheless, Yvonne also expressed the view that: 'The technology means that expectations are very high'. Whereas in the past a patient might have one test now they expect to have multiple tests. This has serious implications for resources: 'I think the amount of money needed is fantastic, isn't it? The funding, it is a bottomless pit, isn't it, really'.

Among our participants there was a shared view that the problems in the NHS were structural due to funding restrictions and increasing workload. While these issues may not have been entirely new, there was a sense that pressure on staff was increasing at a time when recruitment was becoming much more difficult, and, as a result, there was less time to spend with patients. As

---

6 Minister in the Labour government in the 1970s.

our participants age, their relationship with the NHS is changing and many now encounter health services from the perspective of patients and recipients of services. Therefore, the NHS remained highly important in their lives and a subject on which they all had very strong views.

CONCLUDING THOUGHTS

The NHS was a radical and innovative project that has, over the decades, transformed the health and life chances of the British population. It is hard to imagine any politicians today being brave enough to initiate such an ambitious and expensive public service.

However, from the beginning the new service struggled to recruit sufficient local staff and it was quickly apparent that large numbers of workers needed to be attracted from abroad. Thus, as evidenced throughout this book, from its inception in 1948, Irish nurses made up a very large proportion of the staff recruited to work in the NHS. The sheer scale and significance of their contribution deserves to be more widely acknowledged and celebrated.

As this book has shown, the story of Irish nurses is multi-faceted and complex. Using oral history research, we have foregrounded the personal narratives of our forty-five participants. From our earliest participants who arrived in the late 1940s and early 1950s, through to those who migrated in the 1970s, some of whom are still working today, these personal testimonies map onto the history of the NHS over the last seven decades.

Most of our participants profess a great sense of pride in their nursing careers and still care very deeply for the NHS and what it has achieved in terms of advancing health care and disease prevention. From TB, through to AIDS and COVID-19, our participants were at the forefront of nursing throughout some of the biggest challenges in NHS history. Several expressed real concern about the future of the service and were distrustful of government plans around privatization.

This book has focused on the great contribution and achievements of our participants, as individuals but also as part of wider Irish nursing cohorts. Nonetheless, we have also highlighted some challenging experiences. Although actively recruited from Ireland to provide vital health care in Britain, they did not always receive a warm welcome and often encountered anti-Irish hostility.

As nurses, most of our participants felt valued and appreciated by patients and colleagues. Many had long careers within the nursing profession and indeed several are still working today, despite being past retirement age. However, as we have shown, especially in this final chapter, there is also a strong feeling among our participants that the overall contribution of Irish nurses to the NHS is not well known or celebrated in British society more broadly. While in recent years, there is growing recognition of the contribution of other overseas nurses, especially the Windrush generation from the Caribbean, many participants expressed the view that similar recognition is also needed for Irish nurses.

We hope that this book, and the other aspects of our project, including the podcast series, documentary film, portraiture exhibition and our many dissemination events, will start that process of recognizing the enormous contribution of Irish nurses. In this way, we hope to start a national conversation and finally ensure the recognition that Irish nurses so richly deserve.

APPENDIX 1

The anonymous interviewees, ordered by date of interview

	year of migration	training hospital region
Bronagh	1965	Kent
Linda	1972	London
Sheila	1960	Surrey
Veronica	1964	English Midlands
Anita	1963	London
Bridget	1952	London
Orla	1974	London
Fiona	1974	London
Angela	1972	London
Maeve	~1972	London
Aileen	1974	London
Claire	1971	London
Finnuala	1972	London
Mairead	1973	Dublin/moved to London to work
Sinead	1979	London
Carmel	1954	London
Sorcha	1980	Limerick/moved to Britain to study midwifery
Gretta	1948	London
Ruth	1968	Hampshire
Trisha	1969	Essex/London
Miriam	1969	Croydon
Helen	1951	Liverpool
Kathleen	1968	Birkenhead
Jane	1954	Liverpool

APPENDIX 1. The anonymous interviewees, ordered by date of interview (*continued*)

	year of migration	training hospital region
Joseph	1956	Hertfordshire
Dervla	1966	London
Pauline	1974	Kent
Kitty	~1959	Liverpool
Aine	1968	Liverpool
Aoife	1963	Liverpool
Una	1965	Liverpool
Colette	1952	Essex
Aisling	1950	Middlesbrough
Sean	1966	Initial training in Northern Ireland/moved to Yorkshire
Caitriona	1960	Manchester
Deborah	1958	Hertfordshire
Yvonne	1971	Bedfordshire
Fidelma	1966	Hertfordshire
Delia	1961	London
Niamh	1958	Leeds
Eilish	1974	Leeds
Nessa	1957	Yorkshire
Julia	1968	Trained in Belfast/midwifery Glasgow
Jacky	1983	Trained in Limerick/midwifery Glasgow
Ciara	1979	Trained in Dublin/midwifery in Scotland

APPENDIX 2

Undertaking interviews across geographical locations

THE LONDON PARTICIPANTS

We started the London leg of the field work in March 2022 and had undertaken twenty-one interviews by August 2022.

Those twenty-one women were drawn from our existing personal contacts, some had featured in the *Angels of Mercy* (McPolin, 2021) radio documentary, and a few were identified with the support of the London Irish Centre. We are grateful for the support of the centre staff, especially Gary Dunne and Hannah Pender. All the London interviews were conducted in person by Louise and Gráinne together. While some of the interviews were done at the London Irish Centre, in a quiet space to ensure privacy, most interviews were undertaken in the participants' own homes as Louise and Gráinne travelled across all areas of London from the far south-east to the north-west of the city.

The oldest interviewee, aged 92, had been directly recruited from west Cork to train at a London hospital in 1948. The majority of interviewees had been recruited in the 1950s through to the late 1960s and early 1970s. Most participants were aged in their 70s, though several were in their mid-to-late 80s.

The women had trained at a very wide range of hospitals across London and it is noteworthy that many of these hospitals no longer exist. The interviews presented many wonderful, fascinating, funny and sad stories. Beyond the world of work, they also recounted their experiences in swinging London in the 1960s and early 1970s. Their stories of fashion, friendships and the fun of dancing present rare but vivid insights into the leisure activities of Irish women migrants from that era and we heard about their escapades in previous chapters of this book.

Overall, these interviews reveal the enormous contribution of these hard-working Irish nurses not only to the NHS but to wider British society. In retirement, many of these women did voluntary work and continue to make a significant contribution to their local communities across London.

LIVERPOOL INTERVIEWS

Having secured funding from the Irish Abroad Unit and the Liverpool Institute of Irish Studies, we started to plan our visit to Liverpool and the recruitment of participants throughout September 2022. We had various online meetings and phone calls with colleagues at the Liverpool Institute and Irish Community Care.

Louise and Gráinne travelled to Liverpool and undertook interviews on 28 and 29 September 2022. We conducted eight interviews in person – with nine participants as two sisters were interviewed together. Although we did not set out to recruit male nurses, one of the interviewees in Liverpool was an Irish man, a very sprightly 89-year-old, who had worked as a psychiatric nurse.

Our Liverpool participants ranged in age from the youngest at 68 to the oldest at 92. Overall, the average age was 80 years. Of the nine people interviewed, four arrived in the 1950s and five in the 1960s. The earliest arrival was in 1951, only three years after the NHS had been established, and the latest arrival was in 1968. All bar one of our participants were now retired. One, despite being over 70 years of age, was still working part-time in a care home and, indeed, had worked a twelve-hour shift the day prior to our interview.

The Liverpool participants were identified and contacted with the help of Breege McDaid, Irish Community Care, Margaret Lake, Liverpool Irish Centre and Gerry Diver, Liverpool Institute of Irish Studies. We wish to thank them for their assistance. This research would not have been possible without them. All interviews took place at Irish Community Care and we are grateful for the help provided by staff there in organizing taxis for the participants, and providing a nice room, tea/coffee and biscuits to create a relaxed and friendly environment for the research.

MANCHESTER

On 30 September 2022, we were invited by Sarah Mangan, Irish Consul General for the north of England, to address the Conference of Irish Community Organisations in the north of England, at the Irish World Heritage Centre. This event provided us with a valuable opportunity to speak about the Irish nurses project to a diverse range of Irish organizations from across Britain. There was great interest in our research and we collected contact details from several organizations who offered help with recruitment of participants.

We also took advantage of our visit to Manchester to arrange an interview, in-person, with an 88-year-old lady who went to the Irish World Heritage Centre to meet us, accompanied by her daughter and son-in-law.

Moreover, through contacts made at the Irish World Heritage Centre, we later arranged to interview another lady in Manchester. In fact, on the day of our interview it was her 85th birthday and our conversation had to be arranged around the celebrations that the staff at the centre had organized for her. We are grateful to the staff at the Irish World Heritage Centre for facilitating both of the interviews that took place in that venue.

A NURSE IN WALES

Through a personal contact of Gráinne's, we also conducted an interview – on-line – with a retired Irish nurse in Wales in September 2022. Although we had hoped to interview other nurses in Wales, unfortunately that was not possible.

IRISH EMBASSY, 20 OCTOBER 2022

We were invited to attend a reception at the Irish Embassy in October 2022, where we met with the minister for state at the Department of Foreign Affairs, Colm Brophy TD. Interestingly, Minister Brophy told us that his mother had also trained as a nurse in the NHS.

At this event we had the opportunity to network with several Irish organizations across Britain and this was to prove very fruitful in our recruitment efforts. Through contacts made at this event, we subsequently were connected with a retired nurse in Yorkshire. We later interviewed this male participant online. He had also been a psychiatric nurse and thus we have two male participants both of whom worked in the field of mental health.

As a direct result of attending the Embassy event, we received an invitation to speak about the project at the Luton Irish Forum St Brigid's Day event (see more details below).

NETWORKING IN NOVEMBER 2022

In November we started discussions with Vice Consul Jenny Quinn at the Irish Consulate in Scotland about how to recruit Irish-born nurses in that country. We discussed various ways to try to find Irish-born nurses but it was noted that the lack of Irish centres, per se, in Scotland could make recruitment more difficult.

Also in November, Louise was invited to attend the Irish in Britain AGM at the Hammersmith Irish Cultural Centre. Louise spoke about the nurses project and collected contact details from various Irish organizations. This led to a connection with the Leeds Irish Centre – more details below.

LUTON IRISH FORUM, 27–8 JANUARY 2023

Following the invitation to speak at the St Brigid's Day afternoon tea on Saturday 28 January, we engaged in discussions with Noelette Hanley and Elleesa Rushby about recruiting Irish-born nurses to interview in the Luton area. With their help, we arranged to interview three nurses over the weekend of 27–8 January. We also gave a presentation about the project to a packed afternoon tea celebration event at the Golf Club.

FEBRUARY 2023: MORE INTERVIEWS AROUND THE COUNTRY

Arising from communication about our project in the *Irish Post* newspaper and on social media, we were contacted by a lady aged 80 years, now living in the south-west coast of England. After some initial telephone conversations and some concerns about her health, it was decided to interview her online in February 2023.

LEEDS IRISH CENTRE, FEBRUARY 2023

Following a contact made at the Hammersmith Irish Centre event in November, Louise engaged in active communication with Rena Cosgrove at the Leeds Irish Centre to recruit Irish-born nurses in that area. After weeks of communication and planning, three nurses agreed to take part. The interviews were conducted on 23 February 2023.

SCOTLAND

Throughout this time, we continued with our efforts to recruit nurses in Scotland. This proved very difficult. Vice Consul Jenny Quinn suggested that we advertise in the *Irish Voice* newspaper in Scotland. Louise undertook discussions with Mary McGinty, editor of the *Irish Voice*, and this resulted in an advertisement and an article about our study published in February 2023.

As a result, one woman emailed us to arrange an interview. This lady, aged 77 years, was interviewed online on 13 March. She mentioned another Irish-

Appendix 2

born nurse of her acquaintance though she had no contact details for her. Nonetheless, because this nurse had held a senior position in the profession, Louise found her on LinkedIn and began a series of messages before eventually an interview was arranged.

Meanwhile, Mary McGinty got in touch with another Irish-born nurse who was keen to take part. After a few exchanges of emails, this third Scotland-based participant was interviewed online on the 23 March 2023.

We asked our three Scotland-based interviewees if they had any other friends or contacts who might take part in our study. All three noted that their Irish-born colleagues in Scotland had either moved back to Ireland or moved on elsewhere or had now unfortunately passed away. Overall, there was a sense that while many Irish nurses had gone to Scotland, especially to study midwifery (which was a great specialism in Scotland), many had moved on elsewhere and not settled in Scotland.

Moreover, it was noted that unlike other cities in England (e.g., London, Manchester, Liverpool, Leeds, Luton, etc.) that had very active Irish centres, this did not appear to be the case in Scotland. Therefore, our Scottish recruitment endeavour was definitely more challenging than in other parts of Britain. Nonetheless, we are pleased to include the stories of three Scotland-based nurses.

APPENDIX 3

The project outputs

While this book is the main output from our oral history project, it is certainly not the only resource we have produced. The other outputs include the podcast series, documentary film, photographic exhibition and a series of reports and events.

The podcast series:[1] consisting of over nine podcasts (each lasting around 20–30 minutes), produced by Gráinne, this series focuses on specific themes such as recruitment, training, uniform, life in the Nurses' Home, experiences on the wards, perception of Irish nurses, anti-Irish discrimination, social life, career, contribution to the NHS, family and friendships. The initial podcasts in the series were released in July 2023 to coincide with the 75th anniversary of the NHS.[2] We have worked with our partners in the Irish associations, especially the London Irish Centre, the Irish Embassy in London and our funders, to ensure that the podcast series is widely disseminated and promoted.

The film project: a collaboration with Dr Tom McGorrian, Buckinghamshire New University (BNU), has led to a new addition to our project – a documentary film. Tom and Louise have collaborated before on previous research projects. Tom is an established film-maker who teaches media production and has access to studio facilities at his university. Having accessed internal funding from his university, Tom and his colleague Mohammed Ali Elota began work on the documentary in the summer of 2023. The film consists of interviews with nine of the Irish nurses already interviewed by Louise and Gráinne.[3] The 40-minute documentary was premiered at the Irish Embassy in London in February 2024 and screened in Dublin at EPIC, the migration museum, in May 2024. We are most grateful to the staff at both venues for hosting the screenings.

---

1 Acast: https://shows.acast.com/irish-nurses-in-the-nhs.   2 We are very grateful to Kelly Crichton for all her help and guidance in launching the podcast series and her on-going advice on social media promotion.   3 We are grateful to RTÉ and the BFI for permission to use short clips from their archives.

Appendix 3

The portraiture project: supported by funding from the Burdett Trust for Nursing, we have worked with the acclaimed photographer Fiona Freund[4] to produce high quality portraits of twenty-one older women who migrated to London from the 1940s to the 1970s to train and work as nurses. Fiona, along with her colleague Lise Meyrick, produced a beautiful series of high-quality portraits of the ladies as they are now and beside each image she inserted a digitally enhanced old black and white photo of them in their youth, wearing their nurse's uniform. We took extracts from the oral history interviews to create short stories based on the women's biographical narratives. These extracts were added to the pictures and mounted on the boards to present the stories in words as well as pictures.

We are grateful to Fiona for her permission to include some of those photos in this book.

Exhibition at the London Irish Centre, March 2023: the photos and text were displayed at an exhibition at the London Irish Centre, one of our community partners in the research project. We organized a wonderful opening evening on 9 March at their Camden venue. Our research participants and their families were invited to attend. This provided a unique opportunity for the nurses to meet each other for the first time and share stories. The exhibition ran for the month of March 2023, and received widespread attention on social media and across Irish networks in London.

Liverpool dissemination event, June 2023: in partnership with the Liverpool Institute of Irish Studies and Irish Community Care, we took part in a dissemination event on the 19 June 2023 hosted at the University of Liverpool. A diverse range of stakeholders, local cultural groups, our nursing participants, members of the Irish consulate and other interested parties were invited. Following on from our very successful event at the Luton Irish Forum in January 2023 and at the London Irish Centre in March 2023, this Liverpool event was another important opportunity to present our research results back to Irish groups, including retired nurses themselves. We invited one of our Liverpool interviewees to come along and tell her story at the event to ensure that the voice of a nurse was a key part of the event.

Conference at London Metropolitan University, 12 July 2023: we organized a conference on the theme of Migrant Nurses in the NHS which brought

---

4 Fiona has an established career as a professional photographer and specializes in photographing women, particularly working women.

together students, academic researchers, nurses, nurse lecturers/trainers and other practitioners. This event was co-hosted by Dr Julie MacLaren, director of the nursing studies programme at London Metropolitan University. As well as presentations about Irish nurses, the conference also included presentations on African-Caribbean nurses, Filipino nurses and African nurses. This was an important event not only in showcasing the key role of migrant nurses to the NHS but also bringing together different nurses and nurse educators to share their experiences and stories. The event also included an evening drinks reception at which the Irish Nurses in the NHS photos were again displayed.

Royal College of Nursing online seminar, October 2023: throughout this project, we have been maintaining regular communication with the RCN. They have shown particular interest in our research and were keen to help us celebrate and promote the contribution of Irish nurses in the NHS. We worked with Teresa Doherty and Sarah Chaney, at the RCN, to organize an online seminar in October 2023. Hosting this event online ensured maximum reach across the country. At the seminar, chaired by Margaret Graham, we presented our findings through a PowerPoint presentation but also through an illustrated podcast bringing together voices of the different nurses we had interviewed in the project. Moreover, in order to centre the voices of nurses, we invited two of our older participants to join us online and share their stories. In this way, these retired nurses were able to share their stories with the wider audience and provide some important insights from their many years of working in the NHS. This event was well attended and very warmly received.

International Women's Day online seminar, 8 March 2024: in partnership with the London Irish Centre, we also presented an online event to celebrate the contribution of Irish nurses to the NHS but also to discuss experiences of discrimination and anti-Irish abuse, especially during the period of the Troubles and the IRA bombing campaign in England. At the event we launched a special episode of our podcast series and also invited one of our nurse participants to share her own personal story of encountering anti-Irish abuse. Chaired by Mary Kerrigan, from the London Irish Centre, whose mother had been an Irish nurse in the NHS, this event was recorded and is available on YouTube.[5]

Leeds Irish History Month: in March 2024, Louise was invited to speak at Kirkstall Abbey Museum as part of the Irish History Month lecture series. The session was organized by Patrick Bourne from the Abbey House Museum and

---

5 https://youtu.be/oSujHOlMlLo?feature=shared.

Appendix 3

Des Hurley from the Irish Arts Foundation, in cooperation with the Leeds Irish Centre. It was especially fitting to present our research findings in Leeds, as three of our participants had worked in that city.

We plan to continue organizing dissemination events to ensure that the story of Irish nurses in the NHS receives the attention it deserves.

Bibliography

Akenson D. (1993). *The Irish diaspora: a primer*. Belfast: Institute of Irish Studies.
Arensberg C. (1937). *The Irish countryman*. London: Macmillan.
Baker, C. (2022). NHS staff from overseas: statistics, *House of Commons Library* available at: https://researchbriefings.files.parliament.uk/documents/CBP-7783/CBP-7783.pdf [accessed 6 Nov. 2023].
Baxter, C., & Baxter, D. (1988). Racial inequalities in health: a challenge to the British National Health Service. *International Journal of Health Services*, 18:4, 563–71.
Beale, J. (1986). *Women in Ireland: voices of change*. Dublin: Gill and Macmillan.
Beaumont, C. (1997). Women, citizenship and Catholicism in the Irish Free State. *Women's History Review*, 6:4, 563–84.
Beishon, S., Virdee, S., & Hagell, A. (1995). *Nursing in a multi-ethnic NHS* (No. 775). Policy Studies Institute.
Bheenuck, S. (2010). Interrogating identity and belonging through life history: experiences of overseas nurses in post-colonial Britain. *Exploring learning, identity and power through life history and narrative research*, 70–83.
Bornat, J. (1989). Oral history as a social movement: reminiscence and older people. *Oral History*, 17:2, 16–24.
Brannen, J. (2013). Life story talk: some reflections on narrative in qualitative interviews. *Sociological Research Online*, 18:2, 48–58.
Buchan, J. (2002). Global nursing shortages: are often a symptom of wider health system or societal ailments. *British Medical Journal*, 324:7340, 751–2.
Buchan, J. (2007). International recruitment of nurses: policy and practice in the United Kingdom. *Health Services Research*, 42:3p2, 1321–35.
Chamberlain, M. (1997). Gender and the narratives of migration. *History Workshop Journal*, 43, 87–108.
Chaudhry, F.B., Raza, S., Raja, K.Z., & Ahmad, U. (2020). COVID 19 and BAME health care staff: wrong place at the wrong time. *Journal of Global Health*, 10:2.
Commission on Emigration (1955). *Emigration and other population problems, 1948–1954* (Dublin: Government Publications).
Connolly, L. (2001). *The Irish women's movement: from revolution to devolution*. Springer.

Corduff, E. (2021). *Ireland's loss Britain's gain, Irish nurses in Britain – Nightingale to millennium*. Rainbow Valley Books.
Cowley, U. (2001). *The men who built Britain: a history of the Irish navvy*. Dublin: Wolfhound Press.
Daniels, M. (1993). Exile or opportunity? Irish nurses and Wirral midwives. *Irish Studies Review*, 2:5, 4–8.
Delaney, E. (2000). *Demography, state and society: Irish migration to Britain, 1921–71*. Liverpool: Liverpool University Press.
Delaney, E., & MacRaild, D.M. (eds). (2007). *Irish migration, networks and ethnic identities since 1750*. Routledge.
England, P. (1992). *Comparable worth: theories and evidence*. Transaction Publishers.
Fielding, S. (1993). *Class and ethnicity: Irish Catholics in England, 1880–1939*. Buckingham: Open University Press.
Gaffney, G. Irish girl emigrants, *Irish Independent*, 7 December 1936.
Gardner, K. (2002). *Age, narrative and migration: life course and life histories of Bengali elders in London*. Oxford University Press.
Garrett, P. (2000). The hidden history of the PFIs: the repatriation of unmarried mothers and their children from England to Ireland in the 1950s and 1960s. *Immigrants & Minorities*, 19:3, 25–44, DOI: 10.1080/02619288. 2000.9974998.
Gerber, D.A., & Kraut, A. M. (2005). Becoming white: Irish immigrants in the nineteenth century. *American immigration and ethnicity: a reader*, 161–82.
Gray, B. (2004). *Women and the Irish diaspora*. Routledge.
Gray, B. (2006). Curious hybridities: transnational negotiations of migrancy through generation. *Irish Studies Review*, 14:2, 207223.
Gray, B. (2015). Preface to *Models for movers*, O'Carroll, second edition, Attic Press.
Hazard, M., with Sweet, C. (2015). *Sixty years a nurse*. Harper Element.
Henderson, S., Holland, J., McGrellis, S., Sharpe, S., & Thomson, R. (2012). Storying qualitative longitudinal research: sequence, voice and motif. *Qualitative Research*, 12:1, 16–34.
Hickman, M.J., & Walter, B. (1997). *Discrimination and the Irish community in Britain*. London: Commission for Racial Equality.
Hickman, M.J., & Ryan, L. (2020). The 'Irish question': marginalizations at the nexus of sociology of migration and ethnic and racial studies in Britain. *Ethnic and Racial Studies*, 43:16, 96–114.
Hillyard, P. (1993). *Suspect community: people's experience of the Prevention of Terrorism Acts in Britain*. Pluto Press.
Jackson, J.A. (1963). *The Irish in Britain*. London: Routledge and Kegan Paul.

Jinks, A.M., Richardson, K., Jones, C., & Kirton, J.A. (2014). Issues concerning recruitment, retention and attrition of student nurses in the 1950/60s: a comparative study. *Nurse Education in Practice*, 14:6, 641–7.

Jones, E., & Snow, S. (2010). *Against the odds: black and minority ethnic clinicians and Manchester, 1948 to 2009.* Manchester: Manchester NHS Primary Care Trust and University of Manchester.

Kakissis, J. (2018). An anti-immigration speech divided Britain 50 years ago. It still echoes today. *NPR*. Available at: https://www.npr.org/sections/parallels/2018/04/20/603884872/an-anti-immigration-speech-divided-britain-50-years-ago-it-still-echoes-today [accessed 9 Nov. 2023].

Kennedy, R. (1973). *The Irish: emigration, marriage and fertility.* Berkeley: University of California Press.

King, R., & O'Connor, H. (1996). Migration and gender: Irish women in Leicester. *Geography*, 311–25.

King-O'Riain, R.C. (2021). How the Irish became more than white: mixed-race Irishness in historical and contemporary contexts. *Journal of Ethnic and Migration Studies*, 47:4, 821–37.

Kofman, E. (2004). Gendered global migrations. *International Feminist Journal of Politics*, 6:4, 643–65.

Lambert S. (2001). *Irish women in Lancashire 1922–60: their story.* Lancaster: Centre for North West.

Lennon, M.J., McAdam, M., & O'Brien, J. (1988). *Across the water: Irish women's lives in Britain.* London: Virago Press.

Markey, K., & Tilki, M. (2007). Racism in nursing education: a reflective journey. *British Journal of Nursing*, 16:7, 390–3.

McCarthy, A. (2005). *Irish migrants in New Zealand, 1840–1937: 'the desired haven'.* Vol. 3. Boydell Press.

McCarthy, H. (2018). Women, marriage and paid work in post-war Britain. In Tinkler, Spencer and Langhamer (eds), *Women in fifties Britain*, pp 46–61. Routledge.

McCluskey, E. (2017). *I did it my way.* Self-published. Ecclesville Printing Services Ltd, Tyrone, Northern Ireland.

McDaid, M. (2021). Older Irish people living in east London and their stories of migration and dance (PhD, University of Sheffield).

McDermott, S. (2002). Memory, nostalgia and gender in A Thousand Acres, *Signs*, 28:1, 389–408.

McDowell, L. (2013). *Working lives: gender, migration and employment in Britain, 1945–2007.* John Wiley & Sons.

McKenna, Y. (2003). Forgotten migrants: Irish women religious in England, 1930s–1960s. *International Journal of Population Geography*, 9:4, 295–308.

McPolin, G. (14 March 2021) *Angels of Mercy* [Radio broadcast] Newstalk Radio 106–108FM. https://www.newstalk.com/podcasts/newstalk-documentary/angels-of-mercy-documentary-on-newstalk

Muldowney, M. (2007). *The Second World War and Irish women: an oral history*. Irish Academic Press.

Murray, T. (2017) Writing Irish nurses in Britain. In Pierse (ed.) *A history of Irish working-class writing*. Cambridge University Press, pp 195–208.

O'Carroll, I. (1990, 2015). *Models for movers: Irish women's emigration to America*, Dublin: Attic Press.

Okougha, M., & Tilki, M. (2010). Experience of overseas nurses: the potential for misunderstanding. *British Journal of Nursing*, 19:2, 102–6.

Oral History Society (17 April 2021). *Legal and ethical main – Oral History Society*. Oral History Society – Everybody's Story Matters. https://www.ohs.org.uk/legal-and-ethical-advice/

O'Sullivan, P. (ed.) (1997). *Irish women and Irish migration*, London: University of Leicester Press.

Perry, S. (2018). UK public support recruitment of EU nurses post-Brexit, including 'leave' voters. *The Health Foundation*. Available at: https://www.health.org.uk/news-and-comment/news/uk-public-support-recruitment-of-eu-nurses-post-brexit [accessed 10 Nov. 2023].

Phoenix, A., & Bauer, E. (2012). Challenging gender practices: intersectional narratives of sibling relations and parent–child engagements in transnational serial migration. *European Journal of Women's Studies*, 19:4, 490–504.

Redmond, J. (2018). *Moving histories: Irish women's emigration to Britain from Independence to Republic*. Liverpool University Press.

Rudd, J. (1988). Invisible exports: the emigration of Irish women this century. *Women's Studies International Forum*, 11:4, 307–11. Pergamon.

Ryan, B. (2001). The common travel area between Britain and Ireland. *The Modern Law Review*, 64:6, 831–54.

Ryan, L. (2001). Aliens, migrants and maids: public discourses on Irish immigration to Britain in 1937. *Immigrants and Minorities*, 20:3, 25–42.

Ryan, L. (2002a). *Gender, identity and the Irish Press, 1922–37: embodying the nation*. Mellen Press.

Ryan L. (2002b). I'm going to England: women's narratives of leaving Ireland in the 1930s. *Oral History*, 30:1, 42–53.

Ryan, L. (2003). Leaving home: Irish press debates on female employment, domesticity and emigration to Britain in the 1930s. *Women's History Review*, 12:3, 387–406.

Ryan, L. (2003 b). Sexualising emigration: discourses of Irish female emigration in the 1930s. *Women's Studies International Forum*, 25:1, 51–65.

Ryan, L. (2006). Passing time: Irish women remembering and re-telling stories of migration to Britain'. In Burrell, K., & Panayi, P. (eds). *Histories and memories: migrants and their history in Britain*. IB Tauris.

Ryan, L. (2007). Who do you think you are? Irish nurses encountering ethnicity and constructing identity in Britain. *Ethnic and Racial Studies*, 30:3, 416–38.

Ryan, L. (2008). I had a sister in England: family-led migration, social networks and Irish nurses. *Journal of Ethnic and Migration Studies*, 34:3, 453–70.

Ryan, L. (2022). The direct and indirect role of migrants' networks in accessing diverse labour market sectors: an analysis of the weak/strong ties continuum. In Keskiner, Eve and Ryan (eds) *Revisiting migrant networks: migrants and their descendants in labour markets*, 23–40. Springer Open Access available at https://link.springer.com/book/10.1007/978-3-030-94972-3

Ryan, L. (2023). *Social networks and migration: relocations, relationships and resources*. Policy Press.

Ryan, L., & Doshi, N. (2024). 'You would never pick up the thread from where you left off': older Irish women migrants' narratives of non-return, post-retirement. *International Migration*. https://doi.org/10.1111/imig.13321

Ryan, M. (2022). *An Irish nurse*. Self-published (Amazon Great Britain).

Rudd, J. (1988). Invisible exports: the emigration of Irish women this century. *Women's Studies International Forum*, 11:4, 307–11. Pergamon.

Scully, M. (2015). 'Emigrants in the traditional sense'? Irishness in England, contemporary migration and collective memory of the 1950s. *Irish Journal of Sociology*, 23:2, 133–48.

Simpson, J.M., Esmail, A., Kalra, V.S., & Snow, S.J. (2010). Writing migrants back into NHS history: addressing a 'collective amnesia' and its policy implications. *Journal of the Royal Society of Medicine*, 103:10, 392–6.

Snow, S.J., & Jones, E.L. (2011). Immigration and the National Health Service: putting history to the forefront. *History and Policy*. Available at: https://www.historyandpolicy.org/policy-papers/papers/immigration-and-the-national-health-service-putting-history-to-the-forefron [accessed 8 Nov. 2023].

Solano, D., & Rafferty, A.M. (2007). Can lessons be learned from history? The origins of the British imperial nurse labour market: a discussion paper. *International Journal of Nursing Studies*, 44:6, 1055–63.

Sommer, B.W., & Quinlan, M.K. (2018). *The oral history manual*. Rowman & Littlefield.

Spiliopoulos, G., & Timmons, S. (2023). Migrant NHS nurses as 'tolerated' citizens in post-Brexit Britain. *The Sociological Review*, 71:1, 183–200.

Thomson, A. (1998a). Fifty years on: an international perspective on oral history. *The Journal of American History*, 85:2, 581–95.

Thomson, A. (1998b). Anzac memories. In Robert Perks and Alistair Thomson (eds), *The oral history reader*, 300–10. London.
Tilki, M. (2006). The social contexts of drinking among Irish men in London. *Drugs: Education, Prevention and Policy*, 13:3, 247–61.
Trąbka, A. (2019). From functional bonds to place identity: place attachment of Polish migrants living in London and Oslo. *Journal of Environmental Psychology*, 62, 67–73.
Travers, P. (1997). There was nothing there for me: Irish female emigration 1922–71. In O'Sullivan (ed.), *Irish women and Irish migration*, 146–67. London: University of Leicester Press.
Trew, J.D. (2016). *Leaving the North: migration and memory, Northern Ireland 1921–2011*. Oxford University Press.
Trinidad, A.C., & Faas, D. (2024). Upward mobility and class inequities among Filipino migrant nurses in the Republic of Ireland. *Sociology*, 00380385241257488.
Walter, B. (1989). *Irish women in London: the Ealing dimension*, London.
Walter, B. (2002). *Outsiders inside: whiteness, place and Irish women*. London: Routledge.
Whooley, F. (1997). *Irish Londoners*. Published by the Grange Museum.
Yeates, N. (2004). A dialogue with 'global care chain' analysis: nurse migration in the Irish context. *Feminist Review*, 77:1, 79–95.

Index

Abbey House Museum, 218
abortions, 106–7
accents, 75, 105–6, 164–5, 177
    as marker of identity, 162, 172, 178, 179, 183
adoption, 107–8
African nurses, 26, 88, 122, 218
AIDS epidemic, 150–1
Angels of Mercy, 211
anti-immigration rhetoric, 32n12, 82
anti-Irish attitudes, 160, 161, 163–4, 165–7, 169, 170–2, 175–6
    impact of, 175, 183–4
    'no Irish' signs, 172–4
    Troubles, impact of, 177–86
Arensberg, C., 17
Asia, 80, 168
auxiliaries (nursing assistants), 52, 94, 95, 142, 203

Baxter, Carol and David, 168
Beale, Jenny, 19
Beatles, The, 74
Beishon, S., et al., 168
Birmingham, 150, 177–8, 183
    IRA bombings 174, 177n8, 178, 179–80
Bloody Sunday, 185, 185n11
Bornat, Joanna, 29
Bourne, Patrick, 218
Brexit, 33
Britain, 31, 32
    culture shocks, migrants and, 70–6, 102
    Irish migrants, 18, 19–20, 23–4, 25
    Irish women, invisibility of, 22, 26, 33
    journey to, 62–9
    labour shortages, 32
    perception of Irish migrants, 23–4
    reasons for training in, 20, 39
British colonies, 31, 33
Brophy, Colm, TD, 213
Buckinghamshire New University, 216
Burdett Trust for Nursing, 12, 217

Canada, 138, 150
care sector training courses, 158
care system, students from, 42, 56, 65, 94, 129
career change, 157–9, 206
career progression, 136–57
    clinical teaching, 153–4
    family life and, 139–44
    general practice, 145, 155–6
    infection control, 150–1
    marriage, effects of, 137, 139
    nursing officer post, 137
    occupational health, 149
    opportunities to develop, 144–7
    school nurses, 147–9
    senior management roles, 154–7
    sexual health, 148–9
    staff nurse, 136–7
    university sector, 153, 154
Caribbean, 22, 26, 31, 89, 168, 199, 204, 208
Castle, Barbara, 206

Catholic hierarchy, 19–20
Catholic newspapers, 43
Catholics, 25, 39, 75, 106, 131, 149, 162, 171, 177, 195
Celtic Tiger, 28, 28n10
Chamberlain, Mary, 29, 73
Chaney, Sarah, 218
Chinese nurses, 88, 122, 193
Christmas, 108–9, 115, 116, 129, 146
Civil Rights Movement, 28, 185n11
Clarion International Women in Media Award, 11
Commission on Emigration, 21, 42
Common Travel Area, 18, 18n1, 32
Commonwealth Immigration Act (1968), 32
Conference of Irish Community Organisations in the North of England, 212
Corduff, Ethel, 33
  Ireland's loss Britain's gain, Irish nurses in Britain: Nightingale to Millennium, 28
Cork Examiner, 44
Cosgrove, Rena, 214
COVID-19 pandemic, 157, 168, 204
Cusack, Megan, 26
Cusack, Sorcha, 26

Daniels, Mary, 22, 27, 33, 38
de Valera, Éamon, 19, 19n2, 20
discrimination, 168
  Irish nurses and, 28, 163
  religious, 39, 75, 162, 171–2
district nursing, 144–5, 147, 155, 170–1, 172, 181, 191–2
Diver, Gerry, 212
Doherty, Teresa, 218
Doshi, Neha, 14
Dunne, Gary, 211

Eastern Europe, female migration, 22
Elota, Mohammed Ali, 216
Emigrant Support Programme, 12

emigration, 20–1, 24, 25, 28, 32, 42–3, 60
English nurses, 89, 122, 127, 138, 164–5, 174
  scarcity of, 31, 53, 88, 188
Enniskillen bombings, 181
EPIC, 216
Essex, 28, 52, 79, 85, 120
ethnic diversity, 80–2, 88–9, 121, 122, 168
European Union (EU), 32, 33

Filipino nurses, 32, 33, 89, 193, 194
First World War, 28
Freund, Fiona, 217
Fricker, Brenda, 26

Gaffney, Gertrude, 19
General Data Protection Regulations (GDPR), 13
General Nursing Council (GNC), 137
general practice (GP), 145, 155–6, 202
Glasgow, 76, 78, 112, 119, 123, 154
  religious sectarianism, 162, 172, 172n6, 177
Graham, Margaret, 218
Gray, Breda, 24, 25
Guildford bombing, 180

Hammersmith Irish Cultural Centre, 213, 214
Hampshire, 89, 103, 115, 123
Hazard, Mary, and Sweet, Corinne, 33
  Sixty years a nurse, 28
health visitors, 144–5
Hertfordshire, 55, 77, 112, 114, 188
Hickman, M.J., & Walter, B., 18
Hillyard, Paddy, 178n9
hospitals in Britain
  amenities for staff, 112–13, 114
  first impressions of, 71, 72–3, 74, 80
  hierarchy and status in, 97–8
  locations, 89, 123
  matrons, 98, 104

hospitals in Britain *(continued)*
   Nightingale format, 96, 97
   staff canteens, 199–200
   ward sisters, 97–8, 104
   wards as places of encounter, 105–8
   wards, size of, 96–7
Hurley, Des, 219

Indian nurses, 33, 88, 89
infection control, 150–1
infectious diseases, 101–2
Innisfallen (ship), 62, 65
Irish Abroad Unit, 212
Irish Arts Foundation, 219
Irish Community Care, 212, 217
Irish Consulate, Scotland, 213
Irish Embassy, London, 213, 216
Irish Housewives Association, 20
Irish Independent
   'Alarming evil', 20
   'Irish girl emigrants', 19
Irish migrants, 10, 160
   Common Travel Area agreement, 32
   female migrants, 18, 19–20, 22–3, 33
   holidays in Ireland, 128–30
   homesickness, 76–7, 78
   negative stereotypes, 18, 23, 161, 163, 166, 174, 185
   Troubles, impact of, 177–86
Irish nuns, 24, 28
Irish nurses
   anti-Irish abuse/hostility, 161, 163, 166, 167–8, 169, 170–1, 172, 175–9, 180, 182, 183, 184
   appreciation of, 194–6
   cultural stereotypes, 26
   death, dealing with, 190, 191
   decrease in numbers of, 204
   empathy with patients, 192–3
   in hospital dramas, 26
   NHS, contribution to, 187–9, 198–9, 207–8
   professionalism, 163, 164, 186
   special qualities, 190–4
   Troubles, impact of, 177–86
   work ethic, 10, 26, 189–90, 193
Irish Nurses and Midwives Organisation, 12
Irish Republican Army (IRA)
   Birmingham bombings, 174, 177n8, 178, 179–80
   bombing campaign in Britain 10, 161, 166, 177, 177n8, 178–81
   London bombings, 177n8, 178, 180, 182–3
Irish Voice, 214
Irish World Heritage Centre, 212, 213

Jamaican nurses, 31, 81, 88, 123, 189
Jinks, A.M., et al., 31

Kelly, Maeve, *Florrie's girls*, 27n8
Kent, 9, 51, 59, 101–2, 105, 112, 113
Kerrigan, Mary, 218
King, Russell, and O'Connor, Henrietta, 24
Kirkstall Abbey Museum, 218
Kofman, Eleonore, 22

Lake, Margaret, 212
Lambert, Sharon, 24
Lancashire, Irish migrants, 24
Leeds, 53, 55–6, 57, 64, 79, 117, 124, 130
Leeds Irish Centre, 214, 219
Lennon, M.J., et al., *Across the water*, 23
letter-writing, 70, 128, 129
Liverpool, 43, 44, 57, 74–6, 78, 119, 121, 130
   ballroom dances, 130, 131
   Irish dance venues, 114, 120, 123
   Irish migrants, attitude towards, 162, 176–7
   living-out in flats, 127
   religious sectarianism, 162, 176
   Shamrock Irish club, 120

Liverpool Institute of Irish Studies, 12, 212, 217
Liverpool Irish Centre, 212, 217, 218
London, 24, 110–11
    afternoon dancing, 116–17
    Blarney, The, 116, 117, 133
    IRA bombings, 177n8, 178, 180, 182–3, 184
    Irish Centre, 12
    Irish dance venues, 114–15, 119, 123, 132–3
    post-war, 71, 74, 76, 122
    public transport, 77–8
London Irish Centre, 216, 217
London Metropolitan University, 13, 27n7, 217, 218
Luton Irish Forum, 214, 217

MacLaren, Dr Julie, 218
McCarthy, Angela, 23
McCluskey, Elizabeth, 33
    I did it my way, 28
McDaid, Breege, 212
McDermott, Sinead, 29
McGinty, Mary, 214, 215
McGorrian, Dr Tom, 216
McKenna, Yvonne, 24
McNamee, James Joseph, bishop of Ardagh and Clonmacnoise, 19–20
McPolin, Gráinne, 13
    Angels of Mercy, 11, 211
Malaysian nurses, 81, 88, 89, 123, 129, 199
male nurses, 13, 31–2, 52–3, 60, 100, 115
Mangan, Sarah, 212
Manchester, 79, 189
marriage, 130–4
    effect on careers, 137, 139
    mortgages, obtaining, 141
    night duty and, 140–1, 142, 150, 154
    part-time work and, 136, 140–2, 143
Mauritius, 31

Meyrick, Lise, 217
Middlesbrough, 35, 54, 70, 111, 124
midwifery, 36–7, 39, 69, 123, 139, 143
migration/migrants, 17–20
    chain migration, 57, 61
    culture of migration, 21, 47, 61, 69
    female migration, 18, 20, 21–2
    network ties in Britain, 69–70
    see also Irish migrants
Morris, Mary, 27n8
Muldowney, Mary, 24
Murray, Tony, 27n8
Muslims, 186

National Front, 82
National Health Service (NHS)
    business model, move to, 156, 203
    career development, facilitation of, 154
    changes in, 199–207
    COVID-19 pandemic and, 204
    English people in, 188–9
    establishment of, 9
    flexible working, 143
    funding restrictions, 206
    Irish nurses, contribution of, 187–9, 198–9, 207–8
    Irish nurses in, 26–7
    Irish-born nurses in, 187–8
    overseas recruitment, 17, 31–3, 168, 189, 204
    patient care, changes in, 205
    pay and conditions, 205
    privatization, effects of, 204
    recruitment in Ireland, 9–10, 26, 40, 43–54, 190, 204
    role of Irish nurses, 188
    staff shortages, 31, 197, 200, 206, 207
    strikes, 202, 205–6
    working schedules, 203
National Vocational Qualification (NVQ), 157
Nationality Act (1948), 32

New Zealand, 23
Newstalk, *Angels of Mercy* (documentary), 11
Nigeria, 31, 33, 189
night duty
    changes in, 203
    married nurses and, 140–1, 142, 143, 145–6, 150, 154
    nurse training and, 104–5
Nightingale, Florence, 28
Northern Constitution, 43
Northern Ireland, 31, 176, 184
    emigration, 25, 28
    health system 37n1
    nurse training, 10n2, 38–9
    religious discrimination, 39, 75
    see also Irish Republican Army (IRA); Troubles, the
nurse training
    application process, 47–54
    barriers in Ireland, 37–8, 39, 45, 61
    in Britain, 42
    clinical teaching, 153–4
    entrance exams, 52–3
    examinations, 93–6
    female recruits, 31–2
    Intermediate Certificate and, 51
    interviews by NHS, 47–54
    IQ test, 53
    Leaving Certificate and, 47, 48, 50, 51–2
    male recruits, 31–2
    networks, role of, 49, 53–4, 54–60
    newspaper advertisements, 44, 46, 54–5, 58
    night duty, 104–5
    in Northern Ireland, 10n2, 38–9
    pay and status, 32
    postal recruitment process, 49–50
    Preliminary Training School (PTS), 76, 85–6, 87, 96
    in the Republic of Ireland, 10n2, 37–8, 39, 45
    risks, exposure to, 101–3
    salaries, 124–5
    structure of, 84–8
    in the United States, 151, 152
    university-based nurse education, 152–4, 158
    on the wards, 96–104
    working hours, 99
    see also career progression; state enrolled nurse (SEN); state registered nurse (SRN)
Nurses Act (1949), 31
Nurses' Homes, 15, 61, 71–2, 124, 125
    curfews, 117, 118
    ethnic diversity, 81, 122
    friendships, 78–9, 80, 89, 110, 111–12
    rules/restrictions, 73, 117, 118, 126–7
    security of, 79, 82, 117, 170
nursing
    changes in, 200, 202
    geographical mobility, 149–52
    as a pathway to travel, 41, 138, 149–52
    reasons for choosing career in, 35–7, 40–2, 190
    return to nursing course, 159, 200

O'Carroll, Ide, *Models for movers*, 23
occupational health, 149
ophthalmology, 156–7
oral history, 29–30
Oral History Research protocol, 13
Oral History Society, 13
Orange Order, 171, 176

patients
    appreciation of nurses, 194–6
    changes in care, 205
    computerization, impact of, 202
    generational differences, 194
    NHS, experiences of, 200–1
    nurses' perception of, 194

regional differences, 194
turnover of, 201
Pender, Hannah, 211
Philippines, 33, 204
Pioneer Total Abstinence Association, 119n6
Polish nurses, 168
Powell, Enoch, 32
Protestants, 25, 75, 132, 172n6, 184
psychiatric patients, 101, 197
public transport, 77–8, 125

Quinn, Jenny, 213, 214

racism, 82, 94, 164, 166, 167, 168, 172–4, 180
Red Cross, first aid courses, 157
Redmond, Jennifer, 25
Republic of Ireland, 25, 31
   in the 1950s–60s, 41–2, 111
   culture of migration, 21, 47, 161
   decline in emigration, 32
   health system, 37n1
   Intermediate Certificate, 51
   Leaving Certificate, 47, 48, 50, 51–2
   National School education, 94
   nurse training, barriers to, 37–8, 39, 45, 61
   recruitment of Filipino nurses, 32
   women, lack of career opportunities for, 42, 56
Royal Air Force (RAF), 115
Royal College of Nursing (RCN), 153, 158, 218
Rudd, Joy, 21
Runwell Hospital, near Wickford, Essex, 46
Ryan, Louise, 11, 14, 19, 24, 27, 33, 54
Ryan, Maureen, 33
   Irish nurse, An, 28

St Francis Hospital, Haywards Heath, Sussex, 46

school nurses, 147–9
Scotland, 51, 69, 78, 81, 106, 119, 123
   district nursing in, 191–2
   football teams, 192
   religious discrimination, 171–2, 177
Scully, Marc, 24
Second World War, 10, 22, 24, 26, 28
sectarianism, 162, 176, 177, 184
Sligo Champion, 46
social life, 77, 104, 110–21
   ballroom dances, 130–1
   dances, invitations to, 115–16
   Irish dance venues, 114–15, 118, 119–20, 123, 124
Spain, 33
state enrolled nurse (SEN), 50, 53, 94, 96, 145, 168
   conversion to SRN, 146, 153
state registered nurse (SRN), 50, 53, 93–4, 96, 145, 168
   conversion from SEN, 146, 153
strikes, 202, 205–6
Sunday Press, 43

Thomson, Alastair, 29
travel, nursing as a pathway to, 41, 138, 149–52
Trew, Joanne Devlin, *Leaving the North*, 25
Trinidad, 88, 89
Troubles, the, 15, 25, 28, 161, 174, 218
   holidays in Ireland and, 184–5
   impact on Irish migrants, 177–86
TV series, Irish nurses in, 26

uniforms, 15, 84, 90–3, 117, 201–2
United States (US), 17–18, 23
   nursing in, 138–9, 150, 151, 152
Universe, The, 43
university-based nurse education, 152–4, 158

Wales, 150, 158–9, 194
Walter, Bronwen, 22, 23, 26, 27, 33, 186
Walton Hospital, Liverpool, 44
West Indian nurses, 94, 122, 199
White, Maeve, 10
Windrush generation, 31, 199, 208
Winters, Freida, 10

women
    career opportunities in Ireland, lack of, 42, 56
    migration and, 18, 20, 21–2, 23, 33

xenophobia, 82

Yeates, Nicola, 20, 31
Yorkshire, 77, 105, 113, 115, 122, 179